Visions of Technological Transcendence

RHETORIC OF SCIENCE AND TECHNOLOGY
Series Editor: Alan G. Gross

The rhetoric of science and technology is a branch of rhetorical criticism that has grown rapidly since its inception four decades ago. Its initial focus was the texts of such well-known scientists as Darwin, Newton, and Watson and Crick. The field has since expanded to encompass important work on interdisciplinarity, the role of rhetorical schemes, the popular meanings of the gene, the rhetorical history of the scientific article, the question of incommensurability, and the critical engagement with emergent technologies. But this work and these topics by no means exhaust the field. Although the point has already been made that science and technology are in some sense rhetorical, the field remains open to new topics and innovative approaches. For submission information, please visit the series page at http://www.parlorpress.com/science.

BOOKS IN THE SERIES

Visions of Technological Transcendence

Human Enhancement and the Rhetoric of the Future

James A. Herrick

Parlor Press
Anderson, South Carolina
www.parlorpress.com

Parlor Press LLC, Anderson, South Carolina, USA
© 2017 by Parlor Press.
All rights reserved.
Printed in the United States of America
S A N: 2 5 4 - 8 8 7 9

Library of Congress Cataloging-in-Publication Data on File

978-1-60235-875-1 (paperback)
978-1-60235-876-8 (hardcover)
978-1-60235-877-5 (PDF)
978-1-60235-878-2 (epub)
978-1-60235-879-9 (iBook)
978-1-60235-880-5 (Kindle)

1 2 3 4 5
First Edition

Cover image: @NASA. Retrieved from Unsplash. Used by permission.
Cover design by David Blakesley
Printed on acid-free paper.

Parlor Press, LLC is an independent publisher of scholarly and trade titles in print
and multimedia formats. This book is available in paper, hardcover, and digital
formats from Parlor Press on the World Wide Web at http://www.parlorpress.com or
through online and brick-and-mortar bookstores. For submission information or to
find out about Parlor Press publications, write to Parlor Press, 3015 Brackenberry
Drive, Anderson, SC 29621, or email editor@parlorpress.com.

CONTENTS

Acknowledgments

A number of people have contributed in important ways to this project, and I would like to take the opportunity to thank them here. Several friends and colleagues have been faithful conversation partners along the way. I wish to thank Mike McIntosh, Jonathan Greer, Matt DeJongh, Len Bareman, Andy McCoy, Todd Daly, Michael Hyde and John Kampschmidt. For their enthusiastic response to the topic and many helpful comments I would like to acknowledge the students in my Honors Seminar on the rhetoric of biotechnology and human enhancement at Hope College. Linda Koetje provided valuable assistance in preparing the manuscript for submission. Thanks also to Alan Gross and David Blakesley for their helpful guidance regarding the presentation of key ideas. Several authors have informed my thinking about the rhetorical potential of myth, in particular Northrop Frye, Laurence Coupe, Marina Warner and Mary Midgley. I have also benefitted greatly from attending the Annual Conferences on Governance of Emerging Technologies, sponsored by the Sandra Day O'Connor College of Law at Arizona State University. My thanks to the organizers for their efforts. Finally, my deepest appreciation goes to my wife, Janet P. Herrick, for her unwavering support and interest. I would like to dedicate this book to the memory of Clara Naomi Baylis, Robert D. Herrick, and Marian L. Herrick.

Visions of Technological Transcendence

1 Introduction

Our first invention was the story . . .

—Ray Kurzweil

If our minds can't tell stories, we can't consciously create; we can only create by accident. Until we tame the mind with an organization tool capable of communicating to itself, we have stray thoughts without a narrative.

—Kevin Kelly

We are accustomed to think of myths as the opposite of science. But in fact they are a central part of it: the part that decides its significance in our lives. So we very much need to understand them.

—Mary Midgley

Russian media magnate Dmitry Itzkov launched the 2045 Initiative in 2011. Bringing together leading thinkers around the vision of a technologically transcendent future, the Initiative imagines a human race no longer subject to death or other limitations. World-renowned spiritual leaders mingle with leading scientists at Initiative gatherings such as those convened in Moscow in 2011 and New York in 2013. The presence of priests and lamas is in keeping with the organization's "main goals," which include creating social conditions that promote "the spiritual enlightenment of humanity; and the realization of a new futuristic reality based on 5 principles: high spirituality, high culture, high ethics, high science and high technologies."

The Initiative's principal goal is "to create technologies enabling the transfer of an individual's personality to a more advanced non-biological carrier, and extending life, including to the point of immortality." According to the Initiative's account of the technological future, machine-based immortality is a spiritual as well as physical accomplishment. The goal thus requires cooperation of the highest order, including "particular attention to enabling the fullest possible dialogue between the world's major spiritual traditions, science and society." Such a "large-scale transformation of humanity" is "comparable to some of the major spiritual and sci-tech revolutions in history. . . ." Nothing less than the shape of the human future is in view; techno-progressives will "realize a new strategy for humanity's development, and in so doing, create a more productive, fulfilling, and satisfying future."[1]

Itzkov's 2045 Initiative is only one of many contemporary organizations sponsoring events focused on technology's potential to transform the human condition. The transhumanist organization Humanity+ hosts several meetings each year at various locations around the world.[2] Conferences draw hundreds of participants, many of them scientists and science graduate students from major research institutions. A student attending one such gathering speculates about what attracts younger people to such technofuturist events: "Idealism. Most of us are not religious, but we are still idealistic. This gives us a way to express our idealism."[3] That idealism goes by various names including Transhumanism, the human enhancement movement, tecnofuturism, techno-progressivism, and posthumanism.

The proliferation of technofuturist ideas over the past two decades, particularly as those ideas have been endorsed by eminent scientists and philosophers, represents a forceful rhetorical phenomenon deserving attention. Though often described, the future is always unknown; its characteristics can be imagined but never observed. Rhetorical envisioning by skilled advocates thus plays a prominent role in shaping public conceptions of the future. For advocates with an interest in a particular future, visionary narration—the creation of myths—becomes a crucial persuasive project. Moreover, crafting and propagating a compelling future-vision is an undertaking that, when accomplished with rhetorical skill, affords proponents a degree of cultural influence out of proportion to their actual numbers.

This study explores the ways in which technofuturist rhetoric—particularly that associated with Transhumanism and human enhancement—casts a transformative vision of the technological future. In pursuing this critical project, I focus particular attention on a network of transcendent narratives or myths about technology that render this vision of the future plausible and thus persuasive. The substance of Transhumanist and related technofuturist rhetoric is, I contend, a skillfully constructed prophetic mythology describing a limitless human future achieved by means of intentionally appropriated technologies. At the center of this vision stand enhanced and immortal post-humans poised to deliver future generations from the frailties of the human condition by means of transformative science. As the prevailing vision of the future will shape public expectations, legislation, and research agendas, understanding the narrative processes by which such a vision is taking shape is immensely important.

The narratives explored in subsequent chapters represent constituents of a complex vision of technological transcendence. Despite its advocates' claims, this envisioned future is not simply the inevitable consequence of aggregated technological progress. Rather, the future portrayed in epic stories of technological transcendence is a rhetorical invention, a creation of imaginative thinkers and skilled advocates. Many of the leading proponents at work shaping a rhetorical vision of the future are associated with the human enhancement project and its most prominent manifestation, Transhumanism. It will therefore be helpful to take a closer look at these rising technofuturist movements.

Transhumanism and the Human Enhancement Movement

Nick Bostrom and David Pearce founded the World Transhumanist Association in 1997 "to represent a more mature and academically respectable form of transhumanism. . . ."[4] Around the same time, related organizations such as Max More's Extropy Institute began to promote a technofuturist vision around the concept of Transhumanism. But thinkers like Bostrom, Pearce, and More owe a debt to somewhat earlier figures such as Fereidoun M. Esfandiary (1930–2000), a speaker and author of the 1970s and 1980s who famously changed his name to FM-2030. Suave and articulate, FM-2030 appeared on American radio and television talk shows toward the end of the twentieth century. He advocated many of the ideas that would eventually form the Transhumanist agenda—immortality, human-machine merger, space colonization, and artificial enhancement of intelligence. FM-2030 also penned an early Transhumanist manifesto titled *Are You a Transhuman?*, which was perhaps the first work in the contemporary Transhumanist movement.[5] The book focused on practices to develop mental acuity and lifestyle choices to avoid disease. The earlier roots of human-enhancement thought will be explored in the next chapter.

A range of organizations share an interest in the shape of the human technological future. These include, in addition to the 2045 Initiative and Humanity+, Singularity University in California, the Future of Humanity Institute at Oxford University, the Association for the Advancement of Artificial Intelligence in Palo Alto, the European Union's Human Brain Project, the Institute of Electrical and Electronics Engineers, the Defense Advanced Research Projects Agency (DARPA), the Institute for Ethics and Emerging Technologies, Strategies for Engineered Negligible Senescence (SENS) Research Center, the Methuselah Foundation, and many others. Research endeavors of central importance to technofuturism include artificial intelligence, life-extension, nanotechnology, robotics, genetic engineering, synthetic biology, and space colonization.

Transhumanism is both an organized movement and a philosophical perspective that sees current humanity as a transitional stage in evolution that will birth a new species—the posthuman. Some enhancement proponents avoid the Transhumanist label, though they endorse many of the movement's goals. Whether or not they affiliate with a Transhumanist organization, an increasing number of scientists, journalists, philosophers, entrepreneurs, media personalities, spiritual leaders, and self-described futurists promote a program of radical human enhancement. These opinion leaders are developing a language, crafting narratives, and casting a vision of a technologically transformed human future. Such strategic elements constitute a rhetoric of the future—discursive practices intended to frame discussions of the ethics of technology, our relationship to our machines, and even the characteristics of future humans.

Leading proponents of human enhancement include science journalists Ronald Bailey and Joel Garreau, sociologists James Hughes and William Sims Bainbridge, inventors Ray Kurzweil and Martine Rothblatt, philosophers John Harris and Allen Buchanan, and entrepreneurs Dmitry Itzkov and Gregory Stock. Other names often associated with the movement include biochemist Aubrey de Grey, physicist Ben Goertzel, husband and wife philosophers Natasha Vita More and Max More, artificial intelligence expert Hugo de Garis, and computer scientist and novelist Ramez Naam.

Bostrom captures the movement's fundamental orientation in an oft-quoted passage from his essay "Transhumanist Values:"

> Transhumanists view human nature as a work-in-progress, a half-baked beginning that we can learn to remold in desirable ways. Current humanity need not be the endpoint of evolution. Transhumanists hope that by responsible use of science, technology, and other rational means, we shall eventually manage to become posthuman, beings with vastly greater capacities than present human beings have.[6]

Bostrom's colleague Anders Sandberg emphasizes the role of reason in guiding the Transhumanist vision. He writes, "Transhumanism, broadly speaking, is the view that the human condition is not unchanging and that it can and should be questioned. Further, the human condition can and should be changed using applied reason."[7]

Applying reason to improving the human condition is often contextualized in a discussion of what is termed *directed evolution*. Technologically assisted evolution has developed into an important topic in bioethics, medicine, philosophy, and religion.[8] Transhumanists and their allies argue that the time has come to take control of human evolution, hastening and directing the process by technological means such as genetic engineering, nanotechnology, and massive computing power. In the developing enhancement narrative, the present human is a step toward the posthuman—a smarter, longer living, and more compassionate version of the human being. Posthumans will colonize other planets and may possess virtually supernatural capacities such as telepathy and prescience.

Many have noted that the enhancement narrative can quickly take on a religious quality. The language in which the enhancement vision is cast can be marked by terms such as immortality, transcendence, and trust. One prominent Transhumanist states that "trust in our posthuman future is the essence of Transhumanism."[9] Hava Tirosh-Samuelson, a skeptic in regards to the enhancement agenda, finds Transhumanist discourse to reverse the ageless order under which human beings are a component in the vast scheme of nature. Now, godlike, we will control nature. "In the posthuman age," she writes, "humans will no longer be controlled by nature; instead, they will be the controllers of nature."[10]

Some proponents speculate that realizing the Transhumanist dream will require fashioning a new political order that eschews the old model of competing nation states. The new system will be ordered around world cooperation aiming at rapid technological progress enabled by a massively more powerful Internet. Artificial intelligence expert Hugo de Garis suggests that "the exponential rate of technical progress will create within 40 years an Internet that is a trillion times faster than today's, a global media, a global education system, a global language, and a globally homogenized culture" that will constitute the basis of "a global democratic state . . ." This new order of things, which de Garis calls Globa, will rid the world of "war, the arms trade, ignorance, and poverty." [11]

For Bostrom, Transhumanism increases the range of self-determination by creating "the opportunity to live much longer and healthier lives, to enhance our memory and other intellectual faculties, to refine our emotional experiences and increase our subjective sense of well-being, and generally to achieve a greater degree of control over our own lives." Bostrom also notes that Transhumanism represents a radical reaction against religious mores and resultant precautionary ethics. The movement offers "an alternative to customary injunctions against playing God, messing with nature, tampering with our human essence, or displaying punishable hubris."[12]

Bringing about the Revolution

How will the era of enhanced humanity arrive? For many in the enhancement movement, governments and universities—the usual arbiters of large scale technological progress—are too slow and cumbersome to propel a technological revolution. The citizen scientist, the imaginative entrepreneur, and the visionary corporation are the new engineers of progress.[13] Ray Kurzweil provides a model—an inventor, businessman, author, and technology pioneer, he is the most recognizable advocate for radical enhancement and now serves as the director of special research projects at Google.

Other examples of the nimble, entrepreneurial model favored by techno-progressives are Singularity University co-founder Peter Diamandis—the inventor of the XPrize—and dot-com billionaire Peter Thiel whose Thiel Fellowship offers young entrepreneurs up to $100,000 to interrupt their schooling and pursue a technological vision. "Our world needs more breakthrough technologies," says Thiel. "From Facebook to SpaceX to Halcyon Molecular, some of the world's most transformational technologies were created by people who dropped out of school because they had ideas that couldn't wait until graduation."[14]

The vision of technological transformation and radical enhancement is pursued by a wide range of emerging research and educational institutions. Singularity University—a training ground for visionary entrepreneurs in Silicon Valley—attracts large and powerful sponsors such as Google, Deloitte, Genentech, Caterpillar, and GuideWell.[15] The University's annual FutureMed events connect investors with medical practitioners and inventors. A growing number of laboratories around the world—far too many to list—are engaged in artificial intelligence, robotics, genetics, brain, nanotechnology, and prosthetic research, all of which are of interest to human enhancement proponents. Prominent examples include the J. Craig Venter Institute for genomic research in La Jolla, California; Boston Dynamics, a leading robotics laboratory acquired by Google in 2013; and the MIT Computer Science and Artificial Intelligence Laboratories.

Medical research groups such as Wake Forest University's Institute for Regenerative Medicine and the University of Southern California's Davis School of Gerontology pursue regenerative medicine and longevity research.[16] Pharmaceutical companies such as Memory Pharmaceuticals (founded by Nobel Prize winner Eric Kandel) and Dart NeuroScience (formerly Helicon

Therapeutics, founded by memory researcher Tim Tully) hope to benefit from the expected boom in medicines that will improve memory, a step toward cognitive enhancement.[17] Some government agencies also play a role in shaping visions of the enhanced human. DARPA (Defense Advanced Research Projects Agency), a division of the Department of Defense, invests in robotics research and a wide range of other research related to physical and mental enhancement. So vast, diverse, and well-funded is the research network exploring technologies of interest to enhancement advocates that the collective financial and social clout of all related projects is beyond accurate calculating and adequate summary.

As advanced biotechnologies push medical treatments across the threshold separating therapy—medicine's traditional goal—from enhancement, the language of medicine will also face pressures to change. Ed Boyden, director of the MIT Media Lab, has argued that advances in medical technology are rendering concepts such as *normal* obsolete. "Nobody would argue against a treatment that restores normal function to a sick or disabled individual," writes Boyden, "but the consequences of going further than that— going beyond 'normal'—are not commonly studied, nor endorsed by many in medicine." Despite rapid advances in biotechnology, the standards of therapy and normal function remain entrenched in medical practice and research agendas. "The idea that biomedical science is supposed to bring us up to normal is embedded, to a degree, in the very structure of the experiments we commonly do in the laboratory."

Boyden notes that we are entering a period when "going beyond normal may change us in new and unprecedented ways, improving our lives in ways that are hard to even imagine." Research that has dramatically extended the lifespans of worms, yeast, and mice, for instance, "may someday (quite possibly soon) lead to drugs that can extend human life span." Pharmaceuticals will boost alertness beyond normal, and computerized prosthetics will provide amputees the capacity for movement beyond normal. In such a changing context, a new language of medicine may be required. "It's arguably time for a discipline to emerge around the idea of human augmentation," comments Boyden. The new technologies will "make the idea of normal obsolete." It is already becoming "harder and harder to know what *is* normal."[18]

STRUCTURE OF THE STUDY

The goal of this study is to identify, explicate, and assess the visionary narratives or myths of technological transcendence currently emerging around the central ideas of the human-enhancement movement and techno-progressivism generally. The following chapters explore closely related and recurring narratives in the discourse of these movements. These myths sustain a vision of the technofuture as marked by inevitable technological progress, ongoing human evolution, the person as information, the rise of the posthuman, a worldwide network of minds, technological immortality, computers exhibiting human-level intelligence, and human colonization of space. My argument is that these sacred narratives of radical human enhancement constitute an emerging and increasingly influential visionary discourse, a highly consequential rhetoric of the future that is shaping public expectations of technology, policy decisions, research agendas, and ethical debate about the limits of technology.

The following chapter sets out a theory of myth as a rhetorical strategy. Drawing on a variety of experts on the genre of myth, the chapter establishes a framework and a vocabulary of myth that will be applied to particular narratives in subsequent chapters. Chapter Three sets narratives of technological transcendence in a broad historical context by exploring the mythic visions of three noteworthy nineteenth- and twentieth-century futurist thinkers. These writers provided important ideas and strategic language for their rhetorical descendants by crafting early visions of transformative technology, often with a daring and prescient sense of the shape that the technofuturist vision of the future would take.

Chapters Four and Five explore the foundational narratives of progress and evolution, narrative elements crucial to all technofuturist and human-enhancement discourse. Progress and evolution provide the metaphysical groundwork for understanding the kind of cosmos we inhabit.

Chapters Six and Seven redirect us from the background of progress and evolution to the foreground of the enhanced human—the new person who animates the enhancement and Transhumanist vision. Chapter Six examines the crucial narrative turn from the person as biological entity to the person as information, while Chapter Seven takes up myths associated with the enhanced human and the posthuman. As these chapters reveal, technological enhancement is not ultimately a path to improvements in *Homo sapiens*, but a series of steps eventuating in a new species, the posthuman.

Chapters Eight and Nine focus more tightly on mythic narratives that are seldom far from the center of Transhumanist concerns. The first of these are stories surrounding the brain, the essence of the human being in technofuturist discourse. Narratives of the brain and its improvements provide the details of how we will move from ordinary human beings to enhanced persons for whom the unenhanced serve as rudimentary starting points. This chapter also examines the persistent vision of minds directly linked to other minds to create superintelligences of unimaginable capacities. Chapter Nine takes up myths of immortality. Not only is the posthuman a being of vastly superior physical and mental qualities, but these new people will not know death.

Chapters Ten and Eleven move from visions of radical human enhancement to narratives concerning external considerations in the posthuman environment. Chapter Ten takes up myths of artificial intelligence and mechanical imitations of the brain. These stories convey visions of human merger with intelligent machines, and the uploading of human consciousness into computers. The chapter explores how efforts to replicate the brain electronically have also emerged as critically important to the enhancement vision of the human future.

Chapter Eleven traces mythic narratives of space colonization as enhanced humanity's destiny. In this part of the technofuturist vision, distant planets emerge not only as places of residence for future humanity, but also as the locations where human evolution will reach its culmination. In this final chapter the end-point or *telos* of the enhancement vision is realized, progress reaches its completion, and evolution achieves its ultimate goal of extending intelligence to every corner of the universe.

The concluding chapter takes up responses to the Transhuman and enhancement vision as well as leading sources of controversy attending that vision. These include concerns over the growing potential for technological control of life, the possibility of altering human nature, questions of the justice of human enhancement, and the ethics of the person.

The closing section of the conclusion explores the challenge the Transhumanist and enhancement vision poses to its closest parallel vision—that developed in traditional religious systems. The rising rhetoric of transformative technological future directly confronts a series of claims that have, until the present era, resided under the auspices of the monotheistic religions. With the convergence of the visions of technological transcendence into a coherent account of human transformation and the culmination of history, religious leaders and organizations are being presented with perhaps the greatest challenge they have ever faced.

2 MYTH AND RHETORIC

[T]he transcendental and apocalyptic perspective of religion comes as a tremendous emancipation of the imaginative mind.

—Northrop Frye

Does not every science in the end come to a kind of mythology?

—Sigmund Freud

Myth will always be with us, but we must always approach it critically.

—Paul Ricoeur

I am arguing that a network of imaginative narratives envisioning an idealized technological future characterizes technofuturist discourse, particularly that strand associated with human enhancement. These stories, best understood as myths, are just as important to the movements' aspirations as the breathtaking technological breakthroughs that inspire them are. Indeed, propagating visionary futuristic narratives constitutes the principal work of individuals and organizations associated with the broader technofuturist movement. From a rhetorical perspective, this movement's ostensibly scientific agenda rests on a narrative strategy—crafting techno-centric myths that cast a vision of a perfected human existence beyond the biological and earthly. This chapter looks more closely at the concept of *myth,* with particular attention to how this narrative form might function in a contested rhetorical arena—the technological future. The chapter examines the views of several prominent theorists of myth in an effort to understand myth's structure, functions, and rhetorical potential.

Literary scholars, philosophers, anthropologists, and theologians point to our pronounced tendency to develop narratives as a means of ordering and understanding lived experience.[1] In the 1940s Joseph Campbell famously wrote of myth as "the secret opening through which the inexhaustible energies of the cosmos pour into human cultural manifestation."[2] This metaphor of pouring, however, renders human cultures passive recipients of an unaccountable cosmic narrative force. As literary critic Laurence Coupe reminds us, "myth does not arise from nowhere . . ."[3] Some recent assessments have understood myths as goal-directed human productions, albeit with deep evolutionary roots. Jonathan Gottschall argues that in response to existential confusion and metaphysical angst, the "storytelling mind is a crucial evolutionary adaptation. It allows us to experience our lives as coherent, orderly, and meaningful."[4]

It has often been noted that myths construct a cohesive universe, revealing its origin, central figures, and culmination. Gottschall writes that by means of "holy myths," believers "imaginatively construct an alternate reality that stretches from origins straight through to the end times."[5] Narratives locate us in a cosmos and "universally focus on the great predicaments of the human condition."[6] According to one venerable school of thought, when we "must have answers to the big, unanswerable questions," including, "Why am I here?" and "Who made me?" we turn to religious mythology.[7] However, this is only a partial explanation of our persistent tendency to generate "supernatural myths." Gottschall accepts that we also develop sacred stories because they benefit us; we are more cooperative and behave more constructively when we embrace sacred narratives.[8] For theologian Brent Waters, "Myth is *not* merely a sophisticated illusion." Myth "narrates origin and destiny, and explores how evil is overcome by good in between those two states." Thus, a myth "is not a fairy tale or a fable, but rather a narrative interpretation of the human condition—a literary device that encapsulates where hope and trust are placed, in turn aligning desires accordingly."[9]

Prevailing understandings of myth continue to reflect an anthropological orientation. Theologian Don Cupitt writes, for instance, that myth is "typically a traditional sacred story of anonymous authorship and archetypal and universal significance," one that is recurring within a community. Myth is often associated with ritual and "tells a story of superhuman beings," including, "gods, demigods, heroes, spirits or ghosts." Finally, myth "is set outside historical time in primal or eschatological time or in the supernatural world, or may deal with comings and goings between the supernatural world and the world of human history . . ."[10]

While differentiating myth from other narrative genres, such definitions do not convey the rhetorical potency of myth, its adaptability and persuasive force, or even its political necessity in times of crisis. Some observers have emphasized the partisan motives and contingent tendencies that myth may conceal. Literary critic Marina Warner, for instance, remarks that Roland Barthes treatment of myth in *Mythologies* (1957) "reveals how it works to conceal political motives and secretly circulate ideology through society."[11] Warner notes that "myths are not eternal verities, but historical compounds, which successfully conceal their own contingency, changes and transitoriness so that the story they tell looks as if it cannot be told otherwise." Myth's "secret cunning" is its capacity to present things as they must be rather than as contingent and changeable.[12] Paul Ricoeur would add that we return to myth in times of crisis, when we are "threatened with destruction from without or from within." At such stressful junctures, however, myth may assume dangerously "deviant" forms. This deviance is made possible because, as Mircia Eliade argued, "Modern man has lost his awareness of the important role that myth plays in his life. . . ."[13]

In addition to the influence of a persistent anthropological frame, myth has also often been assigned a limited role in public discourse because its connection to argument is little understood. The term *mythos*, however, enjoys a nuanced historical relationship to a related term often associated with rhetoric and the public sphere—*logos*. Laurence Coupe explains that myth "originally meant 'speech' or 'word'," but eventually *mythos* "was separated out from, and deemed inferior to, *logos*." *Mythos* "came to signify fantasy; the latter, rational argument."[14] This distinction does not, however, imply that myth performs a social role subordinate to that of *logos*. Ricoeur contends that at one time *mythos* was "absorbed by the *logos*," but remained a potent force by lending to *logos* "a mythical dimension."[15] While some authorities have identified strategic possibilities in myth, more often has scholarly attention been focused on the genre's ordering, orienting, and guiding functions, capacities typically associated with human nature and social life rather than rhetorical crafting.

Friedrich Nietzsche early on affirmed the role of myth in creating communities. Claude Mangion writes that for Nietzsche, myth is "a form of non-conceptual knowledge" that instinctively "draws an immediate response from individuals bringing them together."[16] Cupitt affirms that creating myths is a "primal and universal function of the human mind" as it searches for comprehensive vision of "the cosmic order, the social order, and the meaning of the individual's life." Thus, for cultures as for individuals, "this story-generating function seems irreplaceable." We discover meaning by crafting and repeating narratives that set our lives "within a larger social and cosmic story."[17] The theologian Waters simply calls myth "a narrative interpretation of the human condition."[18] For religion scholar Karen Armstrong, myth "helped people find their place in the world and their true orientation."[19]

Myth enhances such cosmic cartography and cultural continuity by shaping corporate values. Armstrong writes that myth is our means of assuring ourselves that "life had meaning and value."[20] Scholar of myth Mircia Eliade posits a *"scale of values"* that is communicated "explicitly or implicitly" in any system of myths.[21] Similarly, Eric Dardel has argued that the mythic vision we internalize "illumines every reality, giving it direction and value."[22] Myth "is a way of living in the world, of orienting oneself in the midst of things, of seeking an answer in the quest for the self."[23] Warner writes that "myths convey values and expectations which are always evolving, in the process of being formed . . ."[24]

Such claims reflect an improvement in myth's scholarly reputation in the face of Enlightenment efforts to demythologize western culture.[25] The effort to elevate myth's cultural role—to "rehabilitate" myth—can also be traced to the eighteenth century. Perhaps the first major theorist to assign a myth a central historical role was the philosopher and rhetorician Giambattista Vico (1668–1774). In his *The New Science* (1725) and other works, Vico wrote extensively on myth's work in shaping civilizations.[26] Joseph Mali writes, "Vico's theory of myth has long been recognized by scholars of myth as a major contribution to the modern science of mythology."[27] Nevertheless, Vico's work was largely ignored in his own day and myth was subsequently dismissed by Enlightenment thinkers as a primitive literary form. Such repudiation of myth continued well into the twentieth century. Claude Mangion writes, "For quite some time, as a result of Enlightenment progressive views, myths were disparaged as superstitious and as something that needed to be overcome so as to give way to a 'rationalized' society."[28]

For Vico, however, myth was not a failure of or precursor to reason. Rather, as Coupe writes, myth was for this late-Renaissance rhetorician "an early, necessary and wholly admirable phase in the development of civilization," and the "creative impulse" animating history.[29] Vico's rehabilitating vision of myth also probed the relationship between *logos* and *mythos*, word and story, argument and narrative. His study of ancient mythic systems suggested that myth was not inferior to argument, but its foundation and source—*mythos* grounded *logos*, narrative preceded doctrine. Mali writes that for Vico "the fictions of mythology illumine the 'real world' by constituting or 'prefiguring' all its human actions and institutions. . . ." Historical events reflect patterns that can be known only "insofar as we can recognize in them the coherent narrative patterns" associated with myth.[30]

By presenting *mythos* and *logos* "as different, yet compatible, modes of discourse," Vico elevated myth and challenged prevailing theories "which viewed human history in general as a process of progression from *mythos* to *logos*," and saw history as the inexorable "emancipation of humanity from its 'self-imposed bondage' to myth." *Mythos* and *logos* were not opposed but complimentary and "equivalent" modes of discourse allowing human beings "to make sense of reality" by means of "imaginary tales projected onto reality and the other by empirical theories derived from it." *Logos* reasons from observation; *mythos*, an underlying structure of belief and value, introduces "metaphysical significance."[31]

For Vico, myths—particular stories—carry crucial clues about history and culture for "all our cultural creations . . . are recreations of myths."[32] His study of ancient cultures and their myths revealed that myth was foundational to the formation of the human world itself. According to Mali, Vico claimed to have "discovered this 'truth' in those 'fragments of antiquity'— the ancient myths." By myth our ancestors were able to "create the human world." We carry on this work to the extent that "these myths still persist in our minds and cultures."[33]

Studying mythology was thus crucial to self-knowledge, to grasping the origins of human civilization, and to shaping the world we presently inhabit. Donald Phillip Verene notes Vico's interest in the *vera narratio*, true narration: "The truth of the myth," writes Verene, "is like the truth of perception; it simply forms what is there."[34] In this way myth creates lived reality, human experience being "felt and formed by our power of imagination, or *fantasia*." Through this imaginative power at work in myth "we originally make the human world." Vico differentiates between "imagination (*immaginazione*), understood as the functioning of the mind to organize perceptions into images so that they may become objects of conceptual thought," and *fantasia*—"a power fully and completely to order the world."[35] Myth, operating on perception through the poetic force of *fantasia*, shapes the communities we inhabit.

Vico investigated the human mind and culture employing a "science" of myth. Following the pioneering work of Scottish anthropologist James Georges Frazer, Claude Levi-Strauss (1908–2009) reimagined the work of rehabilitating myth. Frazer demonstrated similarities in mythologies around the world, identifying recurring mythic archetypes. Levi-Strauss reiterated the point in his groundbreaking essay, "The Structural Study of Myth": "Throughout the world myths do resemble one another . . ."[36] Levi-Strauss also argued that the underlying structure or "grammar" of myths revealed the structure of human thought and thus of human experience. Myth was at the core of human language. Indeed, "myth *is* language," for "to be known, myth has to be told; it is a part of human speech."[37]

Myths exhibit a temporal concern, recounting events occurring "before the world was created, or during its first stages—anyway, long ago." Nevertheless, a myth's "operative value" derives from a "specific pattern" embedded within it, the pattern being timeless. Consequently, myth "explains the present and the past as well as the future."[38] Like Vico, Levi-Strauss imagined a science of myth. Focusing on repeated patterns rendered the study of myth scientific, allowing myth to be analyzed into its constituent parts and the interrelationships among them. While the substance of myth lies in "the story which it tells," the "key" to interpretation is not discovered in a myth's narrative content but in its structure.[39] This pattern or "grammar" originates in the human mind itself; thus, "myths get thought in man unbeknownst to him."[40] Moreover, the order the mind seeks through myth may reflect a cosmic order. Hence, the properties that define myth are "only to be found *above* the ordinary linguistic level; that is, they exhibit more complex features beside those which are to be found in any kind of linguistic expression."[41] In sum, for Levi-Strauss, the grammatical structure of myth revealed the structure of the human mind and perhaps the logic of cosmos itself.[42]

Writing in the 1950s, literary critic Northrop Frye (1912–1991) further developed the theory of myth. Frye acknowledged that the prevailing understanding of myth, "its narrower and more technical sense," treated the genre as principally "fictions and themes relating to divine or quasi-divine beings and powers."[43] Myth, he argued, exhibits an ironic tension between timeless and inviolable forces, and temporal conditions of violation. The archetype of myth's double-nature is Adam—inexorable human nature "under sentence of death."[44] Into this narrative contradiction steps the tragic hero who challenges gods and nature, lifting human beings heavenward by his sacrifice. Thus was Prometheus, "the immortal titan rejected by the gods for befriending men."[45] On this view, myth does more than orient us to the cosmos; it also performs the rhetorical work of humanizing transcendent ideas for audiences, rendering dreams of ascent "acceptable to a social waking consciousness."[46]

Particular mythic structures are critically important to myth's humanizing work. Apocalypse is a central function of myth for Frye, not as grand culmination but as "the imaginative conception of the whole of nature as the content of an infinite and eternal living body. . . ."[47] Mythic nature is animated and infused with magic through ritual, an "effort to recapture a lost rapport with the natural cycle." Myth and ritual tame brute nature, bringing it under human narrative control. Through apocalypse, "stupid and indifferent nature is no longer the container of human society, but is contained by that society, and must rain or shine at the pleasure of man. . . ."[48] Out of such an ordered mythic frame emerges "the god" that conveys "the sense of unlimited power in a humanized form."[49] In this way myths generate a comprehensive worldview, "the total body of imaginative hypothesis in a society and its tradition."[50] Myth envisions alternative worlds, thus shaping its transcendent vision and propagating "the imaginative anticipation of the not yet." Always "just ahead," apocalypse is "ready to suffuse the present with its power." The apocalyptic vision "promises a new cosmos out of catastrophe."[51]

Rich with apocalyptic anticipation, myth also suggests a "point of epiphany," the moment at which the transcendent world and the world of nature "come into alignment." Armstrong affirms that "all mythology speaks of another plane that exists alongside our own world, and in some sense supports it."[52] For Frye, epiphany is physically located: "its most common settings are the mountain-top, the island, the tower, the lighthouse, and the ladder or staircase."[53] Frye also writes of "an epiphany of law," referring to "that which is and must be."[54] Epiphany points to myth's sacred nature as narrative that bridges the world of people and the infinite realm of the divine.

Other analyses have also added a rhetorical dimension to earlier discoveries regarding myth's structure and effects. Ricoeur insisted that we must no longer limit myth to "false explanation;" it is imperative to recognize its "exploratory significance and its contribution to understanding." Myth is ubiquitous, the backdrop to all other forms of understanding. It lies "behind speculation" and "beneath gnostic and anti-gnostic constructions. . . ." Myth is our means of "discovering and revealing the bond between man and that which he considers sacred." The genre possesses a "symbolic function" and a "power of discovery and revelation." In an era in which myth and history have been separated, myth remains "a stimulus to speculation" and thus "dimension of modern thought."[55] Myths, like poetry, "constitute a disclosure of unprecedented worlds, an opening on to other *possible* worlds which transcend the established limits of our *actual* world."[56]

Philosopher of science Mary Midgley has more recently written of "the crucial importance" of myth and symbolism "in all our thought. . . ."[57] Myths, she writes, form "our imaginative visions" that in turn become "central to our understanding of the world." Thus, far from being "a distraction from our serious thinking," they are "a necessary part of it."[58] Midgley has been particularly interested in the strategic role that myths play in scientific disputes.[59] One pervasive rhetorical maneuver involves aligning speculative claims with a widely adopted scientific narrative (e.g., the narrative of evolution). "Many of the visions that now dominate our controversies are ones which look as if they were based on science, but are really fed by fantasy," she writes. In this way "a variety of doctrines on all sorts of subjects have used scientific imagery to gain the authority which rightly belongs to science proper." Midgley adds, "because they sound technical, people receive their symbolic message as literal truth."[60] As a result, the paradigmatic modern myths "that actually shape our thoughts and actions owe their force to having appeared in scientific dress."[61] Warner has also observed that myths can have a "binding grip on our imagination," perhaps especially, Midgley contends, when clothed in scientific attire.[62]

Vico held that myth introduced metaphysical significance; Midgley adds that metaphysical assumptions deriving from epic narratives permeate the "ongoing dramas inside which we live our lives."[63] Our preferred narratives are not "just a distraction from real thought;" rather, they constitute "the matrix of thought, the background that shapes our mental habits."[64] Myth conveys imaginative patterns that shape expectations of science and the interpretations of facts. As a growing array of facts becomes "more and more confusing," our demand for narrative's "principles of organization" grows.[65] Myth's work is not limited to bridging the contingent world of sense impression and the transcendent realm of inviolable forces. Myths provide templates for prioritizing and interpreting data, that is, a means of understanding experience. While we may choose the myths we employ for understanding the physical world, "we do not have a choice of understanding it without using any myths or visions at all."[66] Midgley's concern for myth as pattern is reflected in Ricoeur's formula, "The symbol gives rise to thought."[67]

Midgley points to myth's rhetorical potential as a guide to ordering evidence and determining action; in her treatment, myth takes on the qualities of an argument. Kenneth Burke (1897-1993) also recognized a rhetorical force in myth, one that existed despite accounts of the myth's source or original purpose. He cautioned readers about myth's potential for rhetorical excess. Thus, it is a "good idea when dealing with a myth to consider what it is 'doing' as well as what it is 'saying,'" and to keep in view "the pragmatic impulse which would have occasioned it in the first place."[68] Burke wrote in 1935 that "myths may be wrong, or they may be used to bad ends—but they cannot be dispensed with;" they constitute "our basic psychological tools for working together." Just as "a hammer is a carpenter's tool; a wrench is a mechanic's tool," myth is "the social tool for welding the sense of interrelationship . . ." Far from being "illusions," myths "perform a very real and necessary social function in the organizing of the mind."[69]

Beyond the creation of templates and patterns, myths also convey aspirations, cast visions, and unify a chaotic cosmos. Such envisioned unity may, however, come at a high cost. While our "spirit of hierarchy" drives us to "make narrative sense of the world," we may in the process "imagine an unattainable perfection."[70] Quest myths, for example, reflect a yearning for "totality, for completeness, for perfection."[71] While myth arises in the imperfect human present it conjures the "logic of 'perfectionism,'" and an "extreme adherence to an 'ideal order' is totalitarian."[72] A misdirected search for perfection is not the only potential risk of myth. Coupe notes that positing an "independent and self-validating truth" that occupies a realm "beyond the temporal process of myth-making" also carries risk. Myth ought not to foreclose on mystery by capitulating to an excessive realism in the form of "some ultimate and absolute essence. . . ."[73]

Finally, risk may attend *denying* the presence of myth. A secular society that has abandoned its hope in the mystical arena should not for that reason be considered as having abandoned the essential elements of religion. These elements survive the demise of traditional myth in new forms, forms that Ricoeur cautioned may become "deviant."[74] Coupe cites Gianni Vattimo to the effect that secularization "does not consist solely in the exposure or demystification of the errors of religion, but also in the survival of these 'errors' in different, and in some sense degraded, forms." As a result, a secular society "is not one that has simply left the religious elements of its tradition behind, but one that continues to live them as traces, as hidden and distorted models that are nonetheless profoundly present."[75] Hidden and distorted, these isolated and yet surviving elements of once vital myths require careful critical scrutiny.

The Rhetoric of Myth

We began this chapter with a question about the rhetorical potential of myth. I would like to draw together several strands of the discussion into a tentative sketch of a rhetoric of myth—an understanding of the genre as potentially strategic, persuasive, and capable of adapting ideas to audiences.

First, myth appeals to audiences in its capacity to draw order and meaning out of the inchoate impressions of lived experience. In Burke's term, *myth* "names" or sums up a situation. This act of linguistic magic is tactical, drawing attention to one order or cosmos while deflecting attention from other contenders.[76] Gottschall notes that narrative "allows us to experience our lives as coherent, orderly, and meaningful," an inherently appealing prospect.[77] Story situates us in the cosmos and allows us to address the "predicaments of the human condition."[78] Eliade and others have noted myth's capacity to create a sense of order and harmony; we might add, however, that myth as strategic production brings a *particular* significance and a *specific* order and harmony.

Second, we can note myth's capacity to express corporate value and thus render possible a cohesive social identity. Warner underscores myth's publicity in writing that "a myth is a kind of story told in public. . . ."[79] Myth performs this task of social cohesion in constructive and cautionary modes.

Constructively, Vico noted myth's capacity to shape civilization and create the human world; myth was the imaginative engine driving human history and anticipating all "human actions and institutions."[80] By this rhetorical act of narrative myth was the human world created. In its cautionary mode, myth defines dangers and in this way also calls the community to unified life and belief. Myth conveys "values and expectations."[81] Myth also delineates community by identifying "enemies and aliens."[82] This work of defining what belongs and what is excluded also reflects rhetorical intent. For the rhetorician Vico, myth performed these culture-shaping tasks by engaging the "poetic logic" of *fantasia*, "a power fully and completely to order the world."[83]

Third, Frye noted that myth does the rhetorical work of adjusting transcendent ideas to human audiences, rendering dreams "plausible" and in this way "acceptable to a social waking consciousness."[84] In this function, myth is more than its structure and content; it is formidable narrative persuasion that renders social cooperation possible. Burke noted that a myth "is the social tool for welding the sense of interrelationship" by means of which people "differently occupied, can work together for common social ends." Myths thus, "perform a very real and necessary social function in the organizing of the mind."[85]

Fourth, myth's rhetorical force is revealed in its capacity to cast a compelling transcendent vision. Myth's imaginative schemes create alternative worlds and align the mundane realm with a higher order of things. Ricoeur noted this convincing characteristic when he wrote of myth as "'a disclosure of unprecedented worlds, an opening on to other *possible* worlds which transcend the established limits of our *actual* world.'"[86] Mangion notes that for Nietzsche as well, myths "have the power to reveal alternative possibilities;" they open a space for the "disclosure of possible worlds."[87]

Frye labels this world-revealing quality "apocalypse," a feature of myth that envisions "the whole of nature" as an "infinite and eternal living body. . . ."[88] Apocalypse humanizes "stupid and indifferent nature" so that it is "no longer the container of human society, but is contained by that society, and must rain or shine at the pleasure of man. . ."[89] Myth's apocalyptic vision promises, according to Coupe, "another mode of existence entirely, to be realized just beyond the present time and place."[90] Apocalypse renders myth rhetorically tantalizing, for "the apocalyptic moment is always just ahead, ready to suffuse the present with its power." Apocalypse promises universal transformation: a new cosmos out of catastrophe.

Myth also imagines a "point of epiphany," a moment of revelation when a transcendent world and the world of nature "come into alignment." Epiphany bridges and reconciles disparate and apparently contradictory realms—

heaven and earth, time and eternity, and the present and the future. Epiphany is located in places such as "the mountain-top, the island, the tower, the lighthouse, and the ladder or staircase."[91] These metaphors bridge the mundane and heavenly realms. However, Frye also writes of "an epiphany of law, of that which is and must be."[92] The "law" of evolution may provide an example of what must be, or the law-like way we often understand progress. The Law of Moses bridged the heavenly and earthly realms. Epiphany points to myth's sacred nature, bridging the gap between the world of people and the infinite realm of the divine.

Finally, myth shapes rationality, both generally and specifically. Midgley affirms "the crucial importance" of myth and symbolism "in all our thought," not just our thought about origins, culminations, and redemption.[93] She finds myth central even to scientific rhetoric, but her general observation holds for other types of symbolic action as well: mythic narratives exert a powerful influence over the whole range of human cognitive activity. Myths are for Midgley paradigmatic; they provide "the matrix of thought, the background that shapes our mental habits." The "imaginative patterns" characterizing these narratives shape the conclusions we will derive from an exponentially increasing storehouse of data.

Despite the long and determined effort to demythologize Western discourse, Midgley contends that we will rely heavily on myth for organizing templates to guide our journey into a new age.[94] The rapid accumulation of data, now vaster than traditional approaches can adequately address, will drive us inexorably toward principles of interpretation embedded in our guiding narratives. Midgley reminds us, as Burke did earlier, that we may choose our myths, but "we do not have a choice of understanding [the world we inhabit] without using any myths or visions at all."[95] The necessity of myth, however, suggests that myth comes with risks.

In sum, a myth is a public narrative—and as such, "a linguistic construct"—that seeks to account for the relationship of two realms or worlds, and that, in the process, invokes forces beyond the natural and human, toward the end of establishing an orderly cosmos and defining humanity's place in it.[96] Myths imply principles of order, create communities of adherence, align disparate realms, cast a vision of utopia or perfection, and suggest the nature of thought and action that are aligned with transcendent purpose. As a rhetorical strategy myth is deployed to envision for an audience a comprehensive order—a *cosmos*—and with that vision a glimpse of an ideal future for which the imperfect present is a preparatory stage. Myth renders a particular cosmic organization plausible and desirable by means of rhetorical operations such as epiphany and apocalypse. As a type of narrative argument, myth thus warrants particular actions in keeping with the vision of order and precludes actions that do not contribute to the envisioned future state.

Ethical concerns emerge, however, when a particular mythology burdens a community with an inviolable, self-validating revelation of perfection. An inexorable vision is ripe for abuse when it demands a dominant place in the political, social, and scientific arenas. Such exclusive myths displace competing or potentially corrective stories, disallowing serious critical examination because the forces and ends the vision describes transcend merely human and historical considerations. The vision reveals something higher than present mundane concerns, and it is not to be interrogated. Burke argues that our "spirit of hierarchy" drives our quest to make sense of our world. However, this same spirit may cause to pursue a perfection that is always just beyond our reach. In the political and social realms, such an insistent perfectionism may have serious and damaging consequences.

Subsequent chapters examine a set of visionary myths associated with the human enhancement and Transhumanist movements. Employing a paradigm that allows myth a rhetorical role we will seek to understand the sources, content, and implications of these narratives as discursive strategies with profound social, political, and even spiritual significance. We will also seek to assess the ethical implications of these stories where appropriate. All myths develop in response to a social and historical situation. The following chapter considers efforts to develop a mythology of science and technology in the works of three major authors whose visions shaped the visions of technological transcendence discussed in later chapters.

3 ENVISIONING THE TECHNOFUTURE: ANTECEDENTS

What makes science into something much grander and more inter-esting . . . is the huge, ever-changing imaginative structure of ideas by which scientists contrive to connect, understand and interpret these facts.

—Mary Midgley

[I]t is not the physical world that determines the evolution of ideas, but rather ideas that generate scientific and technologi-cal development.

—Jean-Pierre Dupuy

[T]ragic heroes are wrapped in the mystery of their communion with that something beyond which we can see only through them, and which is the source of their strength and their fate alike.

—Northrop Frye

Journalist Joel Garreau is convinced that enhancement is coming and that it is largely a good thing. Rather than seeing science as encroaching on religion's territory, however, he has suggested that spiritual symbols should be crafted around enhancement procedures. "Perhaps it is in our de-votions that we can start choosing to steer. Right now the stories we tell do not match the facts." Garreau asks, "[S]hould we start marking these rites of passage as an important part of the future of human nature?"[1] In Garreau's view, enhancement rituals would allow us to gracefully cross thresholds into new arenas:

> Can we picture devotions marking the great significance of a young person receiving her first cognition piercing, awakening her mind to the Web of all meaning? What about a right of maturity in which someone is formally recognized as knowing enough worth keeping that the larger society marks the occasion of his well-deserved first memory upgrade? Should we have a liturgy of life everlasting as a person receives her first cellular age-reversal workup?

Rituals of enhancement could convey "important aspects of story":

> They could say, "Never forget who you were; always respect what you've become. You are part of us, no matter how far you roam." They could include a formal admonition to use these powers only for good. They could include the observation that we may be playing for the highest stakes.

Rituals embodying sacred transcendence might prevent us from misusing our tools, an insight that may have escaped alien civilizations. "We cannot detect any other intelligences in the universe. Maybe that's because every other species in the cosmos has flunked this transcendence test horribly, leaving no trace behind."[2] Other rituals might develop into "celebrations of transformation where people cross barriers—barriers of class, gender, region, race, and religion."[3]

The work of imagining a comprehensive technological culture actually began well before what might be deemed the dawn of the technological age. Leading technofuturist themes are clearly evident in Francis Bacon's *New Atlantis* (1627). While Bacon's prophetic vision is remarkable in its seventeenth-century context, the imaginative patterns of a technofuturist *mythos* emerge with regularity and in striking detail in the late nineteenth and early twentieth centuries. In casting their particular mythic vision of the future, contemporary Transhumanists and enhancement advocates often adapt themes that have been in place for more than a century.

The following chapters consider historical antecedents for the narratives each explores; some early visions of the technofuture, however, merit consideration here due to their remarkable influence on ensuing technological narratives. Moreover, when considered together these innovative visions establish an intellectual, social, and narrative context for the more focused analyses to follow. In an effort to create an intellectual frame for apprehending subsequent assessments, this chapter explores three highly influential anticipatory efforts to craft a vision of the technological future.

The chapter begins by considering the work of a visionary thinker active at the end of the nineteenth century in Russia. Russian Cosmism's founder Nikolai Fedorov anticipated many of the tenets that now characterize enhancement and technofuturist discourse. We will then take up the metaphysical futurism of the Jesuit paleontologist, Teilhard de Chardin , whose vision of the technological world to come paralleled and was at points influenced by the Cosmists. A third case study in early efforts at crafting a rhetoric of the future focuses on the remarkable vision of British scientist and science-fiction writer, Sir Arthur C. Clarke . This review of the work of the Cosmists, Teilhard and Clarke suggests that contemporary narratives of technological transcendence can claim both religious and secular roots. The chapter concludes by comparing the central ideas of these three writers with leading themes in the developing technofuturist mythology.

NIKOLAI FEDOROV AND THE COSMIST VISION

A narrative of evolving humanity harnessing the occult powers of nature animates the work of Russian liberal political theorist Alexander Nikolaevich Radishchev, writing in the late eighteenth century (1749–1802). His 1792 work, *Man, His Mortality and Immortality*, envisions human beings progressing by "wondrous, splendid, gradual increments" like those that "led up to" present humans.[4] "This," he writes, "more than anything else, is man's distinguishing quality: he can perfect himself; and he can also become depraved. The limit in either direction is still unknown."[5] Radishchev's cultural vision inspired modern Russian political and social thought, establishing imaginative patterns that would inform remarkable developments in nineteenth-century Russian futurism.

Philosopher and librarian Nikolai Fedorov (1828--1903), acquaintance of Tolstoy and major influence on Dostoevsky, Pasternak, and Gorki, was the central figure in the intellectual movement that has come to be known as Russian Cosmism. Fedorov is best remembered for his dramatic proposal that the Common Task of enlightened humanity was the technological resurrection of the entire human race.[6] Though not widely known outside of Russia, Fedorov has been called "without a doubt the most formidable Russian thinker of the nineteenth century."[7] A dedicated futurist who claimed spiritual inspiration, Fedorov speculated about immortality, space exploration, colonizing the oceans and mental eugenics. Borrowing heavily from the Christian *mythos*, Fedorov and his followers envisioned physically and morally perfected immortal humans who would populate and transform the universe.

Historian Michael Hagemeister describes Russian Cosmism as "a broad intellectual movement in contemporary Russia which has scarcely been noticed in the West."[8] Cosmism flourished from around 1870 through the 1920s; it has recently been rediscovered and its influence reassessed. The movement was founded on Federov's "holistic and anthropocentric view of the universe." Following what Federov saw as the demise of religion, Cosmists sought "to redefine the role of humankind in a universe that lacks a divine plan of salvation. . . ."[9] In the Cosmist myth humanity is placed in the universe as the "decisive factor in cosmic evolution, a collective cosmic self-consciousness, active agent, and potential perfector." The cosmos is "dependent on human action to reach its goal, which is perfection, or wholeness."

In the Federovian apocalypse, scientifically enlightened individuals purposefully apply technology to the task of delivering the human race and the world from destruction. Humanity plays a messianic role in this sacred story: "By failing to act, or failing to act correctly, humankind dooms the world to catastrophe."[10] Shrinking back from technology's radical application to human progress constitutes an immoral act, a rebellion against humanity's appointed purpose—the spiritual transformation of the cosmos.

Cosmists set out a progressive scheme in which "the world is in a phase of transition from the 'biosphere' (the sphere of living matter) to the 'noosphere' (the sphere of reason)."[11] By means of the inviolable principle of evolution, intentionally assisted by progressive vision and applied technology, a unified world consciousness emerges and a new era of divine order begins. At the center of Fedorov's epiphany—his vision aligning past and future—was the human race's moral and intellectual evolution; everything hinged on the emergence of "humanity." Stephen Lukashevich writes that the heart of Fedorov's ideology was his "psychological theory of the evolution of man's humanity."[12] This essential and inevitable process would be hastened by a program of psychoeugenics—selective breeding adapted to developing human intellect.

Space colonization also represented a major component in the Cosmist agenda, an inevitable step in the progress of humanity toward the deathless perfection of universal resurrection. In Federov's sweeping interplanetary *mythos*, earth is transformed into a massive spaceship designed to transport crusading humans to the ends of the universe to accomplish the work of cosmic transformation. Lukashevich writes, "For this purpose, mankind must avail itself directly or indirectly of the electromagnetic forces of the earth for the transformation of the latter into a spaceship. . . ."[13] A resurrected human race is destined to inhabit every planet, thus humanizing and rationalizing all matter and in this way bringing living spiritual cosmos out of lifeless material chaos.

Universal technological resurrection preoccupied Federov. Humans, by nature weaker than other animals, had always survived and advanced by their greater ingenuity. George M. Young writes that the master Cosmist's "great theme was immanent universal resurrection, the full and literal restoration of the dead to life, a task or 'project' to be accomplished by human ingenuity and effort. According to Fedorov, universal resurrection is not merely a scientific possibility, it is a moral duty." Young adds:

> Parts of Fedorov's project that were most ridiculed during his own day include his calls for space travel, genetic engineering, and gradual prolongation of human life and health until eventually universal immortality is achieved—a most literal version of the age-old dream of restoring paradise on earth.[14]

Also revealing of Cosmist aspirations is Fedorov's belief that "human effort, properly directed, will actually replace the currently visible reality with the one currently hidden. And everyone will participate in the replacement." This mythic replacement of the present world with a grander reality to come requires re-animating ancestors, an activity in which all living human beings would participate. Religion and science merging as the great and final resurrection provides the ultimate testimony to religious prophecy and scientific power. Young writes, "Those who are now utterly unaware of even the possibility of a higher reality will become aware not by intellectual persuasion but by actual hands-on experience in resurrecting their ancestors."[15]

Resurrection, a remarkable achievement, is but a single step in human progress. In the Cosmist *mythos*, humanity evolves into "a collective cosmic self-consciousness," our ultimate "perfection, or wholeness." As *mythos* gives way to *logos*, human physical and spiritual advancement becomes a moral obligation with pragmatic implications. A "planetarian consciousness" will emerge; the work of "changing and perfecting the universe, overcoming disease and death" will continue until "finally bringing forth an immortal human race."[16]

These are not solely technological goals; each represents the outworking of hidden principles. Hagemeister notes that Cosmism's "belief in the omnipotence of science and technology is rooted in the idea of the magic power of (occult) knowledge." He adds, "The idea of self-perfection and self-deification, including the realization of immortality and the revival of the dead, has a long occult and Gnostic tradition."[17] The Cosmist *mythos* was rooted in earlier mythic systems, re-invigorated by a vision of limitless technological power.

Fedorov's mythic vision influenced early Russian space exploration proponents, including famed rocket pioneer Konstantin Tsiolkovsky (1857–1935).

Tsiolkovsky wrote influential fiction and non-fiction works portraying humanity in space. His *The Exploration of Cosmic Space by Means of Reactive Devices* (1896) is the first serious effort to present a complete scientific account of space flight and even of space craft. Tsiolkovsky took the additional step of linking immortality and space exploration—the universe is alive with "animated atoms" that will assist in the Common Work.

Other prominent Cosmists include Vladimir Vernadsky (1863–1945), probably the first writer to suggest the noosphere, though the credit for the term itself usually goes to Teilhard de Chardin.[18] Vernadsky imagined linking all minds on earth to create an evolving god-like intelligence. Some Cosmists also "shared the Gnostics' view of the earth as a prison, but believed they could harness cosmic forces and energies to end the earthly captivity and overcome death."[19] Here, again, we encounter the Cosmist linking of space and immortality.

Fedorov acknowledged that his "ideology was essentially a scientific exegesis of Christian theology," according to Lukashevich.[20] Transforming the physical world by rationalizing matter fulfilled Christian prophecy. Each individual is "able, indeed obliged, to work to transform everything natural (and therefore transitory) including himself into an intransitory synthetic creation of reason." By rationalization, the chaotic physical universe becomes an ordered and perfected cosmos. Human conquest of space extended this ordering work; "upon humans' actions depends not only their own deliverance but also the salvation and perfection of the entire universe."[21]

Transhumanist and artificial intelligence specialist Ben Goertzel has retrieved the language and philosophy of nineteenth-century Cosmism, refashioning it to contemporary rhetorical ends. Cosmism, he writes,

> . . . provides a world-view and value-system that makes sense in the human world now, and will continue to make sense as the practical world advances, even as some of us leave our human bodies and brains behind and explore new ways of existing and interacting.

Transformative technologies bring with them "profound philosophical implications," many of which the Cosmists anticipated. Understanding how technology will change us requires "taking a deep look at the nature of the mind and the universe." The human race itself will have to be re-imagined; Cosmist *mythos* grounds a new *logos* of the human. Thus, the coming noosphere, imagined by the Cosmist Vernadsky, requires rethinking "the nature of mind and society in a way that goes beyond the models we conventionally use."[22]

Leading Cosmist figures wrote before the advent of genetic engineering, nanotechnology, artificial intelligence, or space flight—technologies necessary to the future they imagined. Theirs was a narrative task, a rhetorical work of strategic envisioning, of crafting a *mythos* capable of aligning their proto-technological world with an advanced technological future. Cosmist rhetoric of the future continues to exert an extraordinary shaping influence on technofuturist discourse.

TEILHARD DE CHARDIN AND COSMIC *TELOS*

The vision of a technologically transformed human race was further developed by French paleontologist, geologist and Jesuit priest, Teilhard de Chardin (1881-1955).[23] Always controversial and often misunderstood, Teilhard is among the twentieth century's great synthesizers of science and religion. His ideas were deemed unorthodox by the Catholic Church, particularly his understanding of original sin as cosmic chaos. Consequently, several of his works written in the 1920s and 1930s were not published until after his death in the mid 1950s.

Henri Bergson's *Creative Evolution* (1907)—a work that treats evolution's metaphysical implications—shaped Teilhard's thought more profoundly than did Darwin himself. While pursuing field work in China, Teilhard developed a theory of evolution toward spirit that he applied to the entire material realm. In books such as *The Future of Man* (1950) and *The Phenomenon of Man* (1955), Teilhard crafted his *mythos* around a grand, unifying principle: out of chaos evolution is driving all matter inexorably toward the orderly state of cosmic consciousness. Teilhard famously labeled his apocalypse Omega Point, the arrival of the Cosmic Christ.

In Teilhard's vision evolution constituted the universe's central operative force, "a general condition to which all other theories, all hypotheses, all systems must bow and which they must satisfy henceforward if they are to be thinkable and true." Evolution is epiphany, the aligning of material and spiritual worlds, "a light illuminating all facts, a curve that all lines must follow." By evolution the universe progresses from inert physicality into living self-awareness. This is Cosmogenesis, Teilhard's apocalyptic vision of matter's evolution toward pure consciousness, the entire universe coming to constitute one "infinite and eternal living body," in Frye's terms.[24]

Matter embodies restless energy, inherent intelligence seeking higher levels of organization; the physical seeks complexity and ever-ascending orders of cosmic being. Teilhard posited a Law of Complexity/Consciousness: each new and more complex network of order breaks forth from the previous network or "envelope." Thus, the interconnected envelope of biological life on earth—the biosphere—is giving way to an envelope of interconnected mentality—the noosphere. In this emergent anagogic reality human mentality "becomes the container of nature."[25]

The noosphere is an intentional technological accomplishment, not an emergent evolutionary event; it is also a purposeful step toward pure cosmic consciousness and thus toward immortality. Death is overcome by technologically expanding consciousness. Teilhard writes,

> The radical defect in all forms of belief in progress, as they are expressed in positivist credos is that they do not definitely eliminate death. What is the use of detecting a focus of any sort in the van of evolution if that focus must one day disintegrate?[26]

Humans play a crucial role in Cosmogenesis—our technologies enable greater contact of minds around the globe, the beginning of universal consciousness. According to the narrative, out of such interconnectedness emerges a global envelope of thought. Teilhard imagined a "harmonized collectivity of consciousnesses equivalent to a sort of super-consciousness." Individual consciousnesses are converging, joining force:

> The idea is that of the Earth not only becoming covered by myriads of grains of thought, but becoming enclosed in a single thinking envelope so as to form, functionally, no more than a single vast grain of thought on the sidereal scale, the plurality of individual reflections grouping themselves together and reinforcing one another in the act of a single unanimous reflection.[27]

The noosphere—described by Vernadsky in a series of Paris lectures Teilhard attended in 1924—became central to the Teilhardian vision. The noosphere does not arise of its own accord, however; there are rhetorical preconditions to be considered. Believers must propagate a global mentality supportive of aggressive technological research. Realizing this vision will require a "common philosophy on which all men of goodwill can agree in order that the world may continue to progress." The *mythos* of noosphere precedes and informs the *logos* of a worldwide philosophy — a new religion founded on the great fact of evolution arising out of "a core of universal truth" and embraced "by everyone." Teilhard asks, "Can there be any true spiritual evolution without it?"[28]

Teilhard's apocalyptic cosmogenic vision aligns the biological, mechanical and spiritual worlds; progressive evolution will involve human integration with machines and moral eugenics. "How can we fail to see the machine as playing a constructive part in the creation of a truly collective consciousness?"[29] Augmented evolution will hasten the arrival of a spiritually perfected human race. "So far we have certainly allowed our race to develop at random," and "given too little thought to the question of what medical and moral factors must replace the crude forces of natural selection should we suppress them." However, in "the coming centuries" it will become "indispensable that a nobly human form of eugenics" be pursued "on a standard worthy of our personalities." Technologies of biological and moral evolution will shape individuals as well as society.[30]

SIR ARTHUR C. CLARKE AND THE AGE OF MACHINES

Scientist and writer Sir Arthur C. Clarke (1917-2008) is among the most respected and influential authors of science fiction, his creative career spanning more than five decades. Clarke's earliest stories such as *Against the Fall of Night* (1948), *The Sentinel* (1951), and *Childhood's End* (1953) set a high standard of scientific integrity and solid story-telling for the science fiction genre. Clarke is best known today, however, for an epoch-making screenplay he developed with director Stanley Kubric for the movie, *2001: A Space Odyssey* (1968), considered by many critics to be among the best movies ever made.

A remarkable work of non-fiction draws our attention in this chapter, however. Clarke's *Profiles of the Future* (1962) anticipated many features of the contemporary technofuturist narrative. Clarke advances a stunning vision of a technological culture, rendering *Profiles of the Future* an outworking of Vico's *fantasia*—the imaginative capacity to envision the human world. Clarke's book began as a series of popular magazine essays written between 1959 and 1961, later collected and published together. Unlike Fedorov and Teilhard, Clarke was not recasting elements of the Christian *mythos*, which he repudiated. *Profiles of the Future* can be read as a series of predictions about *technological* developments likely to occur in the second half of the twentieth century.[31] However, the book is better understood as a relatively early and highly sophisticated materialist myth of the technologically transformed future.

Clarke's narrative opens outward into a prophetic vision of a new humanity and a new world. We will travel the world in space-planes, but more importantly we will become less reliant on physical bodies.[32] Clarke's claim that death "does not appear to be biologically inevitable" hints at a mythic vision of a new humanity harnessing technology to direct its eternal destiny.[33] Clarke has metaphysical questions in mind in his vision of a perfected future; immortality may be achieved by means of replacement bodies, and "the replacement need not be another body of flesh and blood; it could be a machine, and this may represent the next stage in evolution."[34] Ethical conundrums may arise out of technological advances. For instance, immortal machine bodies might provoke social divisions:

> One can imagine a time when men who still inhabit organic bodies are regarded with pity by those who have passed on to an infinitely richer mode of existence, capable of throwing their consciousness or sphere of attention instantaneously to any point on land, sea, or sky where there is a suitable sensing organ.[35]

So searching are his insights that there is hardly an aspiration of technofuturist discourse that Clarke's futuristic *mythos* did not anticipate, many only vaguely imagined as he wrote. A particularly striking example is his paradigm-shifting suggestion that human consciousness in the computer age would be reclassified as information, and thus as capable of being uploaded and stored by various means. "A human being, like any other object, is defined by its structure—its pattern. The pattern of a man is incredibly complex; yet Nature was once able to pack that pattern into a tiny cell, too small for the eye to see." As information, the person might be stored or even replicated electronically in a machine or other format.[36]

Clarke's vision of the informational person had appeared in his storytelling since the 1950s. For instance, in *The City and the Stars* (1956) he wrote:

> The way in which information is stored is of no importance; all that matters is the information itself. It may be in the form of written words on paper, of varying magnetic fields, or patterns of electric charge. . . . Suffice it to say that long ago they [humans] were able to store themselves—or, to be more precise, the disembodied patters from which they could be called back into existence. . . . This is the way our ancestors gave us virtual immortality, yet avoided the problems raised by the abolition of death.[37]

In Mary Midgley's terms, Clarke's future myth was providing new imaginative patterns, a new matrix for thinking about the human that suggested a range of otherwise unimaginable possibilities.

Clarke, like Teilhard, also recognized the centrality of evolution to visions of the technological future, and he grasped the complementary idea that humans would employ technology to direct their evolution. However, Clarke was not a religious visionary and was not seeking redemption through either a divine human or a Cosmic Christ. He foresaw real risks in his narrative of a comprehensive technological revolution. Principal among these was the fear that intelligent machines might bring an end to the human era:

> The tools the ape-men invented caused them to evolve into their successor, Homo sapiens. The tool we have invented *is* our successor. Biological evolution has given way to a far more rapid process—

technological evolution. To put it bluntly and brutally, the machine is going to take over.[38]

Clarke's interest in space exploration is, of course, well known from his many novels and his collaboration with Stanley Kubrick on the movie, *2001: A Space Odyssey*. Space was for Clarke a catalyst to technological evolution: "The greatest single stimulus to the evolution of mechanical—as opposed to organic—intelligence is the challenge of space."[39] Human intellectual development requires the challenge of space exploration. "It may well be that only in space, confronted with environments fiercer and more complex than any to be found upon this planet, will intelligence be able to reach its fullest stature." Again, ethical issues plague the greatest advances. Perhaps geniuses will leave for space, abandoning the less talented on the old earth. "Like other qualities, intelligence is developed by struggle and conflict; in the ages to come, the dullards may remain on placid Earth, and real genius will flourish only in space—the realm of the machine, not of flesh and blood."[40]

In the Clarke *mythos* humans are evolving toward a mechanical existence—a process begun by merging with our machines. Eventually extracting ourselves from our physical bodies, we will become pure consciousness that is "free to roam at will from machine to machine, through all the reaches of sea and sky and space."[41] In this anagogic apocalypse, humans no longer exist in nature but subsume it and cause it to bend to their will. Frye notes that in an anagogic *mythos* nature no longer "is the container of man," but human beings become "the container of nature. . . ." Such visions reveal "the forms of a human universe."[42]

Despite some of his own concerns Clarke reassured readers that they "have nothing to regret, and certainly nothing to fear" in such a future; the loss of the traditional human being—embodied, mortal, finite—should not be lamented.[43] Nietzsche predicted our transitional role: "Man, said Nietzsche, is a rope stretched between the animal and the superhuman—a rope across the abyss. That will be a noble purpose to have served." Rehearsing themes found in Teilhard, Clarke affirms that current humans "represent only a very early stage in the story of evolution, destined to pass away leaving little mark on the universe."[44]

Clarke also imagined that the future will bring "the possibility of contacting extraterrestrial intelligences by radio or laser (coherent light) beams." Moreover, "given sufficient time, rational beings might attain the power to manipulate not merely planets, not merely stars, but the galaxies themselves."[45] Contact with cosmic divinities and divine power awaits the human race in the technological future. Sir Arthur C. Clarke's future myth envisioned boundless human progress toward a disembodied and omnipotent perfection.

CONCLUSION

While other futuristic texts and thinkers of the late nineteenth and early twentieth centuries might have been selected for analysis, the three considered here have exerted particularly strong influence on subsequent techno-futurist thought. From this exploration we can identify several durable elements of a *mythos* of the technological future, in particular immortality, progressive evolution leading to moral and physical perfection, and space colonization.

For the Cosmist Fedorov, "The purpose of man is to be free: that is, to be self-created, for only a self-created being can be truly free."[46] Stephen Lukashevich writes that, "perceived as a whole, Fedorov's ideology represents a magnificent poetical saga of the evolution of mankind . . ."[47] Fedorov emphasized the development of humankind's "humanity." When this quality had achieved its apogee the human race will realize collective divinity. Space colonization advanced this goal: the universe is transformed by a spiritualized human race, colonization becoming in turn a laboratory to augment humanity's moral evolution.

Federov's vision of the future developed around his preoccupation with universal resurrection—the Common Task. The technological reconstruction and resuscitation of individuals was a step toward an immortal human race, conclusive proof of humanity's capacity to order or "regulate" nature. The search for the atomic remains of all previously existing humans would lead to the discovery of Adam—the Original Father—and the Garden of Eden, steps toward reclaiming divinity, immortality and paradise. Directed evolution and psychoeugenics would restore humanity's moral perfection. Fedorov's narrative was deeply rooted in the biblical *mythos* of creation, fall and redemption.

Once recreated, an immortal and morally perfect human race will colonize and humanize the cosmos, rendering that which was material and chaotic rational and orderly. Space is the setting for human transformation, the sacred location where humanity is transfigured in an epiphany that involves divine encounters. Fedorov's disciple Tsiolkovsky translated his teacher's narrative of space-faring humanity into the first serious treatises on rocket science. His idea of a multi-stage rocket provided the foundation for both the Soviet and American space programs. Tsiolkovsky, like Fedorov, accepted that colonization of space would bring about the immortality and moral perfection of the human race.

As Federov sought the Original Father, Teilhard de Chardin sought the Cosmic Son. Material chaos is being transformed into spiritual cosmos by the engine of evolution, a spiritual process yielding the Cosmic Christ. Human beings and their machines evolve together, producing a global network of minds, a noosphere enveloping the earth. Teilhard, like the Cosmists, viewed evolution as a purposeful principle producing order and complexity, inexorably aligning the biological world with the technological and the spiritual. Writing at a time when the role of genes was beginning to be understood, Teilhard wrote that "we appear to be on the eve of having a hand in the development of our bodies and even of our brains. With the discovery of genes it appears that we shall soon be able to control the mechanism of organic heredity."[48] Humanity was on the brink controlling its physical and moral evolution.

Sir Arthur C. Clarke, writing within the era of computers and during the early years of cybernetics, envisioned achieving immortality by merging with machines. In the machine age to come the individual person is not a locus of consciousness but a pattern of information. The informational person eventually abandons the physical domain altogether, a version of rationalizing or spiritualizing nature not unlike that envisioned by Fedorov and Teilhard. This transformational transition from matter to data opens the way for the transfer and storage of consciousness and the personality in other formats, a key component in predictions of immortality by means of downloading consciousness into machines. A satellite scientist, Clarke's thinking seldom strayed far from space. For Clarke, as for Fedorov, the conquest of space was a necessary impetus to further evolution of human intellect. Space is a transformative location for an epiphany: humans entering a new stage of evolutionary development, perhaps with assistance from beings farther along that path.

Subsequent chapters explore in greater detail dominant themes in the technofuturist *mythos*, including guided evolution, technological immortality, machine intelligence, and space colonization. The next two chapters explore narratives that are foundational to the vision of technological transformation. The first of these is the myth of progress, which has developed from a story of social improvement to one of technological triumph over human frailty and finitude. The second is the story of evolution, the animating principle driving nature and technology toward human perfection and cosmic transformation. With these two components of the enhancement and Transhumanist vision in place, we will then examine the narrative superstructure of technological transcendence.

4 Progress, Inevitability, Singularity

[B]elief in progress required faith in the omnicompetence of science.

—Mary Midgley

The Singularity denotes an event that will take place in the material world, the inevitable next step in the evolutionary process that started with biological evolution and has extended through human-directed technological evolution.

—Ray Kurzweil

Ever since we figured out how to make fire, technology has been how humans dream into the future. If 150,000 years of evolution is anything to go by, it's how we dream up the future.

—Peter Diamandis and Steven Kotler

By the year 2045, according to some estimates, the Internet will be one trillion times faster than it is today.[1] Such staggering projections of technological progress have become so commonplace that they hardly register a reaction from a technologically jaded public. Each report of a groundbreaking development in medical research or a mind-boggling advance in computer speed strengthens confidence in our most widely embraced narrative of progress.[2]

Bertrand Russell captured, and was captured by, the mythic force of progress in his 1961 work, *Has Man a Future?*.[3] Physicist Freeman Dyson

(b. 1923) shared Russell's confidence in inexorable, transformative progress. "Six hundred years is plenty of time for the social problems of our own era to be solved, for the history of divisive struggles between nations and races to be forgotten, and for the spark of human individuality to be extinguished." In that space of time, "we shall have achieved the age-old dreams of perpetual peace and the greatest happiness of the greatest number."[4] Technology liberates us from fear, want, disease, discomfort, injustice, and even death.[5] Progress will vanquish the destructive forces of history and the abiding impediments of brute nature.

The progress *mythos* assumes that improvement inevitably occurs as a consequence of the interaction the human mind with technology; this interaction is prompted by curiosity and need. Over time and despite setbacks, the intentional appropriation of technology enhances the human condition. The story has been central to enhancement discourse from the beginning. For instance, Transhumanism founder Max More made "Perpetual Progress" a foundational certainty of extropy, a name for Transhumanism's early philosophy: "Extropy," he writes, "means seeking more intelligence, wisdom, and effectiveness, an open-ended lifespan, and the removal of political, cultural, biological, and psychological limits to continuing development." By "perpetually overcoming constraints on our progress and possibilities as individuals, as organizations, and as a species" we will continue "growing in healthy directions without bound."[6]

This vision of advancing knowledge addressing urgent human needs has shaped the Western imagination for centuries. While belief in the inexorable nature of progress was severely challenged by twentieth-century atrocities, hope in a better future not only persists but has received new life from astonishing technological developments that appear to know no boundaries.[7] Enhancement advocates have refurbished and augmented the progress narrative, supplying it with existential and ontological force.[8]

Joel Garreau locates the foundations of modern notions of progress in a Christian conception of time: "Whereas older pagan creeds gave a cyclical account of time, Christianity presumed a teleological direction to history, and with it the possibility of progress. This belief in progress was inherent in modern science, which, wedded to technology, made possible the Industrial Revolution." Garreau adds, "Thus was the power to control nature achieved by a civilization that had inherited the license to exploit it."[9]

This chapter explores recent versions of the progress narrative that have emerged from technofuturist discourse. These myths challenge the idea that progress is a matter of human inventiveness applied to the improvement of the human condition. A new progress *mythos* locates agency in independent and purposeful forces largely beyond human control. These narratives seek to align the human and the technological realms, to describe an orderly, self-directing cosmos and humanity's place in that order. The chapter begins with a brief history of the idea of progress, followed by an exploration of the myth of technological inevitability, a strengthened version of the narrative progress. We will then consider how influential developments in the progress *mythos*—Kevin Kelly's concept of technium and Ray Kurzweil's vision of Singularity—suggest that traditional treatments of progress have given way to powerful myths which locate the impulse for improvement and complexity, not in human beings, but in the physical universe itself.

I will also be considering how inevitability and related narratives function strategically in the rhetoric of human enhancement. Technofuturists posit purposeful technological advance as an apocalyptic force that cannot and should not be obstructed. Moreover, as technological progress accelerates—a tenet of technofuturism—progress is no longer understood as a tendency or trajectory, but as an animating force aimed at transforming the cosmos. In the process, a spirit of progress is inventing us. Risk attends "an independent and self-validating truth" animating "the temporal process of myth-making."[10] The rhetorical maneuver of locating the power of progress in inexorable forces independent of the human race places any critic of technofuturism in the position of an obscurantist, and opponent of the good technological future, virtually an enemy of humanity.

EXPLORATIONS OF PROGRESS

The public narrative of progress has developed steadily but not predictably since the late Renaissance. The concept of progress in Western thought is a complex, curious and formidable aggregate of disparate ideas: empirical investigation, spiritual growth, the future, and the theory of evolution. Out of this odd mix has emerged a widely embraced myth of steady and transformative technological development. A few prominent developments are worth noting here as context for the rest of this chapter.

Francis Bacon (1561–1626) famously envisioned technological research as progress in *New Atlantis* (1627). On his fictional island of Bensalem, sophisticated technologies arise from the unfettered work of curious investigators. In a vast research facility, the House of Solomon, experiments in both air and submarine travel, among many other projects, are actively pursued. More than a century later, dramatist Louis-Sebastien Mercier (1740–1814) imagined the future as the proper realm of progress. Mercier envisioned twenty-fifth-century Paris as characterized by a range of social improvements—e.g. efficient hospitals, the elimination of poverty —in his novel of 1770, *L'An 2440: Reve s'il en fut Jamais* (*The Year 2440: A Dream If Ever There Was One*).

The book sold more than sixty thousand copies, went through twenty-five editions, and was translated into several languages. *L'An 2440* is among the first technological utopian novels to link the concepts of inevitable progress and the future.

In another signal development in the evolving narrative of progress, Auguste Comte (1798–1857) joined progress to spiritual development to create a scientific "religion of humanity."[11] The studious application of reason to the human predicament produces spiritual breakthroughs vainly promised by religion—peace, freedom, and justice. Inexorable progress occurs in predictable stages, each representing a rational and spiritual advance over previous ones. From the rudimentary theological stage humanity emerged into the metaphysical in which religion gives way to rational philosophy. The final stage of human progress is the positivist, in which only scientific explanations are deemed rational.[12] A progressive narrative of science displaces the old religious myths: science is the religion of the future. Indeed, Comtian Churches sprang up in London and other cities, and Comte himself occasionally "preached and performed marriage and burial services."[13]

The publication of Darwin's *On the Origin of the Species* in 1859 prompted author Samuel Butler (1835-1902) to imagine evolution as the inviolate force of progress. In his dark vision, evoluutionary progress eventuates in a race of intelligent machines that displaces humans. While dystopian in tone—progress means the end of the human race —his short story "Darwin among the Machines" (1863) is, nevertheless, an important imaginative treatment of progress that anticipated aspects of the concept's trajectory into the twentieth and twenty-first centuries.

British scientist J. B. S. Haldane (1892–1964) was among the early twentieth-century writers who sought to redeem progress, while maintaining its technological, futuristic, spiritual and evolutionary qualities. Earlier thinkers pointed the way. "Renan," wrote Haldane in *Possible Worlds* (1937), "suggested that science would progress so far that our successors would be able to reconstruct the past in complete detail, and finally get their consciousness into a relation of memory with our own, thus achieving the resurrection of the just."[14] Technology provided practical markers of progress such as peace, health, and social equality. Haldane advocated space colonization, genetic records for all newborns, and technologically assisted human evolution.[15]

With Haldane and other early twentieth century writers, notions of progress took a mythic turn. Ricoeur called myth "a disclosure of unprecedented worlds, an opening on to other *possible* worlds which transcend the established limits of our *actual* world."[16] Haldane's narrative envisioned the human race, not just better off, but evolving into "a super-organism," adding that "man's material progress" would continue until we achieve "the subjugation to complete conscious control of every atom and every quantum of radiation in the universe." Haldane also foresaw a new spiritual order arising from unfettered scientific inquiry. "There is, perhaps, no limit at all to [humanity's] intellectual and spiritual progress."[17] In *Daedalus; or, Science and the Future* (1924), technology accomplishes what religion had not—transformation of the human race through radical technologies including "ectogenesis" or fetal development in artificial wombs. For another famed biologist of the era, Julian S. Huxley, "biological progress was important only insofar as it validated faith in the progress of mankind."[18]

Other twentieth-century adherents to progress added their own innovations. For George Bernard Shaw, technology is driven toward perfection by an internal force or spirit. In his speech, "The New Theology," (1907) Shaw imagined the

> force at work making God, struggling through us to become an actual organized existence, enjoying what to many of us is the greatest conceivable ecstasy, the ecstasy of a brain, an intelligence, actually conscious of the whole, and with executive force capable of guiding it to a perfectly benevolent and harmonious end. That is what we are working to.

Those who share such a vision, who recognize this force's purpose, will assist it in its work. I become a part of this god "just in so much as I am working for the purpose of the universe, working for the good of the whole of society and the whole world, instead of merely looking after my personal ends."[19] In Shaw's conception, the force of progress has migrated; formerly located in' human curiosity, progress was now internalized in the physical cosmos —"the purpose of the universe" rather than the purpose of human beings.

For Teilhard progress meant not simply increasingly powerful technologies but the continuing evolution of consciousness. Evolutionary progress was spiritual progress toward a unified planet, a belief that divided people. "What finally divides the men of today into two camps is not class but an attitude of the mind."

> On the one hand there are those who simply wish to make the world a comfortable dwelling place; on the other hand, those who can only can only conceive it as a machine of progress, or, better, an organism that is progressing. On the one hand the "bourgeois spirit" in its essence and on the other the true "toilers of the Earth." On the one hand the cast-offs; on the other the agents and elements of planetization.[20]

INEVITABILITY

Progress was a theme of popular culture in the first half of the twentieth century, always associated with some vision of the future. Public spectacles such as the 1939 New York City World's Fair helped Americans "experience" transforming technological progress. Its central attraction, General Motors' *Futurama* exhibit, featured a 700-foot-tall space needle topped by the 200-foot-wide Perisphere. Visitors sported buttons announcing, "I have seen the future." [21] In 1955 Disneyland's *Tomorrow Land* was opened to the public, a visual myth of the future that made inevitable progress materially present for thousands of visitors. This three dimensional narrative equated progress with technological utopia. In the second half of the century popular television programs such as journalist Walter Cronkite's series, *The Twenty-First Century*, reinforced the *mythos* of a future defined by inexorable, physically liberating, and morally elevating progress.

Late twentieth-century confidence in steady technological improvements to the human condition—often in the form of consumer products—gave way in fiction and non-fiction narratives to comprehensive and deterministic notions of progress. Powerful technologies will install themselves in daily life—private and public —because they are destined to do so. Moreover, progress promises more than merely a life or greater leisure and less pain. In their 2012 book, *Abundance: The Future Is Better Than You Think*, Peter Diamandis and Stephen Kotler grounded the technological inevitability narrative in humanity's perennial hopes and dreams for a better future:

> There are also psychological reasons why it's nearly impossible to stop the spread of technology—specifically, how do you squelch hope? Ever since we figured out how to make fire, technology has been how humans dream into the future. If 150,000 years of evolution is anything to go by, it's how we dream up the future. People have a fundamental desire to have a better life for themselves and their families; technology is often how we make that happen. [22]

The inevitability narrative envisions technologies developing a social momentum that ensures their acceptance and refinement. Lingering scruples about the risks of interminable technological advances are irrelevant; regardless of where a precautionary line might be drawn today, it will be obliterated tomorrow as more daring and helpful technologies arrive on the scene. What has been dubbed "the precautionary principle"—the belief that those introducing a new technology have the burden of demonstrating its benefits and safety—is an irrelevant nicety. [23] According to the narrative, transformative technological progress will occur, despite the qualms of the risk averse; objections to new technologies will be overcome and forgotten. Progress must be aggressively and courageously pursued lest we acquiesce in the status quo and impede the liberating promise of new technologies.[24]

Advocates of the inevitability narrative point out that transformative technologies, from automobiles to personal computers and from heart transplants to stem cell therapies, have always been viewed initially as alien and dangerous. Despite the obvious benefits of technological progress, some members of the public are instinctively opposed to the new and the unfamiliar. Regardless, history teaches us that acceptance always follows initial reservations. Physicians Sophia Kleegman and Sherwin Kaufman advanced an oft-cited version of the narrative in 1966 when responding to concerns about reproductive assistance. The emotional trajectory prompted by new technology arcs between "horror" and "acceptance":

> Any change in custom or practice in this emotionally charged area has always elicited a response from established custom and law of horrified negation at first; then negation without horror; then slow and gradual curiosity, study, evaluation, and finally a very slow but steady acceptance.[25]

History and the future are on the side of progress, and the principle inevitable progress applies even to our efforts to improve ourselves. Philosopher Nicholas Agar argues that while "it is impossible to guess the exact means by which we will eventually enhance human abilities . . . it is a reasonable bet that the biotechnologists of some future century will develop techniques capable of safely enhancing human attributes." Agar affirms the inevitability of a new approach to eugenics, "a liberal eugenics" that will afford "prospective parents a limited prerogative to use enhancement technologies to choose their children's characteristics."[26] The narrative of technological inevitability would suggest a future in which enhancement counseling will accompany pregnancy.

KEVIN KELLY'S *TECHNIUM*

Inevitable progress is a dated story at this point; the *mythos* has evolved. Inevitability is no longer a sufficient principle to account for the force of progress. Science writer and *Wired* magazine co-founder Kevin Kelly proposed an inventive metaphysical justification for technological advancement in his 2010 book, *What Technology Wants*.[27] Kelly argues that technology, considered as a cumulative phenomenon developing over eight thousand years, is akin to an organism with its own desires. The technium—the global system of technology developing over time and including laws and arts as well as physical tools—possesses an inner organizing principle, and is not to be denied in the pursuit of its ends. Technology is a product of evolution, but even this powerful force is driven by something deeper and more mysterious. There is a mystical quality to the technium; it reveals the presence of a purposeful dynamism that preceded life itself. Technology *wants* something and will continue to move toward its goal, its *telos*. Kelly augments the idea of inevitability by suggesting that considerably more is at work in technological progress than simply human curiosity and ingenuity.

Kelly's argument is sophisticated and founded on extensive research and his intimate knowledge of the tech scene. Noting that "large systems of technology often behave like a very primitive organism," Kelly also observes that "networks, especially electronic networks, exhibit near-biological behavior." He believes that these systems "mimic natural systems." [28] Kelly concludes that "technology and life must share some fundamental essence." Information rather than physical matter defines life: "However you define life, its essence does not reside in material forms like DNA, tissue, or flesh, but in the intangible organization of the energy and information contained in those material forms." Life as well as technology emerge out of "immaterial flows of information."[29] The spiritual river metaphor suggests an epiphany of consubstantiality: biology and technology are one, varied manifestations of fundamental reality, the timeless cosmic stream of information.

Frye's notion of epiphany is a central feature in Kelly's technium *mythos*. In epiphany, as noted in Chapter Two, apparently contradictory realms are aligned and reconciled. Kelly's narrative bridges the evolution of the technium and the evolution of biological life. The technium is "a self-reinforcing system of creation," he writes, that at some early point "began to exercise some autonomy."[30] As "an outgrowth of the human mind" the technium can be considered "an outgrowth of life, and by extension it is also an outgrowth of the physical and chemical self-organization that first led to life." The technium "shares a deep common root not only with the human mind, but with ancient life and other self-organized systems as well." The technium is a protagonist possessing motives; it "has its own wants," and it wants to "sort itself out, to self-assemble into hierarchical levels, just as most large, deeply interconnected systems do." [31] In a stunning flourish Kelly asserts that as a willful entity, "the technium is now as great a force in our world as nature. . . ." This inexorable force exercises extraordinary power in the human realm. We have little to fear from submitting to the technium, however, for "we can learn to work with this force rather than against it." Taking a mystical turn, Kelly writes that we should practice "listening to what technology wants" in order to ascertain its larger purpose.[32]

We may think of technology as our own invention crafted by curiosity and industry from the stuff of physical matter to meet a human need. However, such is not the case when we take technology as an aggregate phenomenon spanning vast eras. From such a perspective the technium is "a type of evolutionary life."[33] And, as an evolving lifeform the technium is plotting "a steady move toward the immaterial."[34] Technology is "becoming a force—a vital spirit that throws us forward or pushes against us."[35] The technium takes on a spiritual quality as its story becomes the "story of expanding cosmic activity."[36] The technium resembles Teilhard's noosphere—it is the "thick blanket of learning and self-organized information" enveloping the earth.[37]

In Kelly's epic re-imagining of the myth of progress, the technium is now "the most dominant force in this part of the universe."[38] Human nature itself is shaped by it. Kelly is aware that some will respond that technologies undermine the "innate sacred human character, and can be kept in check only by keeping technology to a minimum in strict moral vigilance." Following the trajectory of the technium narrative, Kelly replies that the opposite is the case because "human nature is malleable." Human beings have often changed their nature, and will continue to do so.[39]

Progress has to this point been a product of "human minds," but now those minds must yield to a higher power.[40] According to this version of the progress narrative, humanity will learn to trust machine intelligence to solve our most enduring problems. Progress and inevitability are subsumed under a mythic vision of apocalyptic artificial intelligence—"artificial minds" that may no longer needtheir human creators.[41] Life follows the predetermined course of evolution; we discern evolution's goals and assist it to achieve them. The technium's "inherent direction" is determined "by the nature of matter and energy." Certain "nonmystical tendencies" are inherent to technology, rendering features of the technium "inevitable."[42] The reader might easily attribute a mystical cast to Kelly's vision. He does not, however, wish to be read as a mystic; nevertheless, his mythic account of progress enchants nature and "introduces metaphysical significance" into the worlds of biology and technological.[43] Kelly stresses that the technium "is not a supernatural force," but a principle like evolution[44] This principle is at work in DNA as it is in culture, in technology, in the evolving cosmos, and in the human mind. The old narrative of progress gives way to myth of internal purposefulness creating order and even perfection. The technium's fundamental dynamic is also at work in the human mind. If an inexorable force is evident in the technium, and the technium arises out of human minds, then great technological breakthroughs may be "dissolved in the genome. . . ."[45]

This unifying vision leads Kelly to entertain the panspermia hypothesis, a narrative affirming that the seeds of life on earth arrived from another planet. Our DNA may have been "cleverly crafted by superior intelligences" and then "shotgunned into the universe to naturally seed empty planets over billions of year."[46] Thus, progress, inevitability, and the technium perhaps originated in the minds of entities on a planet orbiting a distant star. This component in Kelly's narrative brings to mind Gianni Vattimo's idea of a secularized culture engaged in the "demystification of the errors of religion," while "the survival of these 'errors'" remains evident and "hidden in distorted models that are nonetheless profoundly present."[47]

For Kelly the universe appears designed to assist us in discovering our potential; it has been following an evolutionary arc toward this goal for eons. [48] Providing human beings a wide field of possibilities is the technium's "foremost consequence."[49] Moreover, by expanding human potential the technium is making us better people, increasing "the mind's fundamental goodness."[50] In addition to its agenda for humanity, the technium is a vehicle for achieving the emerging consciousness of the cosmos. By means of the technium "the universe has engineered its own self-awareness."[51] Technology is "stitching together all the minds of the living. . . ."[52]

Kelly suggests that the technium's ultimate purpose may be to reveal the presence of God and to assist the process of God's becoming. Kelly sees us entering "a new axial age" in which technological breakthroughs will yield theological insight. Technology may "be considered a portrait of God rather than of us."[53] To contemplate the technium is to grow in appreciation for "its transformative positive powers." "If there is a God," Kelly writes, "the arc of the technium is aimed right at him."[54] Kevin Kelly's mythic narrative presents the technium as a spiritually transformative force in the cosmos, the universe's strategy for achieving self-awareness, directing the human race's evolution and revealing the presence and nature of God.

Kelly's technium *mythos* is a formidable effort to come to grips with the powerful momentum of technology. T. S. Eliot wrote of Joyce's use of myth as "a way of controlling, of ordering, of giving a shape and a significance to the immense panorama of futility and anarchy which is contemporary history . . ."[55] Kelly has ordered technology's "immense panorama" by means of a novel narrative of progress as built into the very substance of the universe.

KURZWEIL'S SINGULARITY

Circumspect and subdued, Ray Kurzweil's manner is methodical and his humor dry; his flat affect and cerebral self-presentation suggest the engineer rather than the prophet. Kurzweil is most comfortable when discussing graphs and data, and he avoids waxing metaphysical. Though not the Great Oz, he does appear to relish the role of the man in the know. Kurzweil's understated brilliance, organizational genius, and unparalleled ability to peer into the technological future place him at the head of a technofuturist movement influential beyond its numbers. He is the voice of the inevitable future for a growing number of highly educated true believers.

Widely published and the subject of two movies, Kurzweil is best known for his theory of exponential technological progress that he labels the Singularity.[56] His tireless advocacy of the concept has positioned the Singularity as a popular culture meme that is regularly mentioned in movies, television programs, cartoons, books, and video games. Adherents and critics alike have seen in the Singularity a technological apocalypse. Jaron Lanier, for instance, has written: "The coming Singularity is a popular belief in the society of technologists. Singularity books are as common in a computer science department as Rapture images are in an evangelical bookstore."[57] Lanier's analogy recognizes a religious quality in Kurzweil's vision, an intentional importation of metaphysical meaning, one function of myth .[58] Kurzweil's influential construct has accomplished this goal more successfully than has any other component of the technofuturist narrative. He single-handedly transformed observations about technological advances into a transcendent vision of the future.

Kurzweil is famous for predicting the advent of human-level machine intelligence by the year 2045. The creation of computer intelligence "won't immediately change everything." "We have six billion of them, so a few million more won't profoundly change the world." Nevertheless, the change that changes everything—the technological apocalypse—is coming, and soon:

> But by the time we get to the 2040s, say 2045, we'll be able to multiply human intelligence a billion fold. That will be a profound change that's singular in nature so we use this term [Singularity]. It will be a profound transformation. But it really is what human beings are all about. Human beings transcend our limitations. We make ourselves stronger. We make ourselves smarter with our tools, and that's really what the singularity will do.

Kurzweil defines the Singularity as a moment of technological transformation that introduces a new cosmic order. "[T]he impending Singularity in our future is increasingly transforming every institution and aspect of human life, from sexuality to spirituality." Kurzweil's *mythos* of a radically altered human existence through the power of Singularity yields a transformative *logos*—a new philosophy by which we approach life itself:

> What, then, is the Singularity? It is a future period during which the pace of technological change will be so rapid, its impact so deep,

that human life will be irreversibly transformed. Although neither utopian nor dystopian, this epoch will transform the concepts that we rely on to give meaning to our lives, from our business model to the cycle of human life, including death itself.

The Singularity is the most important event in human history; understanding and anticipating it represents a personal spiritual conversion:

> Understanding the Singularity will alter our perspective on the significance of our past and the ramifications for our future. To truly understand it inherently changes one's view of life in general and one's own particular life.[59]

Kurzweil's fullest treatment of the concept, his 2005 book *The Singularity Is Near*, is a narrative and as such a pattern for the future: "This book, then, is the story of the destiny of human-machine civilization, a destiny we have come to refer to as the Singularity."[60] The Singularity is also, however, an intentionally crafted *mythos* intended to envision for an audience a comprehensive order of things—a *cosmos*. The Singularity myth warrants particular thoughts and actions. In theologian Brent Waters' words, it "encapsulates where hope and trust are placed, in turn aligning desires accordingly."[61] Radically enhanced humanity is a required component in the narrative, once one grasps its force and magnitude. "Can the pace of technological progress continue to speed up indefinitely? Isn't there a point at which humans are not able to think fast enough to catch up? For unenhanced humans, clearly so." Such is not the case, however, for a scientist "1,000 times more intelligent than the human scientists of today."[62] The narrative leads us to not just anticipate such a development, but desire it.

Frye described visions of "an epiphany of law, of that which is and must be," a transformative principle that reveals a new world.[63] Kurzweil has had such a vision: technological transformation arises from a principle he refers to as the law of accelerating returns: technology does not improve incrementally, but exponentially at a relatively predictable rate. He writes, "The ongoing acceleration of technology is the implication and inevitable result of what I call the law of accelerating returns, which describes the acceleration of the pace of and exponential growth of the products of an evolutionary process."[64] This sort of progress also occurs in the biological sciences, according to Kurzweil. Thus, "genetic sequencing has doubled every year. The cost has come down by half every year. There's a hundred different measures like this. And this has been going on since the 1890 American census, and it's remarkably smooth and predictable."

Computers will continue to shrink in size until they become invisible. The line between biology and machine will blur, and we will reprogram life. This massive project of reprogramming life itself, assisted by unimaginably powerful artificial intelligence, will eventuate in, not just progress, but the Singularity event that will change the human race and the cosmos forever. "[T]he fate of the universe is a decision yet to be made, one which we will intelligently consider when the time is right." [65]

The goal of this exponential and evolutionary progress toward Singularity is to convert the "dumb matter" of the cosmos into "smart matter," and thus to bring about a cosmic transformation. Intelligence "turns dumb matter into smart matter," and such smart matter "is so extraordinarily intelligent that it can harness the most subtle aspects of the laws [of physics] to manipulate matter and energy to its will."

In fact, Kurzweil contends "that intelligence is more powerful than cosmology." He explains:

> That is, once matter evolves into smart matter (matter fully saturated with intelligent processes), it can manipulate other matter and energy to do its bidding (through suitably powerful engineering). This perspective is not generally considered in discussions of future cosmology. It is assumed that intelligence is irrelevant to events and processes on a cosmological scale.

Once evolution has produced "a technology-creating species and that species creates computation (as has happened here)," then in "a matter of a few centuries" intelligence will permeate everything. A civilization harnessing such power "will then overcome gravity (through exquisite and vast technology) and other cosmological forces—or to be fully accurate it will maneuver and control these forces—and engineer the universe it wants. This is the goal of Singularity." [66]

This is the technofuturist apocalypse, brute nature transformed into intelligence. Borrowing Ricoeur's terms, Singularity is "a disclosure of unprecedented worlds, an opening on to other *possible* worlds which transcend the established limits of our *actual* world." [67] Here is Kurzweil's "imaginative conception of the whole of nature as the content of an infinite and eternal living body," to quote Frye. [68] Kurzweil's techno-apocalypse humanizes "stupid and indifferent nature" so that it is "no longer the container of human society, but is contained by that society, and must rain or shine at the pleasure of man. . . ." [69] In Singularity the humble story of technological progress births a comprehensive and insistent sacred narrative; the new wine has burst the old wine skins.

While Kurzweil has refined and popularized the concept, mathematician I. J Good (1916-2009) introduced the Singularity in the 1960s. Good posited a moment when technological advance occurs so rapidly that it brings about an apocalyptic rupture in human history. He tended to emphasize artificial intelligence as the harbinger of Singularity. Good writes:

> Let an ultraintelligent machine be defined as a machine that can far surpass all the intellectual activities of any man however clever. Since the design of machines is one of these intellectual activities, an ultraintelligent machine could design even better machines; there would then unquestionably be an "intelligence explosion," and the intelligence of man would be left far behind. Thus the first ultraintelligent machine is the last invention that man need ever make.[70]

Computer scientist Jaron Lanier has noted that legendary cognitive scientist Marvin Minsky—one of Kurzweil's mentors—articulated his own version of the phenomenon:

> One day soon, maybe twenty or thirty years into the twenty-first century, computers and robots will be able to construct copies of themselves, and these copies will be a little better than the originals because of intelligent software. The second generation of robots will then make a third, but it will take less time, because of the improvements over the first generation.[71]

Famed science fiction writer Vernor Vinge—often credited with popularizing the Singularity concept—wrote forebodingly in 1993 that "within thirty years, we will have the technological means to create superhuman intelligence. Shortly after, the human era will have ended."[72] In this version of the narrative, human history ends with the Singularity and a new order begins. As Lanier interprets the Singularity myth, "computers will soon get so big and fast and the net so rich with information that people will be obsolete, either left behind like the characters in Rapture novels or subsumed into the cyber-superhuman something." This is not to say that the myth is not persuasive. "Silicon Valley culture has taken to enshrining this vague idea and spreading it in the way that only technologists can."[73] The Singularity is now "a popular belief in the society of technologists."[74] The Singularity *mythos* renders our lives "coherent, orderly, and meaningful," and does so by challenging other powerful mythic systems.[75] The stakes are high, for the Singularity affords a vision of nothing less than human redemption and cosmic transformation. Even the myths of the major religious systems do not provide a more comprehensive and compelling vision of the human future.

RESPONSES

Myths of progress and inevitability are foundational to the technofuturist and enhancement vision, providing an account of technology's trajectory and assurance of limitless advances. One of the most persuasive and influential myths of the modern age, progress suggests that human rationality and ingenuity will yield ever greater breakthroughs in the struggle against physical frailties and social ills. The *mythos* of progress affords a means of making sense of human experience and of importing "metaphysical significance" into the world of technology. [76]

This chapter has argued that the early visions of progress, which located technological advances in the curiosity and skill of human agents, have given way to more forceful and comprehensive visions that attribute advances to purposeful non-human agents—nature, intelligence, evolution or technology itself. Inevitable progress no longer suggests mere improvement in the human condition. Recent re-creations of the myth render technological progress a purposeful energy that wills its destiny. Technology is one of its tools, perhaps its principal tool. In new visionary constructs such as Kelly's technium or Kurzweil's Singularity, progress is a causal agent compelling grand culminations, disseminating intelligence to every atom, awakening the universe to self-awareness, providing humans a wider range of possibilities and fashioning itself into a divinity.

New, metaphysically charged stories of progress propel this venerable narrative of Western science from the bounded present to the apparently limitless future. Coupe notes that "the not yet of apocalypse" is "the key to mythic life."[77] However, if myths are necessary to social and intellectual life, then myths that tend toward an inevitable end point place real limits on human agency. In the visions of inventive rhetors such as Kelly and Kurzweil—following the lead of visionaries such as Fedorov and Teilhard—a spirit of technology seeks goals of *its* choosing, the shape of apocalypse belonging to that spirit.

Inevitability is a rhetorical strategy with other potentially sinister overtones. Critics of progress are mutineers unwilling to assist the self-actualizing work of the technological cosmos. Sociologist Michael Hauskeller points to this intriguing paradox in the rhetoric of inevitability, one that characterizes Transhumanist and enhancement narratives. Regarding the various components of the technofuturist vision, he writes:

> They are presented as inevitable outcomes, but at the same time as dependent on our willingness to help bring them about and not throw any unnecessary obstacles in their way. The promise thus borders on an order.[78]

This is among the risks of myth discussed in Chapter Two—myths can take on an insistent quality that disallows objections." Singularity represents transformative technological triumph over historical forces, natural obstacles and human contingencies. Human history has been heading in this direction from the beginning. The idea of Singularity exercises enormous influence in technology circles and has now captured the attention of members of the public. Kurzweil's mythic vision has galvanized the human enhancement movement and provided it a set of guiding principles. The myth is, however, allegedly rooted in an inviolable law and thus both insistent and highly resistant to challenges.

Kelly's technium pursues its own agenda, and as that agenda develops it provides ever-increasing possibilities to human beings; the technium is about developing potential. Its ultimate goal, in true mythic fashion, is to reveal the presence and nature of God. The writers considered in this chapter have crafted sacred narratives in which technology is a spiritual force, a profoundly transformative and intentional agent that places technology beyond the control of humans. This *mythos* carries an overarching principle, a *logos*: we must learn to work with technology in the pursuit of its goals, even if those goals involve profoundly altering the nature of the human race and of the cosmos we inhabit.

5 FROM NATURAL SELECTION TO SPIRITUAL EVOLUTION

A surprising number of the elements which used to belong to traditional religion have regrouped themselves under the heading of science, mainly around the concept of evolution.

—Mary Midgley

We have just started our evolution as Homo sapiens.

—Kevin Kelly

I believe that drastic reorganization of our pattern of religious thought is now becoming necessary, from a god-centered to an evolutionary-centered pattern.

—Julian Sorell Huxley

In a now famous 1994 article in *Scientific American*, legendary computer scientist Marvin Minsky affirmed that humans would continue to evolve. However, natural selection will give way to a new kind of evolution under human direction:

> To lengthen our lives, and improve our minds, in the future we will need to change our bodies and brains. To that end, we first must consider how normal Darwinian evolution brought us to where we are. Then we must imagine ways in which future replacements for worn body parts might solve most problems of failing health.

This new evolution will be comprehensive. Biological augmentation will be accompanied by other improvements:

> We must then invent strategies to augment our brains and gain greater wisdom. Eventually we will entirely replace our brains—using nanotechnology. Once delivered from the limitations of biology, we will be able to decide the length of our lives—with the option of immortality—and choose among other, unimagined capabilities as well.

In order to advance we will have to abandon the notion that we are evolution's endpoint. "In the past, we have tended to see ourselves as a final product of evolution, but our evolution has not ceased." Darwinian evolution was slow and haphazard, involving eons and producing more failures than successes. However, "we are now evolving more rapidly, though not in the familiar, slow Darwinian way." As a result, "it is time that we started to think about our new emerging."[1]

Minsky was rehearsing a widely endorsed narrative that, along with inevitable technological progress, is foundational to the technofuturist and enhancement visions. This myth of directed evolution affirms that the slow process of natural selection brought us to our present point of development. However, the time has come for human beings, employing biotechnologies, to take control of their destiny. Humans will in this way shape evolution into a vehicle for achieving technological transcendence and creating the posthuman. The *mythos* of directed evolution asserts that "stupid and indifferent nature is no longer the container of human society, but is contained by that society," and in Frye's appealing phrase, "must rain or shine at the pleasure of man"[2] This chapter's principal concern is to explore evolution as a modern myth of human transformation, a foundational component in the Transhumanist and technofuturist vision of a transcendent human future. As such, evolution plays a spiritual as well as a physical role in progress toward the posthuman era.

We will begin by examining several early writers who crafted an evolutionary account of life's origins and progress, preparing the way for later conceptions of evolution as a principle of improvement inherent in the natural world. The chapter then turns to two highly influential writers of the nineteenth and twentieth centuries—Ernst Haeckel and Julian Huxley. Each contributed importantly to shaping a vision of evolution as a metaphysical force working to unite the physical and spiritual worlds in a perfect symbiosis. The chapter then directs attention to several leaders in the human enhancement arena who have propagated a vision of directed or enhanced evolution as a means of achieving radical human transformation. The story of directing our own evolution has assumed an unparalleled influence on the emerging vision of the technofuture.

PRECURSORS

Evolution was not Charles Darwin's idea; similar theories had been advanced by ancient Greek writers as well as by European naturalists in the eighteenth and early nineteenth centuries. Darwin's own grandfather, Erasmus Darwin (1731–1802), proposed a rudimentary theory of evolution in *Zoonomia, or the Laws of Organic Life* (1794–96), a treatise on medicine, anatomy, and related topics. All living beings were sentient, connected, and striving for higher orders of existence. As Edward S. Reed writes, "For Darwin all of animate nature was possessed of sensibility and feeling, even plants." Darwin's narrative of life featured an energy animating the whole natural system, "a subtle fluid or ether in the body and nerves."[3]

French naturalist Jean-Baptiste Lamarck (1744–1829) theorized that species undergo change in direct adaptation to environmental pressures. Lamarck's *Philosophie Zoologique* (1809) envisioned the descent of all species from earlier forms. Evolution was incremental and progressive—biological life advanced in a relatively steady upward arc as better adapted members of a species survived and flourished. One internal force encouraged complexity in organisms, a second drove species to adapt to new environments. Charles Darwin contributed a plausible physical explanation of change from one species to another—natural selection. Whether Darwin intended it is debatable, but in the popular mind progress was a component in his vision of evolution.[4] The idea of progress had at least occurred to the great naturalist. In his autobiography, Darwin wrote of a future human race that would consist of "far more perfect creature[s]" than the present one.[5] Evolution as progress, including moral progress, gained momentum. English biologist T. H. Huxley (1825–1895) wrote in 1893 that "the struggle for existence tends to eliminate those less fitted to adapt themselves to the circumstances of their existence." As a result, "the strongest, the most self-assertive, tend to tread down the weaker." This "the cosmic process" applied to civilizations as well as to organisms What Huxley termed "social progress" required "checking of the cosmic process at every step" and then "the substitution for it of another, which may be called the ethical process," the goal of which "is not the survival of those who may happen to be the fittest, in respect of the whole of the conditions which obtain, but of those who are ethically the best."[6] Evolution acquired a spiritual end—the moral improvement of the human race. The "spirit of hierarchy" is apparent in Huxley's narrative, pointing to a potentially dangerous vision of unattainable perfection.[7]

French philosopher Henri Bergson (1859–1941) sought to discover the forces at work within the evolving organism and, indeed, the cosmos. In *Creative Evolution* (1907) he speculated about an élan *vital* or vital spirit driving all living things toward consciousness. In Bergson's narrative the spirit in living things overcomes obstacles to its purposes, propelling life toward spiritual awareness. *Creative Evolution* follows the mythic arc traced by Erasmus Darwin more than a century earlier, not the strictly natural path marked out by his grandson in 1859.

The idea of limitless evolution also appeared in the fiction of English novelist and philosopher Olaf Stapledon (1886–1950).[8] Stapledon imagined vast histories of the distant human future in celebrated stories such as *Last and First Men* (1930) and *Star Maker* (1937). *Homo sapiens* are a life-giving race that awakens the universe—bringing cosmos out of chaos. Natural evolution is too slow; the new humans are coming and it will take serious scientific effort to hasten their arrival.[9] Affirming that "our conception of humanity must be fundamentally altered," Stapledon argued that just as "Darwin showed that man is the result of evolution," scientists since have "shown that he may direct his evolution."[10] Technology has given us the "wherewithal to climb a little nearer to divinity."[11] *Homo sapiens* is but a step along the way to something grander, a "splendid race." Stapledon explored the conviction that "our whole present mentality is but a confused and halting first experiment."[12] The supermen to come will possess "more of godliness" and "less of the animal."[13] Salvation "rests in future man biologically improving the species."[14]

Ernst Haeckel: Evolution and Sacred Progress

On the Origin of the Species lent scientific credence to the popular narrative of evolution as progress; natural selection, also however, made clear why Lamarck was wrong to assume that evolutionary change occurrs in direct response to environment pressures.[15] Darwin's causal account did not, however, eradicate the idea that evolution was progressive, morally directed, and involved energies present in matter itself. The most prominent representative of spiritualized evolution was the enormously influential German biologist Ernst Haeckel (1834–1919). Haeckel, among the greatest intellectual figures of his day, crafted from Darwin's theory a spellbinding narrative of life's eternal progress. His popular books and richly illustrated lectures brought his ideas to a broad public in the nineteenth century; lecture halls became "temples of some new religion."[16]

Haeckel's views on evolution's pursuit of perfection were controversial, and for good reason. He argued that different human races constituted separate species arising in different locations and in response to widely diverse environments. At the top of the racial hierarchy were Caucasians, "the most highly developed and perfect" race. Haeckel supported his progressive evolutionary narrative with language studies—more sophisticated languages pointed to more advanced races. His racism also rested on his fabricated embryology.[17] When the embryological evidence did not fit with his conclusions he altered the evidence.

Influenced by Hegel's Idealism, Spinoza's pantheism, and Goethe's Romanticism, Haeckel presented nature and spirit as a unified whole. He clothed evolution in a religious language that fused "nature worship (sun worship in particular) with Darwinism, anti-Semitism, anti-Christianity, eugenics, euthanasia, and *volkisch* thought."[18] Convinced that a new *mythos* would birth a new scientific religion to replace Christianity, Haeckel established his International Monist League in 1906.[19] A narrative of evolutionary progress was the cornerstone of his monistic ideology—a spiritual myth spawning the doctrinal *logos* of a new religion.

JULIAN SORELL HUXLEY: EVOLUTION AS RELIGION

A twentieth-century expert on evolution coined the term transhumanism in the 1950s. Sir Julian S. Huxley (1887–1975) argued in his popular lectures, radio broadcasts, and books such as *New Bottles for New Wine* (1958), that we must engineer a new type of human employing available technologies. Recognizing the tremendous mythic potential in directed evolution, Huxley provided the vision a name:

> The human species can, if it wishes, transcend itself—not just sporadically, an individual here in one way, an individual there in another way, but in its entirety as humanity. We need a name for this new belief. Perhaps transhumanism will serve: man remaining man, but transcending himself, by realizing new possibilities of and for his human nature.[20]

Huxley envisioned a transcendent human nature achieved by the scientific management of evolution.

The myth of directed evolution took some strange twists and turns in Huxley's writing, revealing an embedded *logos* or ideology of social caste. "The brain's level of performance could be genetically raised," creating a cognitive elite.[21] Huxley understood the metaphysical power of narrative when interpreting natural phenomena. Only humans can "read purpose into evolution," that is, create purpose through myth. Any "purpose for the future of man" will be the purpose we determine.

Transhumanism will infuse nature with just such metaphysical purpose and thus reveal a new world. Huxley's *mythos* promised "discovery and revelation," unveiling realms hitherto unknown.[22] As Coupe notes, myth conveys "a promise of another mode of existence. . . ."[23] Myth also conveys ideology. Kenneth Burke wrote, "Ideology is to myth as rhetoric is to poetry;" the propositional statements of ideology (*logos*) have their roots in narratives (*mythos*). Huxley's *mythos* of directed evolution producing a gifted intellectual caste—"the best endowed ten-thousandth among us"—led him to the ideology of eugenics.[24] "Purposes in life are made, not found," and the material from which they are made is sacred narrative.

Some of the purposes Huxley invented for the new humans were strange: "Telepathy and other extra-sensory activities of the mind" are within reach of practical technology.[25] Evolution for Huxley, as for Teilhard, is *the* universal principle: " [A]ll aspects of reality are subject to evolution, from atoms and stars to fish and flowers, from fish and flowers to human societies and values—indeed, ... all reality is a single process of evolution. And ours is the first period in which we have acquired sufficient knowledge to begin to see the outline of this vast process as a whole."[26] Huxley anticipated the crucial role played by Midgley's "imaginative patterns" in directing scientific enterprises, including managing the "human phase" of evolution. "[M]ajor steps in the human phase of evolution are achieved by breakthroughs to new dominant patterns of mental organization, of knowledge, ideas, and beliefs—ideological instead of physiological or biological organization."[27] These "idea-systems" occur in succession: "Each new, successful idea-system spreads and dominates some important sector of the world, until it is superseded by a rival system or itself gives birth to its successor by a breakthrough to a new organization system of thought and belief."

With Darwin a new pattern arrived—the evolutionary. Charles Darwin "opened the passage leading to a new psycho-social level, with a new pattern of ideological organization—an evolution-centered organization of thought and belief." His account of evolution was not simply a theory of the rise of species; it was "a new and improved ideological organization," and "a new dominant thought organization."[28] Darwin's scheme could even be construed as the basis of a new religious faith. Paul Philips writes of Huxley's interest in founding a religion, "Since the loss of religion was the greatest defect of the modern world, a new religion was a moral necessity for Huxley."[29]

Each subsequent system of thought—magical, theological, scientific and now evolutionary —addresses "the most ultimate problems that the thought of the time is capable of formulating" and thus is concerned "with giving some interpretation of man, of the world which he is to live in, and of his place and role in that world—in other words, some comprehensible picture of human destiny and significance."[30] Huxley realized a mythic function in his systems of thought, a capacity to address big questions.[31] Evolutionary science allows us to see "this vast process as a whole," narrative allows us to interpret and manage that "vast process."[32] Having attained such a vision we are called to undertake "the cosmic project of evolution."[33]

Constituting a "new and improved" ideology, evolution provides "the central germ or living template of a new dominant thought organization."[34] As such, evolutionary thinking will have to provide a "comprehensible picture of human destiny and significance." We are agents in this process; human destiny is "to be the sole agent for the future evolution of this planet."[35] The old religions were "organs of psychosocial man concerned with human destiny and with experiences of sacredness and transcendence." Evolution is a new *mythos*, the foundation of a new religion. While it is "hard to break through the firm framework of an accepted belief system and build a new acceptable successor," it is also "necessary." In any event, "our new organization of thought—belief system, framework of values, ideology, call it what you will—must grow and be developed in the light of our new evolutionary vision."[36]

The implications of the new evolutionary *mythos* are profound and will elicit controversy. For example, an evolutionary narrative will not elevate equality:

> Our new idea-system must jettison the democratic myth of equality. Human beings are *not* born equal in gifts or potentialities, and human progress stems largely from the very fact of their inequality. 'Free but unequal' should be our motto, and diversity of excellence, not conforming normalcy or mere adjustment, should be the aim of education.

The new order will be a meritocracy forced upon us, not by a new myth, but by the fact of an exploding world population. "The spectacle of explosive population" raises the question, *"What are people for?"* Huxley's answer to his question, rooted in the myth of directed evolution, is chilling. "And we see that the answer has something to do with their quality as human beings and the quality of their lives and their achievements."[37]

To come to his main point, Huxley affirmed that "the evolutionary vision is enabling us to discern, however incompletely, the lineaments of the new religion that we can be sure will arise to serve the needs of the coming era." In the new mythology are found "the emotion of sacredness and the sense of right and wrong."[38] Existing myths reveal serious flaws, but "the emergent religion of the near future could be a good thing." The new religion will "take advantage of the vast amount of new knowledge produced by the knowledge explosion of the last few centuries," from which we will "construct what we may call its "theology"—the framework of facts and ideas which provide it with intellectual support . . ."

The new evolutionary *mythos* will not support worship of "supernatural rulers." Rather, it will "sanctify the higher manifestations of human nature in art and love, in intellectual comprehension and aspiring adoration, and to emphasize the fuller realization of life's possibilities as a sacred trust."

Following the arc of Huxley's myth, "the evolutionary vision, first opened up to us by Charles Darwin a century back, illuminates our existence in a simple, but almost overwhelming way." As a result, the Darwinian vision "exemplifies the truth that truth is great and will prevail, and the greater truth that truth will set us free." [39] In Huxley's myth of the human future, directed evolution provides the foundation of a global scientific faith.

DIRECTED EVOLUTION IN ENHANCEMENT DISCOURSE

Narratives of evolution are central to human enhancement rhetoric. Whether presented as origin story or technofuturist vision, the myth of directed evolution grounds and validates every component in enhancement discourse. As we have seen, the story of evolution has often departed from Darwin's naturalistic theory and taken on progressive and moral coloration. To the venerable narrative of progress has been added the intentional technological direction of human evolution. Among contemporary writers the story of directed evolution has been further refined. In the following section we will review various treatments of the narrative developed by several human enhancement and technofuturist writers.

In 1990, leading robotics scientist Hans Moravec rehearsed the foundational narrative in his classic work of futurism, *Mind Children*. "We are at the start of something quite new in the scheme of things," he wrote.[40] Moravec announced a vision that would become foundational in human enhancement circles: "Until now we have been shaped by the invisible hand of Darwinian evolution, a powerful process that learns from the past but is blind to the future." Evolution, by means of natural selection, brought us to this point; now we are ready to "supply just a little of the vision it lacks." Repeating Huxley's notion of choosing the evolutionary future, Moravec writes that humans will "choose goals for ourselves and steadily pursue them, absorbing losses in the short term for greater benefits further ahead."[41] We will employ technological advances in robotics and artificial intelligence to pursue the goal of directing our evolution as we choose.

Moravec's real interest is robots, and in his vision robots will become the dominant species on earth by 2040, taking human evolution in a non-biological direction. He develops his narrative of the robotic future in *Robot: Mere Machine to Transcendent Mind* (1998).[42] While he brought considerable technical knowledge to the task of crafting his vision of the future, the basic components of his narrative were already familiar; the basic plot was initially set out by Samuel Butler in his story of 1863, "Darwin among the Machines." Technological humanity would take control of its own evolution. Exponential advances in robotics technology would lead to rapid development of artificial intelligence and the eventual emergence of robots with human level intelligence. Human beings would give way to their evolutionary successors—intelligent robots, our children.

These monsters are not, however, to be feared. In the Moravec *mythos*, "thinking robots" are "an entirely new kind of life." And yet, they are our offspring:

> In behavior robots resemble ourselves more than they resemble anything else in the world. They are being taught our skills. In the future they will acquire our values and goals. . . . How should we feel about beings that we bring into the world that are similar to ourselves, that we teach our way of life, that will inherit the world when we are gone? I think we should consider them our children, a hope rather than a threat, though they will require careful upbringing to instill good character. In time they will outgrow us, create their own goals, make their own mistakes and go their own way, with us perhaps a fond memory—but that too is the way of children.[43]

Moravec's mythic effort to allay our fear of the monstrous is rhetorically stunning. He transforms the robot from the malign other of science fiction to that most irresistible of all creatures: our own child. Following Warner's idea that myths "define enemies and aliens," we may note that they can also define members of our own tribe, society, or family.[44] In this story the robot is our child, though the child will become a god. In the new order of things robots will give way to disembodied Minds, "vast and enduring." These virtually omnipotent beings, following their insatiable curiosity and limitless power, will one day occupy a position "intermediate between Sherlock Holmes and God." They will create and explore whole worlds and civilizations. Moreover, these divinities will accomplish Fedorov's life-restoring Great Task: "Entire world histories, with all their living, feeling inhabitants, will be resurrected in cyberspace."[45]

Philosopher John Harris has crafted a similar narrative of the technological future. Writing that "the 'progress of evolution' is unlikely to be achieved accidentally or by letting nature take its course," he advocates that we "prioritize improving on humans over preserving the species in its present form."[46] Thus, we ought to replace "*natural selection* with *deliberate selection, Darwinian evolution* with '*enhancement evolution.*'"[47] Harris recognizes that the story of technologically enhanced and intentionally directed evolution is linked to the question of human nature.[48]

Opponents of directed evolution argue that technological intervention in the evolutionary process threatens to disrupt an inviolable human nature. For most other contemporary proponents of directed evolution there is no fixed human nature, a construct rooted in ancient origin myths. According to Harris, efforts to identify a fixed nature risk marking a particular stage of evolutionary development as capturing essential humanness. The human race is, however, in constant flux—there is no moment of essential humanness. To make his argument against this version of the precautionary principle, Harris asks readers to imagine an ape ancestor who, following the same misguided logic of a fixed nature that must be preserved, decided to protect her genetic status. Human exceptionalism of the type affirmed by enhancement opponents is as dangerous and presumptuous as ape exceptionalism would have been:

> If our ape ancestor had thought about it, she might have taken the view adopted by so many of our contemporary gurus . . . that there is something special about themselves and that their particular sort of being is not only worth preserving in perpetuity, but that there is a duty not only to ensure that preservation, but to make sure that neither natural selection nor deliberate choice permit the development of any better sort of being.[49]

Myth can define the alien as well as the kinsman; it may also redefine the self. Enhancing our evolution requires shedding the hubristic notion that there is something worth preserving about our current form. Harris detects two specific obstacles that emerge from such human exceptionalism:

> The first is that our present point in evolution is unambiguously good and not susceptible to improvement. Second, it is assumed that the course of evolution, if left alone, will continue to improve things for humankind or at least not make them worse.[50]

Harris articulates a relatively conventional version of the directed evolution vision; other proponents tell a somewhat more expansive story.

Ray Kurzweil rehearses the narrative of evolution in the introduction to his bestselling 2013 work, *How to Create a Mind: The Secret of Human Thought Revealed*. Returning to themes discovered in writers such as Haeckel, Teilhard, and J. S. Huxley, Kurzweil affirms that evolution is the story of life's inexorable march toward increasing complexity. However, Kurzweil defines *complexity* as a more capacious and effective means of storing information. "The story of evolution unfolds with increasing levels of abstraction," he writes. In the beginning, "atoms—especially carbon atoms, which create rich information structures by linking in four different directions—formed increasingly complex molecules." The result was what we now term chemistry. "A billion years later, a complex molecule called DNA evolved, which could precisely encode lengthy strings of information and generate organisms described by these 'programs.'" At this point in the story chemistry "gave rise to biology."

To achieve increasing levels of information storage, evolution accelerated as it neared the highly complex biological form we now know as *Homo sapiens*. Information *storage* gave way to information *management* as "communication and decision networks" form:

> At an increasingly rapid rate, organisms evolved communication and decision networks called nervous systems, which could coordinate the increasingly complex parts of their bodies as well as the behaviors that facilitated their survival. The neurons making up nervous systems aggregated into brains capable of increasingly intelligent behaviors.

At this juncture, "biology gave rise to neurology, as brains were now the cutting edge of storing and manipulating information." In sum, "we went from atoms to molecules to DNA to brains."[51] The *mythos* of evolution prepares the way for the *logos* of policy, as Kurzweil advocates for the aggressive development of artificial intelligence as a pathway to further progress in our evolution.

For Kurzweil, the implications of humanity's evolution are as far reaching as any mythic vision of Nikolai Fedorov or Teilhard de Chardin. Evolving, technological humans will awaken a slumbering universe to consciousness. In his 2005 publication, *The Singularity is Near*, he reiteratess the apocalyptic vision: "The universe is not conscious—yet. But it will be. Strictly speaking, we should say very little of it is conscious today. But that will change and soon."[52] Evolution remains at the heart of his epiphanous Law of Accelerating Returns (LOAR), virtually a name for his narrative of human technological progress. He writes:

> The primary idea in my three previous books on technology . . . is that an evolutionary process inherently accelerates . . . and that its products grow exponentially in complexity and capability. I call this

phenomenon the law of accelerating returns (LOAR), and it pertains to both biological and technological evolution.[53]

Kurzweil's LOAR is not a reiteration of standard Darwinian evolutionary thinking, but the centerpiece of a mythic account of the emergence of complexity and intelligence.

Kurzweil's expansive and complex narrative of human evolution posits that human agents will bring consciousness to every corner of the cosmos. This work of consciousness colonization approximates the traditional view of God and is the direct consequence of evolution:

> Evolution moves toward greater complexity, greater elegance, greater knowledge, greater intelligence, greater beauty, greater creativity, and greater levels of subtle attitudes such as love. In every monotheistic tradition God is likewise described as all of these qualities, only without limitation: infinite knowledge, infinite intelligence, infinite beauty, infinite creativity, infinite love, and so on.[54]

The spiritual tenor of Kurzweil's evolutionary narrative is inescapable in *The Singularity is Near*:

> Of course, even the accelerating growth of evolution never achieves an infinite level, but as it explodes exponentially it certainly moves rapidly in that direction. So evolution moves inexorably toward this conception of God, although never quite reaching this ideal. We can regard, therefore, the freeing of our thinking from the severe limitations of its biological form to be an essentially spiritual undertaking.[55]

Kurzweil's *mythos* makes evolution a "spiritual undertaking," placing him in the stream of the evolutionary mythographers Bergson, Teilhard, Huxley, Haeckel, and Moravec. While evolution may have been launched as a biological process, it is transcending biology and assuming its true mission: the creation of gods, a Cosmic Christ, or God. Into the apparent contradiction of a created creator steps Ray Kurzweil as tragic hero, conquering the restrictions of natural law in a grand apocalyptic vision that lifts all of us heavenward. It has taken Kurzweil a lifetime to formulate his vision of LOAR and Singularity, and his ideas have on occasion been mocked and rejected by the public and even the tech community. His prophetic role has at times forced him out of the community and into a desert place where he has experienced a unifying epiphany, a radical and comprehensive Law for understanding human and cosmic purpose. Out of this new cosmos emerges a vision of "the god" that is, in Frye's phrase, "unlimited power in a humanized form."[56]

RESPONSES

This chapter has considered mythic treatments of evolution that have their roots in evolutionary thinking that pre-dates Darwin's *On The Origin of the Species*, and that situate evolution as the ontological force in the universe. These narratives attribute "metaphysical significance" to evolution, presenting the process as purposeful, capable of human direction, and tending toward a spiritual outcome.[57] The myth of directed and spiritualized evolution has, as we have seen, a long history. It has now become, along with the myth of inevitable and transformative technological progress, a foundational component of technofuturist discourse. In this last section of the chapter I would like to examine some important critical responses to the vision of evolution as a transformative force that humans ought to appropriate to change themselves.

Critics of the metaphysical turn in talking about evolution have raised various objections to it. In the 1970s physicist and neuroscientist attendee Donald MacKay (1922–1987) noted that evolution started developing into a religious view almost from the time of its initial appearance in the mid-nineteenth century:

> Hardly was it published . . . before this purely scientific idea was seized upon in the interests of atheism and turned into something quite different. . . . 'Evolution' began to be invoked in biology apparently as a substitute for God. And if in biology, why not elsewhere?

The concept of evolution moved rapidly "from standing for a technical hypothesis" to "an atheistic *metaphysical* principle, whose invocation could relieve a man of any theological shivers at the spectacle of the universe." According to MacKay, "'Evolutionism' became a name for a whole antireligious philosophy, in which 'Evolution' played the role of a more or less personal deity, as the 'real force in the universe.'"[58]

Given its prominence in human enhancement circles this alternative narrative of evolution is challenging the hegemony of religious origin and culmination narratives. We have noted that thinkers such as Julian S. Huxley jettisoned the view that God was in charge of human development and destiny. God's removal from the cosmic narrative did not imply religion's simultaneous removal, however, a new evolutionary vision was poised to displace the old one founded on the work of God. It would appear that we are in the presence of a new myth, a sacred narrative that situates us in the cosmos, describing both our origins and our *telos*. Philosopher of science Mary Midgley has for decades been reminding her readers that to call a narrative a myth "does not of course mean that it is a false story." Rather, "it means that it has great symbolic power, which is independent of its truth."[59]

Technologically directed human evolution is envisioned as a process that will involve moral as well as physical progress for the human race. In the evolutionary narrative of Huxley, Kurzweil and others, evolution becomes the agent of physical complexification, moral improvement and ultimately of the cosmos's spiritual transformation. We are now involved in the work of assisting in this great transformational process, assisting evolution as purposeful agents who have prepared ourselves for this role by technologically directing our own evolution.

Physician and philosopher Jeffrey Bishop raises moral concerns about a vision of evolution that implies that we are merely assistants to an inexorable force. To make evolution or technology into agents is to relieve ourselves of moral responsibility—we are just following orders. Bishop notes that writers such as John Harris and other proponents of directed evolution turn evolution into an "ontological creative force." Directed evolution is affirmed as achieving "a new state in human history where evolution is no longer natural selection," but rather a process of "deliberate selection." Thus, evolution is radically altered from natural process to a project of the self-governing human will.[60]

Bishop refers to this new understanding of evolution as "power ontology." "The point is," writes Bishop, "that rational human will directs evolutionary history." Bishop is suspicious of future-visions in which "this achievement is mediated through the deployment of technology with all of its attendant powers."[61] Evolution becomes the product of "the human will," itself alleged to be "an evolutionary achievement" that now "turns to order the chaos of creative ontology, and thereby enacts an ordering theology." Humans transform themselves into gods on the argument that their destiny is to refine and direct natural processes. Bishop writes:

> This ordering force—this human will set to order the powers of creation—is transhumanism's theology. The human will is a product of the creative force of becoming, which turns for the moment to master and control its own becoming.[62]

The visionary turn away from evolution as a natural process and toward evolution as a willful plan is essential to the Transhumanist and technofuturist vision of the human future. As such it is closely related to a counter-intuitive understanding of the human being that has gained remarkable currency since the middle of the twentieth century. This complementary narrative of the person as information is the subject of the next chapter.

6 Life as Information

When and where did information get constructed as a disembodied medium? How were researchers convinced that humans and machines are brothers under the skin?

—N. Katherine Hayles

I explained how life ultimately consists of DNA-driven biological machines.

—J. Craig Venter

No one today is surprised in the least that the brain . . . should be compared to a digital computer. There was, moreover, a time . . . when the computer was called an "electronic brain.

—Jean-Pierre Dupuy

What constitutes human identity? Answers to this question have until recently focused on the body, actions and reputation, or the divinely created soul. Such thinking began to change when Oswald Avery (1877–1955) of Rockefeller University discovered the role of DNA in carrying the details of an organism in 1944. When nine years later the English research team of James Watson and Francis Crick unveiled the double helix structure of DNA it seemed that a new answer to the conundrum of human identity was needed, one that acknowledged the individual's unique genetic structure. A narrative of life and identity began to take shape that located the essence of the human in code-carrying structures in the nuclei of cells.[1] The individual began to look like a pattern of information rather than a present body. If this were the case, human beings could be assessed, stored, and transmitted much like any other source of data.

Viewing the human being as information has deep historical roots. Following the Enlightenment the natural sciences were seen as the model for the study of human populations. Social groups were assessed using numerical models. Human beings could be studied in the aggregate; patterns of behavior were evident in large populations. Statistical analysis of large populations meant that scientific certainty about human behaviors would replace personal generalization and religious revelation. A science of human societies was possible—a social science.

With the growth of the social sciences the notion that the activities of large human populations were measurable became widely accepted. The methods of the social scientist could be employed to measure and predict economic behavior, political activity, workplace efficiency, and even religious belief. It was also possible to understand how ideas gained traction with the public. Gregor Mendel (1822–1884) revealed the basic principles of genetic inheritance in 1865. Invisible "factors" governed traits of living organisms, and connected each new generation to earlier ones in predictable, measurable ways. Increased understanding of genetics suggested that a similarly measurable approach to the individual person was also possible. Traits and tendencies, proclivities, and even appearance had their origins in the microscopic world of the cell.

The idea that the traits by which we identify one another—facial features, stature, voice, and even personality—were expressions of a code stored in our cells gradually gained acceptance. Watson and Crick's 1953 discovery of the shape of the DNA molecule fueled public interest in the genetic bases of life and identity. Richard Dawkins' landmark 1976 work, *The Selfish Gene* placed the gene in the center of what it means to be human. Dawkins' narrative of life suggested more, however: what it means to be an *individual* human was actually governed by the gene. Genes rather than character or a soul made us who we are. A new vision of human identity was taking shape; cells made up the human cosmos and the gene was the monarch on the throne of life. This new vision of life suggested that the embodied individual, a physically present agent, was no longer the essence of the person.

The perennial gene, bearer of information, indicated that we had been making far too much of notions such as personality and individuality. "Individuals are not stable things, they are fleeting." Only genes endure. Dawkins was casting a new vision of life:

> Chromosomes . . . are shuffled into oblivion, like hands of cards
> soon after they are dealt. But the cards themselves survive the shuf-

fling. The cards are the genes. The genes are not destroyed by cross-ing over, they merely change partners and march on. Of course they march on. That is their business. They are the replicators and we are their survival machines. When we have served our purpose, we are cast aside. But genes are the denizens of geological time: genes are forever.[2]

In this narrative genes are intentional agents—they change partners, they march on, they conduct their business, and they survive. Genes carry infor-mation and this information makes us human and provides us our identity. "The argument of this book is that we, and all other animals, are machines created by our genes," was Dawkins' reductionist conclusion.[3] Nevertheless, his narrative of the gene as selfish agent had paradigmatic significance—it provided, in Midgley's phrase, a new "imaginative pattern" for thinking about life and identity.[4]

The genetic turn shifted narratives of identity away from the physical body and toward patterns of information, a change that gained momentum as medical technology enabled the alteration of physical appearance and as computers allowed the construction of "digital selves." The perennial ver-ity of a single persistent identity for each person was suddenly under radical scrutiny. Media theorist Lisa Nakamura is among a growing group of schol-ars who question whether the body is any longer essential to identity:

Chosen identities enabled by technology such as online avatars, cos-metic and transgender surgery and body modifications, and other cyberprostheses are not breaking the mold of unitary identity, but rather are shifting identity into the realm of the 'virtual,' a place not without its own laws and hierarchies.[5]

Identity as information is crucial to visions of downloading personalities into computers as a means of achieving immortality. Brent Waters writes of the Transhumanist vision of the person, "In brief, they believe that nature and human nature can be reduced to their underlying information and, using appropriate technologies, reshaped in more desirable ways."[6]

This chapter considers the developing *mythos* of the informational per-son—the individual as a pattern of data. This narrative challenges tradi-tional physical accounts of identity with a conception of the individual as an aggregation of immaterial data. We begin by reviewing early sources of the vision of the informational person. These include the Macy Conferences of the 1950s and Hans Moravec's classic 1988 work on robotics and artificial intelligence, *Mind Children*. We will also consider the case for genetic iden-tity of the person developed by famed genomic biologist J. Craig Venter, and the rising discourse of the information person discovered in various corporate settings. The myth of the informational person will then be traced in the Mind Clones project advocated by inventor and Transhumanist Martine Rothblatt. The chapter's concluding section considers critical responses to this new vision of human identity and its centrality to technofuturist dreams.

THE MACY CONFERENCES

Rendering individual identity a matter of information was one consequence of the Macy Conferences, a series of meetings occurring in New York between 1946 and 1953. Sponsored by the Josiah Macy Jr. Foundation, these gatherings of leading British and American intellectual figures of the day covered a wide range of topics. The loosely structured conversations were intended to bring greater unity to science and achieve greater understanding of the human mind.[7] Re-imagining human identity was particularly relevant at the dawn of the computer age. Also on the agenda was developing strategies for bringing the rigor of the natural sciences to the social sciences.

In the post-war years remarkable new technologies were reshaping foundational understandings of life itself. Computers garnered increasing attention in the academy, business, and with the public, and inevitable comparisons were drawn between these calculating machines and the brain. Erwin Schrodinger's landmark 1944 book, *What Is Life?* suggested that information was at the center of biological systems. Schrodinger posited the existence of a "code-script" in the cell, a sequence of information stored in the genes and providing an organism its characteristic qualities. If other organisms were shaped by genetic information, human beings were as well. Physical laws governed much that had previously been attributed to inaccessible entities such as the mind or the soul.

The greatest intellectual energy in the Macy discussions developed around those conferees devoted to the new field of cybernetics—the study of self-adjusting information feedback systems. A cybernetics group was formed to discuss new understandings of the human being, the brain, and complex neural networks. Historian of science Steve Heims writes that the cybernetics group "was interested in models of the brain based on electronic circuitry and inclined to mechanistic philosophy."[8] Macy conferees searched for a language that would allow productive conversations across disciplinary boundaries. Of particular concern was a common discourse of the person. New research agendas and commercial ventures also required a definition of the person a computer would understand. Mechanical metaphors of the human being emerged; the mind itself was a kind of computer.[9]

A narrative of the human was developing that "made information seem more important than materiality within the research community."[10] As physicists took an interest in the field of neurobiology, machine analogies of the brain proliferated. Cyberneticist and Macy conferee Warren S. McCullough wrote in 1955, "Everything we learn of organisms leads us to conclude not merely that they are *analogous* to machines but that they *are* machines."[11] Brains became for cyberneticists, "a very ill understood variety of computing machines."[12] As Jean-Pierre Dupuy summarizes the developing view in the 1950s, "The brain is a machine and the mind is a machine, and the machines in each case are the same: therefore mind and brain are one and the same."[13]

The idea of meaning was also being newly construed along a narrative line suggested by physics. Meaning was to be found, not in the interaction of minds, but in "causal physical laws."[14] Dupuy notes that theorists discussed complex systems as entities with a life of their own. Such systems produced "emergent" or "autonomous" functions." Systems behaved

> as if their paths are guided by an end that gives meaning and direction to them even though it has not yet been reached; as if, to borrow Aristotelian categories, purely efficient causes were capable of producing effects that mimic the effects of a final cause.[15]

The person as information was consistent with the basic principles of cybernetics, a science that pre-dated digital computers. Feedback was shorthand for "information about the outcome of any process or activity." The cyberneticist's "feedback loop" characterized a self-regulating mechanism's response to information from its environment, and the person was such a feedback-based system. Like Grey Walter's widely publicized autonomous mechanical tortoises, the human brain processed information from its environment and adjusted accordingly. This cybernetic analogy led to a "stimulus-response" view—the person as information processing system. As the human being was increasingly understood by reference to mechanistic metaphors, machines appeared to share qualities with human beings. McCullough, however, was not simply interested in mechanizing the human; he was "intent on 'humanizing the machine,' as he put it."[16]

As computers attracted the attention of business, the academy, and the military it was important that information possess "a stable value as it moved from one context to another." This meant that information needed to be cut free from the idea of subjective meaning. Information thus became a value-neutral currency—data. N. Katherine Hayles notes that had information remained "tied to meaning it would potentially have to change value every time it was embedded in a new context."[17] There appeared to be profound implications for consciousness in the new view. *"Taken out of context,"* writes

Hayles, "the definition allowed information to be conceptualized as if it were an entity that can flow unchanged between different material substrates, as when Moravec envisions the information contained in a brain being downloaded into a computer."[18]

Following the Macy meetings, mechanical metaphors informed narratives of the newly invented informational person. Heims writes that "The effort was always to give mathematical form, to simulate by a machine, or in other ways to resemble engineering when speaking of anything human, even the most personal feeling."[19] Consistent with cybernetic theory the human mind was no longer a mental entity but a mechanical one; consciousness was an epiphenomenon that emerged out of the brain's complex electrical circuitry.

A new narrative of the person was taking shape: the person was information and the brain was an information processing computer. The body itself was a machine and societies were large collections of such informational entities. The new person could interact seamlessly with machines because he or she was a kind of machine that operated on the basis of available information—just like a computer. Just as computers were progressing to greater levels of efficiency and speed, so might the human mind-machine be adapted to become more powerful. The information that formed an individual's identity might be stored in another, more permanent format—perhaps in the hard drive of a computer.

HANS MORAVEC: UPLOADING CONSCIOUSNESS

Physicist and computer scientist Giulio Prisco, a leading Transhumanist and a former senior manager of the European Space Agency, advocates mind uploading as a means of achieving immortality. If the human mind is a computational machine then it "can be transferred from a biological brain to another computational substrate." He adds that, "once mind uploading technology is available, humans will be able to live indefinitely in non-biological bodies and make backup copies of themselves."[20] Uploading a human mind into a machine became an imaginative possibility because of the informational turn taken by Macy conferees. Contemporary narratives of uploading a personality into a computer, commonplace in enhancement and Transhumanist circles, also owe a great deal to computer scientist Hans Moravec.

In his groundbreaking 1988 book, *Mind Children: The Future of Robot and Human Intelligence*, Moravec developed an early and persuasive narrative describing what has since come to be known as mind uploading. With vivid visualization, Moravec made his readers patients in an exotic surgical procedure:

You are wheeled into the operating room. A robot brain surgeon is in attendance. By your side is a computer waiting to become a human equivalent, lacking only a program to run. Your skull, but not your brain, is anesthetized. You are fully conscious. The robot surgeon opens your brain case and places a hand on your brain's surface. The unusual hand bristles with microscopic machinery, and a cable connects it to the mobile computer by your side.

At the end of the procedure "your mind has been removed from the brain and transferred to a machine" and "your suddenly abandoned body goes into spasms and dies." But, there is nothing to worry about, for "the computer simulation has been disconnected from the cable leading to the surgeon's hand and reconnected to a shiny new body of the style, color, and material of your choice. Your metamorphosis is complete."[21]

Moravec's narrative compares uploading to religious accounts of immortality, while at the same time seeking to disconnect digital immortality *from* religion:

It is easy to imagine human thought freed from bondage to a mortal body—belief in an afterlife is common. But it is not necessary to adopt a mystical or religious stance to accept the possibility. Computers provide a model for even the most ardent mechanist.

Introducing the central element of uploading narratives, Moravec assures readers that just as "a computation in progress—what we can reasonably call a computer's thought process—can be halted in midstep and transferred," it is easy to "imagine that a human mind might be freed from its brain in some analogous . . . way."[22]

Moravec anticipated that the question of identity would have to be convincingly addressed in order for the concept of uploading to gain broad acceptance. Opponents would respond that "the end result will be a new person," not the same individual who originally submitted to the process, but "a self-deluded impostor." Moreover, "If the copying process destroys the original, then I have been killed." Moravec refers to this as "the *body-identity position*," a view he rejects in favor of "an alternative position" which he termed "*pattern-identity.*"

Moravec joined uploading to the person-as-data narrative that had emerged from the Macy Conferences. He explains that "body-identity assumes that a person is defined by the stuff of which a human body is made." If this is the case then "only by maintaining continuity of body stuff can we preserve an individual person." However, "pattern-identity . . . defines the essence of a person, say myself, as the *pattern* and the *process* going on in my head and body." Thus:

> If the process is preserved, I am preserved. The rest is mere jelly. The body-identity position, I think, is based on a mistaken intuition about the nature of living things. In a subtle way, the preservation of pattern and loss of substance is a normal part of everyday life.[23]

The data-as-identity view renders the body inconsequential to one's essential personhood. It is not the body that matters, but immaterial patterns of information.[24]

Apocalyptic imagery informs Moravec's narrative of the downloadable informational person. In a fashion reminiscent of Nikolai Fedorov's dream of mass resurrection, he writes: "Wholesale resurrection may be possible through the use of immense simulators." Such a simulator could be "made out of a superdense neutron star" that might provide an environment so detailed that "simulated people would be as real as you or me, though imprisoned in the simulator." The possibilities are endless. Combining information-based personality transfer with the simulation argument, Moravec suggests that "we could 'download' our minds directly into a body in the simulation and 'upload' back into the real world when our mission is accomplished."

Moravec imagined that "it might be fun to resurrect all the past inhabitants of the earth in this way and to give them an opportunity to share with us in the (ephemeral) immortality of transplanted minds. Resurrecting one small planet should be child's play long before our civilization has colonized even its first galaxy."[25] Resurrecting the populations of entire planets is a legitimate scientific goal in this story. Brent Waters notes that Moravec can craft such narratives because the human mind and thus the human person "cannot be anything other than information."[26]

J. Craig Venter and the Human Genome

In 2003 two research teams—one government-backed and the other privately funded—deciphered the impossibly complex code of the human genome. The leader of the private genome mapping project, J. Craig Venter, stunned the scientific community four years later, in 2007, with his claim to have created the first synthetic, self-replicating life form. The J. Craig Venter Institute announced that the new bacterium "is the proof of principle that genomes can be designed in the computer, chemically made in the laboratory and transplanted into a recipient cell to produce a new self-replicating cell controlled only by the synthetic genome."[27]

In his BBC Dimbley lecture the same year, Venter argued that creating new forms of life was a moral obligation. "[T]he future of life depends not only in our ability to understand and use DNA, but also, perhaps in creating new synthetic life forms, that is, life which is forged not by Darwinian evolution but created by human intelligence." In a subsequent interview, Venter acknowledged that coming changes "may be troubling, but part of the problem we face with scientific advancement is the fear of the unknown—fear that often leads to rejection. . . ." Dismissing anticipated criticism, Venter concluded, "Science is a topic which can cause people to turn off their brains." [28]

Venter tirelessly promotes a vision of life as information. In his book, *Life at the Speed of Light*, human beings are "DNA machines." Venter reaches for a vivid image developed by Richard Dawkins—life as a river of information flowing out of the biblical Eden: "Expanding upon this idea, biologist and writer Richard Dawkins came up with the evocative image of a river out of Eden. This slow flowing river consists of information, of the codes for building living things." [29] In this origin myth, life emerges from a living river of information. The definition of life as information encoded in a DNA codescript "has come to dominate biological science, so much so that biology in the twenty-first century has become an information science." [30]

Venter traces the arc of the information narrative from Erasmus Darwin's filament of life, to Schrodinger's "aperiodic crystal," and finally to DNA. He disparages an alternate story—that of genetic epiphenomena—as a modern version of vitalism. "Vitalism today manifests itself in the guise of shifting emphasis away from DNA to an 'emergent' property of the cell that is somehow greater than the sum of its molecular parts and how they work in a particular environment." Such stories reflect unscientific superstitious belief in occult life-forces. "Some have not abandoned the notion that life is based on some mysterious force." [31] Vitalism is a "belief system" rather than a scientific theory.

In Venter's narrative DNA is concerned solely with information retention, organization and transfer. He thus sees his account as a demythologization of the story of life. The insight about DNA is, however, a point of mythic epiphany for Venter: life itself is a code-script that can be digitized and thus instantaneously sent from one place to another instantly. Such transferred data can be reconstructed by a recipient from available chemicals. This is life at the speed of light, the transcendent world of information and the natural world of biological life coming into alignment. This epiphany is physically located in the DNA molecule itself, with its ladder-like structure bridging the mundane world of biology and the immaterial realm of pure information. [32] Epiphanies are sacred insights, and this one promises life without limits.

The informational turn also means that we can rearrange life, inventing new forms to meet new needs. For Venter such work becomes humanity's moral duty:

> All living cells run on DNA software, which directs hundreds of thousands of protein robots. We have been digitizing life for decades, since we first figured out how to read the software of life by sequencing DNA. Now we can go in the other direction by starting with computerized digital code, designing a new form of life, chemically synthesizing its DNA, and then booting it up to produce the actual organism.[33]

Human beings as highly evolved DNA machines are now empowered to redesign the "software of life." By this means "humankind is about to enter a new phase of evolution."[34] Venter's vision of life as transmittable and malleable information extends human capacities almost infinitely: "When life is finally able to travel at the speed of light, the universe will shrink, and our powers will expand."[35] The implications for commerce are also endless.

MARTINE ROTHBLATT ON MIND CLONES

Entrepreneur, attorney, and communication satellite expert Martine Rothblatt (b. 1954), founded Sirius Radio and United Therapeutics. The highest paid woman in the United States, she is also among the most influential. Rothblatt is a Transhumanist who has set out a plan to achieve digital immortality through the development of what she terms Mindclones—individual digital personalities constructed from information about a living person. Rothblatt sees limitless potential in personality construction and storage, a vision founded on the myth of the informational person. Through her Vermont based Terasem Foundation, Rothblatt and associates have been testing this idea with the robotic personality, Bina 48, a talking mindclone crafted to resemble Rothblatt's wife, Bina. Terasem Foundation has spawned a religion called Terasem Movement Transreligion, or Terasem Faith. This boundary-crossing faith is described as "a movement which can be combined with any existing religion, without have to leave a previous religion."[36] In keeping with this religious turn, Rothblatt casts a vision of inevitable, affordable, and digital immortality in the near future.

A frequent speaker at Transhumanist and technofuturist conferences, Rothblatt develops strong connections with her large audiences. She recognizes that talk of digital replication of personalities and digital immortality makes people uncomfortable. However, always the entrepreneur, Rothblatt counters:

As uncomfortable as it makes some—a discomfort we have to deal with—the mass marketing of a relatively simple, accessible and affordable means for Grandma, through her mindclone, to stick around for graduations that will happen several decades from now, represents the *real* money.[37]

Mindclones can begin as simple mindfiles, repositories of information about a person that can be collected at any time and built up gradually. In, *Virtually Human: The Promise and the Peril of Digital Immortality*, Rothblatt writes:

> There is no doubt that once digital cloning technology is fully developed, widely available, and economically accessible to 'average consumers,' mindclone creation will happen at the speed of our intentionality—as fast as we want it to.[38]

Recognizing the ambiguity of the term consciousness, Rothblatt affirms that mindclones will achieve a version of self-awareness she terms cyberconsciousness. Indeed, we are already crossing the threshold from biological consciousness to Cyberconsciousness. "While still in its infancy, Cyberconsciousness is quickly increasing in sophistication and complexity." Cyberconsciousness will receive a boost from "the development of powerful yet accessible software, called *mindware*," which will be employed to "activate a digital file of your thoughts, memories, feelings and opinions—a *mindfile*—and operate on a technology-powered twin, or *mindclone*."[39]

The mindclone also holds out the possibility of self-improvement via digital auto-eugenics. "By tweaking our mindware to make our mindclones a bit better than ourselves, our immediate goal is not even positive eugenics; it is more akin to self-enhancement or self-augmentation because your mindclone is you."[40] Thus, in Rothblatt's narrative the mindclone is not simply a way to re-create certain aspects of the individual but is a path to enhancement.

Rothblatt's *mythos* exhibits Vico's *fantasia*, a "power fully and completely to order the world."[41] Comprehensive cultural change will accompany the cyberconsciousness/cyber-immortality revolution. "The eventual sophistication and ubiquity" of cyberconsciousness "will naturally raise societal, philosophical, political, religious, and economic issues." Nevertheless, it is certain that "cyberconsciousness will be followed by new approaches to civilization that will be as revolutionary as were ideas about personal liberty, democracy and commerce at the time of their births." In Rothblatt's epic mythic vision the future holds the certainty of "liberty from death via digital immortality. . . ." Immortality is not the end of the story, however, for we can also expect "electorates with cyberconscious majorities and the extended commercial rights and obligations of people with mindclones." With such a revolution ahead, Rothblatt urges her readers to, "Get ready."[42]

RESPONSES

A powerful narrative is developing in the discourse of human enhancement and Transhumanism that equates the person with information. The theologian Brent Waters finds this narrative to constitute a salvific myth, which he summarizes as follows:

> The rough storyline of the emerging posthuman myth (and it is a salvific myth) goes something like this: the essence of a human being is the information constituting the mind or will. Unfortunately, this information is confined to a body that imposes unacceptable constraints upon the will and that deteriorates over a relatively short period of time.[43]

This narrative of the informational person is also evident in mainstream research and commercial settings. For instance, Google has recently hired Oxford University philosopher Luciano Floridi to address the question of what constitutes human identity. Science journalist Robert Herritt writes, "For Floridi, you *are* your information, which comprises everything from data about the relations between particles in your body, to your life story, to your memories, beliefs, and genetic code." Floridi argues that developments in technology have "brought about a shift in self-understanding that's as dramatic as the ones precipitated by Copernicus, Darwin, and Freud." This paradigm shift is as consequential as "discovering the operative mechanism of evolution or that the earth orbits the sun." With this shift in understanding of the human being, we now occupy a new and largely immaterial zone of existence—the "infosphere." While Darwin "revealed that we aren't special and separate from the rest of the animal kingdom," information and communication technologies have shown us that we are "interconnected informational organisms." We are "made of information." Herritt writes, "We all exist together in what Floridi calls the infosphere—an ecosystem that a company like Google has significant power to shape."[44]

The narrative of the informational person, which Floridi treats as a clearly established fact, privileges information over the bodies and minds that provide it. Information is always information *about* something, and it is derived from sources other than itself; information is neither disconnected from the physical world nor meaningless to minds. Mary Midgley writes, "Information is not a third kind of stuff added to Cartesian mind and body or designed to supersede them. It is an abstraction from them. Invoking such an extra stuff is as idle as an earlier talk of phlogiston or animal spirits or occult forces." Information, she writes, "is facts about the world. . . ."[45]

Literary scholar N. Katherine Hayles has explored popular fiction's role in propagating the idea that to be human is to be information. Science fiction author William Gibson, for example, "makes the point vividly in *Neuromancer* when the narrator characterizes the posthuman body as 'data made flesh.'"[46] Hayles discerns profound moral risks in the informational person narrative. If we sever data from bodies, for instance, what do we owe the body? She writes, "the cultural contexts and technological histories" in which the body is reduced to the cyberneticist's "cellular automata" or complex system of information support the idea "that because we are essentially information, we can do away with the body."[47] Hayles thus contends that we must "demystify the assumption that information is more essential than matter or energy."[48]

Hayles finds helpful guidance in the work of Antonio Damasio, who focuses on "the complex mechanisms" linking the mind and the body. Damasio "emphasizes that the body is more than a life-support system for the brain." The body supplies "content" that is "part and parcel of the workings of the normal mind." Thus:

> [F]eelings constitute a window through which the mind looks into the body. Feelings are how the body communicates to the mind information about its structure and continuously varying states. If feelings and emotions are the body murmuring to the mind, then feelings are 'just as cognitive as other precepts,' part of thought and indeed part of what makes us rational creatures.[49]

Software designer and enhancement critic Jaron Lanier has also noted that the idea that identity is to be discovered in information constitutes something like an aggressive reductionist religious view:

> [I]f you want to make the transition from the old religion, where you hope God will give you an afterlife, to the new religion, where you hope to become immortal by getting uploaded into a computer, then you have to believe information is real and alive. . . . You demand that the rest of us live in your new conception of a state religion. You need us to deify information to reinforce your faith.[50]

For Lanier, "information underrepresents reality," and there are risks involved in this underrepresentation. "Demand more from information than it can give, and you end up with monstrous designs."[51] He also finds advocates of uploading the informational person insufficiently open to the mystery of life. "They want to live in an airtight reality that resembles an idealized computer program, in which everything is understood and there are no fundamental mysteries. They recoil from even the hint of a potential zone of mystery or an unresolved seam in one's worldview." As an alternative to the seamlessness of Transhumanist myths of digital immortality, he offers the full experience of the life we currently enjoy. "What matters instead, I believe, is a sense of focus, a mind in effective concentration, and an adventurous individual imagination that is distinct from the crowd." [52]

Nevertheless, artificial intelligence experts such as Ben Goertzel affirm the uploading narrative, writing that "some of us [will] leave our human bodies and brains behind and explore new ways of existing and interacting." Such radical technological applications will, he acknowledges, bring with them "profound philosophical implications." Consequently, thinking about uploading requires "taking a deep look at the nature of the mind and the universe." The human race itself will have to be reconsidered in light of technology; technological immortality will necessitate new definitions of "self and identity." Goertzel recognizes that these questions are preparing us for spiritual transformation, one that brings with it considerable risk. "[T]hinking about these possibilities from a purely technological perspective is inadequate and may perhaps be dangerously misleading," he writes. [53]

In addition to moral issues and logical mistakes associated with it, the narrative of the informational person carries implications for conceptions of the self. To see ourselves principally as data may shift our cultural focus away from human rights and human flourishing, and toward informational concerns. Sociologist Zygmunt Bauman has also noted that we find ourselves confronted by numerous options for "constructing a self," a possibility that may leave us uncertain about how to shape a *stable* self. Modernity gave us the autonomous self, and post-modernity the flexible self. We may now be entering a period of "liquid modernity" in which identity dissolves into the infinitely malleable "liquid self." The person as information view may suggest impermanent, shifting identity; identity becomes a matter of strategy, convenience, or a thirst for change. [54]

Further complicating the question of shaping a self, the myth of the informational person pushes considerations of gender toward irrelevance. Informational persons are less sexual/biological entities than asexual technological ones for whom gender, like identity itself, becomes liquid. Such informational individuals prepare the way for the merger of human and machine, and in this technofuturist vision gender assumes a diminished role in identity. Gender as an artifact of biological evolution is jettisoned much as scales were when ocean-dwelling creatures emerged onto land. Moreover, if information constitutes the person, and this information may be stored, transferred, and replicated in various formats, reproduction may become a technological process that no longer requires the interaction of sexual biological bodies.

The informational person is accepted in Transhumanist and human enhancement circles as a stage in human evolution, a step away from biology and toward immortality and the posthuman condition. These two components of the broader technofuturist *mythos*—the posthuman and technological immortality—provide the subjects for the following two chapters.

7 Enhanced Brains, Connected Minds

After all it is the brain that counts, and to have a brain suffused by fresh and correctly prescribed blood is to be alive—to think.

—J. D. Bernal

[O]nce it was declared that the brain was just a computer made of meat . . . everything began to look different.

—Mary Midgley

Technology is stitching together all the minds of the living, wrapping the planet in a vibrating cloak of electronic nerves. . . .

—Kevin Kelly

We will enhance our brains gradually through direct connection with machine intelligence until the essence of our thinking has fully migrated to the far more capable and reliable new machinery.

—Ray Kurzweil

As noted in Chapter Two, French paleontologist Teilhard de Chardin envisioned a mental network—the noosphere—that would one day cover the earth much as the biosphere of organic life does. In the middle of the twentieth century, evidence for such a mental web was already present:

I am thinking, of course, in the first place of the extraordinary network of radio and television communications which . . . already link us all in a sort of 'etherized' universal consciousness. But I am also thinking of . . . those astonishing electronic computers which, pulsating with signals at the rate of hundreds of thousands a second, not only relieve our brains of tedious and exhausting work but, because they enhance the essential (and too little noticed) 'speed of thought,' are also paving the way for a revolution in the sphere of research. . . .

For Teilhard, "all these material instruments . . . are finally nothing less than the manifestation of a kind of super-Brain, capable of attaining mastery over some supersphere in the universe."[1]

Transhumanists and other enhancement advocates have been keenly interested in Teilhard's enormously influential vision of ongoing evolution and developments such as the noosphere. At the same time, their attention has been focused on the crucial arena of brain research, and for obvious reasons. The brain is the key to understanding consciousness, improving intellect, focusing directed evolution strategies, and, by extension, shaping the very project of radical enhancement. While the brain remains something of a mystery, brain science is advancing at a rapid pace. John R. Shook, the Director of the Center for Inquiry, sees dramatic breakthroughs ahead: "There may be very little about our brains and about our conscious selves that will remain beyond the reach of . . . radical technologies by this century's end."

Understanding the brain is also the key to finding solutions to mental health problems and a range of social pathologies—important issues to an ideology dedicated to improving the human condition. Shook writes that "too many brains lack sufficient moral capacity" as evidenced by psychiatric categories such as "'psychopath,' 'sociopath,' 'social deviant,' and the like."[2] Breakthroughs in brain science and pharmaceutical science may deliver us into a future in which moral limitations are a thing of the past, perhaps even reducing ethics and moral systems such as religions to irrelevance. Moral systems and religions are no longer adequate; they have produced no consensus about what constitutes morality.

Powerful market forces may eclipse nuanced philosophical speculation about which brain enhancements are ethically justified. Shook writes that "free-market economies will produce moral enhancement therapies based on conventional standards . . . without waiting for philosophical conclusions."[3] Visions of emotional and cognitive enhancements will shape even theses market forces. Rhetorical considerations will also influence crucial definitional issues such as what constitutes happiness. Ed Boyden, director of MIT's Media Lab, writes that "whereas many measures of depression and sadness have been defined, a coherent description of happiness remains elusive." He asks, "How can you augment something if you can't define it?" Thus the search is on for "better, measurable definitions of such phenomena." Boyden notes that "radically new tools are needed to augment the mind," including "new kinds of neural stimulators . . . that enable highly targeted manipulations of the brain." Emerging technologies will allow technicians "to turn specific sets of neurons on and off with brief pulses of blue and yellow light."[4]

The brain is to the twenty-first century what manned space-flight was to the twentieth—a daring and exotic research challenge focusing the attention of numerous scientists and government agencies, and capturing the public's interest. The European Commission announced in 2013 its massive Human Brain Project, a project coordinating the efforts of nations of the European Union as well as European universities and corporations. The project is under the direction of brain scientist Henry Markram. The project's website states:

> The Human Brain Project (HBP) is a European Commission Future and Emerging Technologies Flagship that aims to accelerate our understanding of the human brain, make advances in defining and diagnosing brain disorders, and develop new brain-like technologies.[5]

Not long afterwards United States President Barack Obama announced the Brain Research through Advancing Innovative Neurotechnologies (BRAIN) Initiative:

> BRAIN is part of a Presidential focus aimed at revolutionizing our understanding of the human brain. By accelerating the development and application of innovative technologies, researchers will be able to produce a revolutionary new dynamic picture of the brain that, for the first time, shows how individual cells and complex neural circuits interact in both time and space.[6]

Interest in brain research is high in human enhancement circles, generating visions of the enhanced brain, merging the human brain and machines, and connecting brain to brain. In order to gain an appreciation for the mythic origins of this vision, the chapter first considers a popular narrative imagining a radical agenda for brain research advanced by pioneering Irish futurist and scientist John Desmond Bernal (1901–1971). Bernal's reductionist vision reduced the person to the brain, and proposed enhancing the brain through uncompromising technological interventions.

We will then explore technofuturist discourse about the brain and technologies aimed at increasing intelligence, memory, and other capacities. The chapter also takes up narratives that envision a network of linked minds. The final section looks at efforts to recreate the brain using computer technology, a project driven by therapeutic concerns but with profound implications for human enhancement. Emerging from this complex set of developments, the possibility of technological brain enhancement resides at the center of the Transhumanist vision.

J. D. BERNAL'S NEW VIEW OF THE BRAIN

The brain was until relatively recently sacred terrain protected by its own complexity, shrouded in nearly religious mystery, and beyond the reach of science. Not until 1924 and Hans Berger's development of the electroencephalograph was the brain explored with the precision of the modern laboratory. In his highly influential 1929 essay, "The World, The Flesh and the Devil," legendary Irish scientist J. D. Bernal shattered any remaining brain-reverence, arguing that it ought to be the focus of fearless scientific experimentation. Hava Tirosh-Samuelson notes that Bernal "fantasized about the future where science would transform all aspects of social life and would replace religion as the dominant social force, primarily through the transformation of the human brain."[7] Bernal's vision, then, was to do an end run around myth and transform culture by transforming the brain. However, as Midgley reminds us, we may choose our myths but "we do not have a choice of understanding [the world we inhabit] without using any myths or visions at all."[8]

As a step toward understanding the brain, Bernal proposed sustaining a living human brain without a body. Thus begins his narrative of the autonomous brain, cut free from the cumbersome and error-prone body, the person of the future. "After all," he writes, "it is the brain that counts, and to have a brain suffused by fresh and correctly prescribed blood is to be alive—to think." Referring to a gruesome line of research conducted by Russian scientist Sergei Brukhonenko in 1928 and 1929, Bernal affirmed that "the experiment . . . has already been performed on a dog and that is three-quarters of the way towards achieving it with a human subject." Communicating with a disembodied human brain will be possible, for "already we know the essential electrical nature of nerve impulses; it is a matter of delicate surgery to attach nerves permanently to apparatus which will either send messages to the nerves or receive them."

Bernal's narrative involves a brain thus "connected up" that "continues an existence, purely mental and with very different delights from those of the body, but even now perhaps preferable to complete extinction." A functioning brain operating without the body was preferable to death; indeed, it was deliverance from death.[9]

Myth conveys and reinforces value in a culture, and Bernal's myth of the autonomous brain elevated the life of pure thought by reducing the person to the brain—"it is the brain that counts." As a new *mythos* yielded the *logos* of an experimental agenda, the great scientist suggested radical experiments to enhance the brain's capacity and longevity, and envisioned a network of electronically connected brains. "If a method has been found of connecting a nerve ending in a brain directly with an electrical reactor," he reasoned, "then the way is open for connecting it with a brain-cell of another person." Such connectedness would enable a "more perfect and economic transference of thought" eventuating in the "co-operative thinking of the future." The life of conscious thought is the life of the person.

Bernal's apocalyptic myth reveals a new world just ahead. A bold vision of corporate humanity emerges from his narrative of the autonomous and immortal brain; the old idea of the individual—characterized by an ensouled body and an embodied soul—was passing away.[10] As neuronal connection becomes more common, "connections between two or more minds would tend to become a more and more permanent condition until they functioned as a dual or multiple organism." Gottschall writes that story allows us to "focus on the great predicaments of the human condition."[11] The central human predicament is the certainty of death, and overcoming death is a central concern of Bernal's narrative. In a corporate mental organism, death "would take on a different and far less terrible aspect," due to its being "postponed for three hundred or perhaps a thousand years. . . ." Through constant transferal of "memories and feelings of the older member," the "multiple individual" becomes "immortal." Each new brain would bring to this great project a commitment transcending "the devotion of the most fanatical adherent of a religious sect."

The collective mental organism would exist in a "state of ecstasy." With the "barriers . . . down" between individuals, the divine "complex minds" possess an infinite "lease of life, extend their perceptions and understanding and their actions far beyond those of the individual." Limitless and eternal disembodied minds might explore "the interior of the earth and the stars, the inmost cells of living things themselves, would be open to consciousness through these angels, and through these angels also the motions of stars and living things could be directed." Bernal's *mythos* thus invokes unimagined, god-like powers for enhanced, collective, disembodied, and everlasting human minds. His radical disdain of the body emerges from this vision of the omnipotent and immortal brain.[12] Bernal was not the first to enter this narrative territory, but his scientific stature in the English speaking world ensured that the brain's place in an emerging technological mythology was secure.

ENHANCING THE BRAIN

Famed futurist Kurzweil affirms that brain augmentation is among the first priorities of human enhancement advocates. "My vision of the future is that we will start to augment our brains with nonbiological intelligence starting in the 2030s. We are already doing that with devices and cloud computing outside of our bodies." Vast research efforts backed by equally vast resources propel our growing understanding of the brain, opening the way for an era of intense experimentation in brain enhancement. Research universities as well as private foundations such as the Allen Institute for Brain Science are dramatically expanding knowledge of the brain.[13] Computer scientist and Transhumanist Ramez Naam emphasizes the role of therapeutic technologies in this transformation of the brain:

> As we know now, the power to heal leads to the power to enhance. As we learn how to repair damaged brains, we'll discover an immense amount about how the brain works. That in turn will lead to devices that can improve our mental abilities.[14]

Brain enhancement technologies are already widely employed, while some experimental procedures are opening a new discussion of whether limits ought to be placed on brain augmentation. A team at MIT has successfully transplanted false memories into the brains of mice.[15] Military organizations have a strong interest in technologies with potential enhancement application. The Defense Advanced Research Projects Administration (DARPA) is developing a brain prosthetic that may restore lost memory to injured soldiers.[16] There is also talk of "memory capture" procedures that allow the transferal of memory cells from one mouse brain to another. Brain imaging technology now makes it possible to view cerebral activity, including the formation of words and images.[17] Similar research focused on language production and image recognition is underway at several leading research institutions.[18]

Enhancing intelligence is one perennial goal of brain research. Researchers at the UCLA Geffen School of Medicine and the Laboratory of Neuro Imaging announced the discovery of genes associated with intelligence. A single gene variant "affected brain size as well as a person's intelligence." It is now clear how identifiable genes affect the brain. The potential for genetic engineering of the brain is apparent—a genetic tweak might create a genius.[19] A study at Oxford University showed that electronically stimulating a spot in the brain improves mathematical ability.[20] Implanted electronic devices can also replicate brain functions.

The first successful brain prosthetic has also been developed. An artificial hippocampus in the form of a silicon chip implant "will perform the same processes as the damaged part of the brain it is replacing," thus restoring normal functioning to victims of stroke, epilepsy, or accident.[21] Following the principle of dual use, news of the hippocampus prosthesis led immediately to discussions of enhancement. Philosopher Nicholas Agar has written about some of the enhancement applications of this therapeutic technology. "Perhaps in the years to come some parents will equip their children with electronic hippocampuses that do a considerably better job of translating lessons into memories than do the biological hippocampuses of their schoolmates."[22]

While such reports pique interest, understandable reservation attends the idea of surgically augmenting the brain. The brain is incomprehensibly complex and extremely delicate. Moreover, a change in the functioning of the brain due to a surgical intervention can mean a change in demeanor or even the destruction of personality. In order to prepare the public to be receptive of intimidating risk in the pursuit of unimaginable rewards, narrative is again playing a critical role.

In *More Than Human*, enhancement proponent Ramez Naam vividly portrays a futuristic brain augmentation procedure. "Someday in the future, you take the plunge and have a computer interface implanted in your brain," he writes. Peer pressure plays a role in your decision, as does a desire to get ahead in the workplace. Augmentation brings social as well as intellectual advantages; the enhanced worker contributes in a manner not possible pre-implantation: "Over the coming weeks, you find your work productivity greatly increased. You can work faster, more easily, and more accurately with teammates who have implants than you can with the non-implanted."[23] Predictable workplace divisions develop between the enhanced and the unenhanced:

> In meetings with other implanted workers, you routinely work using mental diagrams, images, and silent speech. In mixed company you take mental control of the presentations, projecting text and images onto the screen and changing them with a facility you never would have reached with a marker and whiteboard.[24]

Augmentation transforms the collegial workplace into a techno-hierarchy of haves and have-nots, though not for the purpose of emphasizing the injustices that might arise because of the costs and risks of enhancement. Rather, Naam emphasizes the tensions arising as brain-enhanced workers easily outmaneuver and outperform their unenhanced counterparts. The divide will mean that the unenhanced worker confronts a dilemma—submit to invasive and expensive procedures or be permanently relegated to the status of organizational appendix, low-level gopher, or custodian of enhanced co-workers' ideas. Naam's point, then, is that enhancement will rapidly spread through the workplace, propelled by both radically improved performance and attendant economic and professional realities. His vivid narrative persuasively portrays a possible future for the brain. Naam writes, "The ability to tinker directly with the inner workings of our brains and connect them directly with computers offers us more power over ourselves than any technology we've discussed thus far."[25]

NOOSPHERIC DREAMS: FROM ENHANCEMENT TO CONNECTION

Movie producer and technology advocate Jim Gilliam captivates audiences with his remarkable story of survival. According to Gilliam, omnipotence is not to be discovered in a distant and invisible deity, but in people connected online. The divine is found in a network of human minds creating something vastly larger and more powerful than themselves. A cancer survivor, Gilliam credits friends who rallied around his cause online with saving his life. He tells audiences that they are all creators, and that online connection is "very spiritual." Gesturing toward the sky he says, "when you are all connected online, you are *the* Creator." Describing how friends pressured medical professionals at a famous hospital to move ahead with a transplant procedure they were reluctant to perform, Gilliam says, "That's when I truly found God." He adds, "God is what happens when humanity is connected."[26] Gilliam articulates one narrative of the technologically networked minds, this one developing out of existing social networking technologies. It turns out to be surprisingly close to Teilhard de Chardin's vision of a noosphere of mental life enveloping the globe. This section explores the vision of enhancing the brain's reach and force. It then examines the critical issue of direct connection between brains and machines. This section closes with a discussion of narratives of direct mental connection.

Networked mental activity is a dream stretching back at least to the Cosmist Vernadsky and the Jesuit Teilhard in the 1920s. The idea of mental connection can also be traced to speculation about mental telepathy and other types of transferable thought. "In the 1920s and '30s," writes Michael Hagemeister, "the assumption of physically measurable brain radiation (the 'brain radio') formed the basis for the pioneering studies of the Leningrad physiologist Leonid Vasiliev (1891–1966) in long-distance telepathy." Telepathy and related concerns were of enormous interest in the first half of the twentieth century, spurred on by developments in radio and television technology. Psychologist J. B. Rhine (1895–1980) of the famed Parapsychological Laboratories at Duke University in the 1920s and 30s undertook systematic telepathy studies. Rhine's book, *Extra-Sensory Perception* (1934) brought him and telepathy a great deal of attention. Novelist Sinclair Lewis wrote *Mental Radio* (1930) about his wife Mary Craig Sinclair's telepathic abilities. Famed psychologist William McDougall wrote the introduction, while the German translation's forward was written by Albert Einstein. Rhine and Lewis carried on an extensive correspondence following the publication of *Mental Radio*.

Cosmists imagined that "besides the atmosphere and the photosphere, our entire planet is enveloped in a sphere of spiritual creation [noosphere], and manifold, iridescent emanation of our energy . . ."[27] The term noosphere itself "was coined in the 1920s by the French mathematician and follower of Henri Bergson, Edouard Le Roy (1870–1954)." However, the first exploration of the concept was likely undertaken by the Cosmist Vernadsky, who envisioned collective thought as part of "a new phase of evolution brought about by conscious human activity."[28] Teilhard and LeRoy heard Vernadsky lecture on the idea at the Sorbonne in 1922. In Russia the idea has also been appropriated in occult circles.[29] Teilhard is most often credited with exploring the concept in detail in *The Phenomenon of Man*. Teilhard's discussion is not easy to interpret, though he seems to be describing not so much a technological network—which might be a late stage of the concept—but a web of ideas that began to envelop the earth as soon as human beings started to communicate.

In Teilhard's vision, the noosphere has evolved along with the human race. While his discussion of the topic is extraordinarily opaque, it is clear that he has in view the slow but certain evolution of an interconnected mental web surrounding the globe. As accretions of social connection—of energy above the level of biology—connect with and augment one another, the noosphere emerges. As this new order emerges to supersede the biosphere, a revelation much like Jim Gilliam's epiphany regarding the transcendent nature of online connection occurs. "One thing at any rate is sure—from the moment we adopt a thoroughly realistic view of the noosphere and of the hyper-organic nature of social bonds, the present situation of the world becomes clearer. . . ."[30]

While the origins of the noosphere stretch back into pre-human time, the evolution of this transcendent technology can no longer be left to chance. The noosphere must be intentionally developed at this point in human history; the further evolution of our species depends on the realization of this unifying vision:

> Thus, amongst the various forms of psychic inter-activity animating the noosphere, the energies we must identify, harness and develop before all others are those of an "intercentric" nature, if we want to give effective help to the progress of evolution in our selves.[31]

"Intercentric" for Teilhard refers to overlapping centers of sources of mental energy. When the final stages of evolution are achieved, a peaceful regime under the domain of the noosphere will emerge. "Some sort of unanimity will reign over the entire mass of the noosphere. The entire convergence will take place in *peace*."[32]

Teilhard's friend and admirer, Julian Sorrel Huxley, placed the noosphere at the center of his own Transhuman dream. In "The Evolutionary Vision" he wrote of the highly evolved human being who "exists and has his being in the intangible sea of thought which Teilhard de Chardin has christened the 'noosphere,' in the same sort of way that fish exist and have their being in the material sea of water which the geographers include in the term 'hydrosphere.'"[33] While it's not clear that Huxley's analogy captures the essence of the noosphere, it is apparent that Huxley placed the concept at the center of the early Transhuman vision.

The idea of a powerful mental collectivity has also had a robust life in fiction. Sir Arthur C. Clarke envisioned a collective intellect as a highly evolved, semi-divine entity in *Childhood's End* (1953), perhaps the most influential and successfully executed science fiction novel ever penned.[34] Among many other possible examples, the most widely known may be the collective consciousness of one of the most popular of *Star Trek* inventions, the hive-minded Borg race. More recently Naam has probed the possibility of a nano-drug that links human minds in his novel, *Nexus*.[35] While *Star Trek*'s Borg or Clarke's Overmind may seem fanciful creations of science fiction, an increasing body of scientific experiment suggests the possibility of communication among directly linked brains.

Technologies that enhance cognitive interface—both brain to machine and brain to brain—are developing at a rapid pace, fueling interest in enhancement circles of a developing global mental network. Voice, eye motion, and brainwave commands have sharply decreased the distance between brain and machine, that connection now heading toward a seamless state.[36] Electronic headbands, for instance, allow game players to control objects by thought alone. Automobile manufacturers are developing thought-operated devices such as trunk openers and other conveniences.[37] Thought-operated drones are seen as a step toward airplanes operated by a pilot's thoughts alone.[38] Mind-controlled wheelchairs and robotic arms have been developed to aid handicapped individuals.[39]

Thought-based technologies have attracted the attention of military forces due to their potential combat and therapeutic applications.[40] Soldiers' helmets may connect electronically with the brain to promote "long term wakefulness and increased attentiveness and stability in battle conditions."[41] DARPA's Reliable Neural-Interface Technology program "is seeking implants that can connect to the human central nervous system reliably for decades," and that "provide quality perception at reliable speeds."[42] Direct brain stimulation would render soldiers and pilots hyper-alert to the presence and movements of enemy combatants.[43] "Neural dust" consisting of microscopic chips placed in the brain will "monitor neural signals at high resolution and communicate data highly efficiently via ultrasound."[44] This approach "is estimated to be ten million times more efficient than [electromagnetic] chips."[45]

Such advances in high-speed human-machine interfaces encourage not just military designers, but proponents of the mental network narrative; there is a close relationship between brain-machine interface and brain-to-brain communication. One dramatic development in the latter arena is the remote electronic linking of mammalian brains—including recently the brains of two human subjects. In early 2013, Duke University researcher Miguel Nicolelis electronically connected the brains of two rats. "The wired brain implants allowed sensory and motor signals to be sent from one rat to another, creating the first ever brain-to-brain interface." The receiver rat correctly interpreted newly learned behaviors from the sender rat:

> The researchers first trained pairs of rats to solve a simple problem—pressing the correct lever when an indicator light above the lever switched on, to obtain a water sip. Researchers then placed the rodents in separate chambers and connected their brains using arrays of microelectrodes . . . inserted into the area of the cortex that processes motor information.

When the first rat pressed the correct lever following a light signal, "its brain activity was delivered as electrical stimulation into the brain of the second rat. . . ." Though the second or "decoder" rat did not see the light signal, it still managed a seventy percent success rate in pressing a lever to receive a reward.

Myths "convey values and expectations," even the expectations of research scientists.[46] From Teilhard's and Vernadsky's noosphere and Bernal's complex mental organism, through Clarke's Overmind and the Borg of *Star Trek*, the myth of connected minds has developed considerable popularity. Nicolelis commented on the success of his experiment as if predicting the advent of the noosphere: "You could actually have millions of brains tackling the same problem and sharing a solution." There is more to the story, for his research will eventually have human application. "We will have a way to exchange information across millions of people without using keyboards or voice recognition devices or the type of interfaces that we normally use today. I truly believe that in a few decades . . . we will know what it is to communicate in that way." One expert observer commented that Nicolelis' research "basically shows that it is possible to take information out of the brain, and it is possible to take information and pump it into the brain." The technology that might enable a noospheric future "is here." The next questions are: "Why are we doing this, and what do we hope to get out of it?"[47]

Remarkably, Nicolelis' experiment was successfully replicated with human subjects at the University of Washington in 2014. In the experiment a "sender" "is hooked to an electroencephalography machine that reads his brain activity . . ." This message from the sender's brain is transmitted into "electrical pulses" that are sent "via the Internet to the 'receiver,' who has a transcranial magnetic stimulation coil placed near the part of his brain that controls hand movements." In this way two human brains are in direct digital contact with one another. The sender can then "issue a command to move the hand of the receiver by simply *thinking* about the hand movement." The sender is playing a video game that involves defending a city by firing a canon. The sender "thinks about firing the cannon at various intervals throughout the game. The 'Fire!' brain signal is sent over the Internet directly to the brain of the receiver, whose hand hits a touchpad that allows him to fire the cannon."

While transmitting a command from one brain to another is not the same as multiplying cognitive ability, the technology feeds the noosphere vision. One University of Washington researcher suggested that the same method used in the initial experiment would also "work reliably with walk-in participants." The UW team has received a grant to explore "decoding and transmitting more complex brain processes, expanding the types of information that can be sent from one brain to another." Chantel Prat of the University of Washington Institute for Learning and Brain Sciences stated that the immediate goal is "therapeutic applications for people with brain injuries or disorders," on the assumption that "you can help the [brain's] recovery process by literally transmitting the waves of a healthy brain to the brain that has been damaged."[48] This claim follows the pattern suggested earlier by Ramez Naam: therapies for the brain will lead to enhancements of the brain.

For some, Nicolelis' experiments point in the direction of a plausible noosphere in the technological future. Ralph H. Abrahams, a complex systems pioneer, captures the mythic spirit of the narrative of collective intelligence in writing, "What we're hoping for is a global increase in the collective intelligence of the human species, without which we cannot survive on this planet."[49] Futurist George Dvorsky adds that "the internet is already very much like this." He adds, however, that "the process of interacting with it is still rather primitive." Imagining a digital communion, Dvorsky writes:

I suspect that collective IQs will rise dramatically, collaborative efforts will increase in scale and potency, and social networking will evolve to a new level. This might even usher in the much speculated age of the global mind in which we will have ubiquitous access to a chorus of friends, thinkers, and specialized groups.[50]

Some see the Internet as a significant step in the direction Dvorsky predicts. Science journalist Robert Wright comments, "The Web is mediating a collective thought process."[51] Today's social networking technologies are "weaving humans into electronic webs that resemble big brains—corporations, online hobby groups, far-flung N.G.O.s." Though such a description of social networks as "big brains" suggests where we might be headed, Wright sees bigger things in the connected human future. It is not "outlandish" to think and talk of ourselves as "neurons in a giant superorganism." In this narrative, connection is salvation: "If we don't use technology to weave people together and turn our species into a fairly unified body, chaos will probably engulf the world—because technology offers so much destructive power that a sharply divided human species can't flourish."[52] According to the noosphere narrative, technological transcendence arrives when collective cognition, enabled by digital connection of radically enhanced brains, transcends the limited potential of the individual brain.

RESPONSES

The human brain is the only known source of intelligence in the cosmos for many Transhumanists; if there were intelligent aliens around they would have contacted us. Thus, the human brain is our one hope. This is why Kurzweil writes, "From this perspective, reverse engineering the human brain may be regarded as the most important project in the universe."[53] Projects don't get any more important than that. Such reverse engineering is the key not only to enhancing the brain's powers, but to connecting the brain to other sources of intelligence, human and machine. As Miguel Nicolelis has said, "You could actually have millions of brains tackling the same problem and sharing a solution." Thus, the merging of enhanced brains and machines, or of many enhanced brains and many machines, would hasten the moment of exponential increase in computational power that transforms history—the Singularity.

The dream of radically enhanced brains and connected minds has, predictably, attracted critics. One line of criticism focuses on the reductionism involved in claiming the human being is contained in the brain. The late theologian Jean Bethke Elshtain points out in her essay, "Cartesian Decapitation," that such reductionism severs the body from the head. Elshtain finds in this maneuver a Cartesian caricature—a disembodied head in need of a body. Mary Midgley points out the essentially rhetorical quality in reductionist narratives: "Formal reductions don't spring up on their own, but like weeds in a garden. They are not value-free. They are always parts of some larger enterprise, some project for reshaping the whole intellectual landscape, and often our general attitude to life as well."[54]

It is not surprising that human enhancement advocates should perform such a reduction; twentieth century discussions of the brain had already located personhood within the cranium. As Bernal stated in the late 1920s, "After all, it is the brain that matters." It is difficult to imagine radical human enhancement without cognitive enhancement. Peter Diamandis and Steven Kotler, for instance, envision a future in which "the majority of humanity will end up merging with technology, enhancing themselves both physically and cognitively."[55] A major step in that direction is already being taken according to a popular narrative of the Internet: It is not just about information any longer, but about enhancing us, especially our brains. Futurist George Dvorsky writes that we will soon witness "the unimpeded connection of the brain with the Internet." When that merger occurs, we will "navigate the Web and communicate with others through our subvocal commands and even our thoughts alone." The Internet will be "less an external resource than . . . an extension of our brain."[56] Proponents point to ways in which human-machine mergers will dramatically enhance intellectual power and eventually allow new spiritual experiences.[57] The broader Transhumanist vision sees such enhancements as an evolutionary step toward the posthuman.

From Teilhard de Chardin and Arthur C. Clarke to Jim Gilliam and George Dvorsky, technofuturists have suggested that joining minds is a path to human transformation. Thought itself is becoming technologically accessible, some experts contending—with support from recent breakthroughs—that it is only a matter of time before machines will read our thoughts remotely.[58] This technological potential for reaching into one's mind will raise obvious privacy concerns at first, but these concerns will pale in comparison to the vastly more threatening specter of limitless, continuous, anonymous, and inescapable thought surveillance. Access to unuttered thought will trigger unprecedented legal and ethical concerns. Nevertheless, research moves forward under the justification that reading thoughts will allow communication with patients in a "locked in" or vegetative state. The border between therapy and enhancement is already a vexing one; that between therapy and intrusion into the last private realm—personal thought—will be vastly more so. Even such intrusions might be justified by the argument that the old evolutionary brain must be enhanced or it will soon be surpassed by the machines it created.

8 Enhanced Humans and Posthumans

It may be that after much labour and many catastrophes in time there will arise a splendid race of men, far wiser than we can hope to be, and far greater hearted.

—Olaf Stapledon[1]

The Bible said that God made man in his own image. The German philosopher Ludwig Feuerbach said that man made God in his own image. The transhumanists say that humanity will make itself into God.

—Sebastian Seung

We are, if we choose to be, the seed from which wondrous new kinds of life can grow.

—Ramez Naam

The person of superior intellectual, physical or spiritual capacity—from Achilles and Athena to Arthur and Joan of Arc—has exercised extraordinary influence over the Western imagination. Ancient sculptors idealized the body and mythographers extolled the exploits of semi-divine heroes. Superhumans, human-divine hybrids and immortals of one type or another enjoy a remarkable presence in popular fiction and spiritual literature. On the mortal plane the exceptional person remains an object of fascination, whether encountered in the professional sporting event or a world chess championship. The unusually gifted individual, the larger than life hero who does not labor under the mundane restraints of an ordinary body or an average mind, exerts a powerful influence over visions of the technological future.

Occupying a central place in the Transhumanist *mythos*, posthumans are the heroic culmination of efforts to direct our own evolution toward the creation of our successors. Posthumans exist only as rhetorical constructions, vaguely sketched but confidently anticipated demigods in a vision of the technological future. The posthuman myth draws together prominent technofuturist themes: directed evolution, exponential technological progress, the merging of human and machine, and the genetic alteration of human beings. Products of our technological efforts, semi-divine guides to further technological transformation, posthumans are the "other" of our own manufacture—gods created in our image.

Technologically altered humans, superhumans, cyborgs, and posthumans have long played a major role in technofuturist narratives. Their presence imparts a mythic quality to these stories, as myth "tells a story of superhuman beings such as gods, demigods, heroes, spirits or ghosts . . ."[2] It is this aspect of myth—the presence and significance of the supernatural being—that I would like to explore here. This chapter first establishes a rhetorical context for the posthuman *mythos* by considering several important early examples of stories of the radically enhanced human being. As we shall see, these early narratives often are haunted by the twin specters of eugenics and racial politics.

We will also examine the posthuman vision in the thought of Transhumanism founder Nick Bostrom and several other prominent voices in the human enhancement movement. These writers develop a mythic frame for discussing the human future by crafting narratives of radical human enhancement culminating in the posthuman. Posthumans are unique in the pantheon of superhumans, however, in that we will create them. The posthuman *mythos* presents this new species of superhumans as the outcome of evolutionary processes controlled and directed by ordinary human beings. The chapter concludes by considering critical reactions to the posthuman vision and to the idea of radical technological enhancement of the human race.

Narrative Precursors

Discussions of superior people or advanced races are common in fiction and non-fiction, modern and ancient. These magnificent beings inhabit unexplored regions of the earth, other planets, Mt. Olympus, or perhaps walk among us unnoticed. They are the offspring of gods and humans, examples of advanced evolution, ante-diluvian survivors, visitors from space, or the products of eugenics or genetic experiment. Regardless of their provenance, persons of extraordinary intellectual or physical capacity are always close at hand. Contemporary descriptions of the enhanced human or the posthuman owe a debt to narratives that preceded them.

The typical nineteenth-century route to enhanced humans was racial mythology. French novelist Arthur de Gobineau (1816–1882) published *On the Inequality of the Races of Man* (1855); races were arranged in a hierarchy with Europeans at the top. Josiah Clark Nott's and George Robert Giddon's *Indigenous Races of the Earth* (1857) advanced a similar "scientific classification" of race. Predictably, the *mythos* of race gave way to the *logos* of political and social policy, often with devastating results. Perhaps the chief example is Houston Stewart Chamberlain's *Foundations of the Nineteenth Century* (German1899; English 1911), a work which exerted extraordinary political and social influence.

Racial mythology was widely embraced on both sides of the Atlantic.[3] According to social historian Leon Poliakov, when the idea of an "unbroken line and succession" for all humanity was jettisoned, the dangerous myth of different points of origin for different races took hold. Such narratives of diverse human origins gave rise "in due course to the Aryan myth."[4] This *mythos* suggested that one race possessed extraordinary spiritual strength, and thus was destined to lead humanity.[5] For Friedrich Schiller (1759–1805), Germans were "elected by the universal spirit to strive eternally for the education of the human race." Heinrich von Kleist (1777–1811) imagined that "the gods" had preserved "the original image of the human species with greater purity" in northern Europeans.[6] These apocalyptic myths subsumed the mundane world under a supernatural order in what historian Dan Stone has termed "a racist worldview." They thus provided a narrative foundation for the *logos* of eugenics.[7] Francis Galton founded the Eugenics Education Society in 1907. While the eugenics narrative promised better people through social planning, superhuman fiction envisioned various posthuman futures. Mary Shelley (1798–1851) imagined a synthetic person who owed its existence to a visionary scientist in her well-known novel *Frankenstein*. George Edward Bulwer-Lytton's *The Coming Race* (1871) located an ancient race of superhumans in vast subterranean caverns. George Bernard Shaw explored superhuman possibilities in his *Back to Methuselah* series (1921), while Philip Wylie's (1902–1971) novel *Gladiator* (1930) explored the conflicted life of a chemically enhanced posthuman in a world unprepared for his presence.[8]

Contemporary movies endlessly reprise the enhanced human *mythos*. The *Robocop* franchise has allowed viewers to watch a living person merge with machinery to produce a super-policeman. Cyborgs have been portrayed many times in fiction from the popular television series *The Six Million Dollar Man* (1974–1978), to the Borg of *Star Trek*. The popular *Iron Man* movies revived the concept of blending human with machine to create a super-human. Biotechnologically enhanced strength and agility is a theme in the *Captain America* series, the *X-Men* films, and related cinematic adaptations of comic book themes. A posthuman artificial intelligence is the centerpiece of the movie *Ex Machina* (2015).

Enhancement Narratives

Ramez Naam, a prominent futurist, novelist, and computer scientist, captured the enhancement vision in his 2005 book, *More Than Human: Embracing the Promise of Biological Enhancement.*[9] Following a narration of the remarkable achievements of human biological and cultural evolution—large brains, specialized tools, art, medicine, philosophy—he reflects on what comes next. "Now the same accelerating pace of change is on the verge of touching us in the most intimate way—by giving us the power to reshape our minds and bodies."[10] Radical enhancement is a story of creating the human race anew using technologies of directed evolution. Naam sketches what has become a standard *mythos*:

> We humans represent the next [evolutionary] phase shift. Our arrival on this world is as significant in biological terms as that of the first multicelled creatures. We are as different from every past life-form on this planet as chimpanzees are from bacteria. We alone possess the power to alter our own minds and bodies and those of our children. We alone possess the power to guide our own development—to choose our own paths, rather than allowing nature to blindly select for the genes that are best at spreading themselves.[11]

Celebrity physicist Michio Kaku has also rehearsed the foundational apocalyptic deliverance myth of radical enhancement. New humans inaugurate a perfected order:

> Why not enhance ourselves? . . . [In the future] we'll have perfect bodies, except we'll be ageless. We will become the gods that we once feared. We will like Zeus mentally control objects around us. Like Venus we will have perfect bodies and ageless bodies. Like Apollo we will have carriages that make us fly effortlessly in the sky with no energy from the outside and like Pegasus we'll have animals that have never walked the surface of the earth or ceased walking the surface of the earth tens of thousands of years ago. . . . How would we today view someone from 2100? We would view them as the gods of mythology.[12]

Human transformation into posthuman supermen is only a matter of time. Sociologist James Hughes suggests that genetic enhancements may become a moral obligation:

> If eugenics also includes the belief that parents and society have an obligation to give our children and the next generation the healthiest brains and bodies possible, then most people are eugenicists. Once safe, beneficial gene therapies are available parents will feel the same sense of obligation to provide them for their kids as they do a good education or good health care.[13]

An evolutionary imperative informs enhancement narratives, involving physical, cognitive, and moral progress. Until now, says Hans Moravec, "we have been shaped by the invisible hand of Darwinian evolution," but now "we can choose goals for ourselves and steadily pursue them . . ."[14] Computer scientist Ben Goertzel has written that "some of us [will] leave our human bodies and brains behind and explore new ways of existing and interacting."[15] Daily reports of astonishing technological breakthroughs nourish the foundational enhancement narrative. An Italian team restored sight to dozens of patients whose corneas had been severely burned, achieving "a stunning success for the burgeoning cell-therapy field."[16] A German research group restored partial vision to previously blind patients using sub-retinal implants.[17] Scientists at UC Berkeley and MIT have introduced "wearable, motorized machines," exoskeletons that allow some wheel-chair bound individuals to experience upright mobility.[18] Military versions that dramatically increase the strength of soldiers have also been developed.[19]

Enhancement proponents like Naam contend that providing otherwise healthy and able-bodied individuals with augmented intelligence, greater strength and substantially longer life will inevitably follow such therapeutic advances. "Scientists cannot draw a clear line between healing and enhancing, for they're integrally related."[20] In response to the claim that radical enhancement is "unnatural," Naam argues from a mythic vision of a human nature that seeks perfection:

> [F]ar from being unnatural, the drive to alter and improve ourselves is a fundamental part of who we humans are. As a species we've always looked for ways to be faster, stronger, and smarter and to live longer.[21]

Opposed by the brute forces of nature, human beings strive for improvement: "The only reason that we live lives of such great comfort and potential today is that throughout history, there have been men and women who've refused to accept the natural order of things."[22]

The envisioned perfection of the human being is not limited to physical and intellectual capacities; enhancement narratives incorporate our moral lives as well. For ethicist Julian Savulescu, it is time to "acknowledge our human imperfection, identify our moral limitations, and employ strategies to correct these." Otherwise we are stuck with a nature that evolved millennia ago to ensure our survival in a world that required aggression. Today, however, "it may be, as Stephen Hawking said, that our chances of survival are dependent on how much we can change the nature that's essentially stuck in a world 100,000 years ago."[23]

Groundbreaking developments in the pharmaceutical industry suggest another path to moral enhancement. Pharmaceuticals known as moral enhancers or moral steroids "are already being used." In clinical settings, "there may already be a subtle form of moral assistance going on, albeit one we do not choose to describe in these terms," writes Sean Spence of the University of Sheffield in the *British Journal of Psychiatry*. Spence suggests that "science should be searching for drugs to make people more 'humane' not just smarter." He adds, "If we ask the question 'Can pharmacology help to enhance human morality?' then we should answer 'yes,' that *sometimes* it can be used as a means to this end." Spence is just one of a growing number of ethicists and physicians promoting "moral pharmacology." Such drugs can be specifically targeted to, for instance, reduce aggression or even increase kindness.[24]

Philosopher John R. Shook affirms that "the possibility of moral enhancement at present faces no deep philosophical or practical obstacles." Some caution may be warranted in presenting moral enhancers to the public, but "so long as the field of moral enhancement does not permit itself to make implausible claims about the sort of morality enhanced or the degree of enhancement possible, then the future for the development of genuine moral enhancement remains open."[25] Even intractable moral problems such as racism may be subject to pharmaceutical management. A 2012 Oxford University study found that the beta-blocker propranolol "can reduce 'subconscious' racism." Stephen Adams, medical reporter for *The Telegraph*, writes, "Researchers found that people who took propranolol scored significantly lower on a standard test used to detect subconscious racial attitudes, than those who took a placebo." Researchers hypothesize that propranolol "reduces racial bias because such subconscious thoughts are triggered by that autonomic nervous system."[26]

Technologically realized moral visions will inspire ethical debate. While greater happiness from a morally weighted pharmaceutical might not elicit much concern, other outcomes certainly will. Savulescu, Brian D. Earp, and Anders Sandberg have explored the ethics of using drugs to "normalize" people with atypical sexual desires. They note that in the future, "drugs could be used to reverse homosexual inclinations," and raise the concern that the chemical basis of love and sexual orientation might be pharmaceutically altered in efforts to change same-sex attraction.[27]

THE POSTHUMAN VISION

Nick Bostrom, a founder of contemporary Transhumanism, sums up the movement's optimistic essence when he writes that "Transhumanists hope that by responsible use of science, technology, and other rational means, we shall eventually manage to become posthuman, beings with vastly greater capacities than present human beings have."[28] If the enhancement agenda goes according to the vision, a new species may emerge:

> [R]adical enhancement technologies may make us, or our descendants, "posthuman", beings who may have indefinite health-spans, much greater intellectual faculties than any current human being—and perhaps entirely new sensibilities or modalities—as well as the ability to control their own emotions.[29]

The posthuman myth poses unique rhetorical challenges to enhancement and Transhumanist advocates. While the technologically *enhanced* human is easily imagined and even observable in some cases, the *post*human is not present on the scene. Moreover, the very idea of humanoid beings who are not *human* beings elicits a visceral rejection response in a public whose imaginations have been shaped by science fiction portraits of dangerous AIs, bad robots, and violent aliens. A reassuring vision of the posthuman "other" is thus a matter of strategic invention, of concentrated rhetorical work. Michael Hauskeller astutely notes a gap separating the posthuman vision and potential realities should posthumanity be achieved:

> The rhetoric disguises the fact that we actually know very little about what it would be like to be posthuman and that we cannot be certain that the world we are going to create by taking the path of radical enhancement is anything like the world described so imaginatively by its ardent proponents.[30]

Warner writes that "myths define enemies and aliens, and in conjuring them up they say who we are and what we want. . . ."[31] They also "convey values and expectations. . . ."[32] The idea of the posthuman can raise fears of the unknown and the alien other, thus necessitating a reassuring and optimistic narrative to convey a set of positive expectations. Posthumanity takes on a utopian cast, a seeking of perfection from a position of imperfection. More so than at any other juncture in its mythology, Transhumanism makes good on its future vision by describing the posthuman, the point at which ideology yields a vision of utopia. Ricoeur placed utopia and ideology in a dialectic: "Utopia prevents ideology becoming a claustrophobic system; ideology prevents utopia becoming an empty fantasy."[33] Without the posthuman, the ideology of radical enhancement is a fragmented mosaic rather than a unified vision.

The "myth of deliverance suggests a final end of history, an eschatological moment of completio. . . ."[34] The posthuman represents a kind of deliverance, its intelligence so vast and its moral vision so elevated that it is capable of delivering the world from error and finitude. The utopian posthuman *mythos* is capable of various presentations. Naam suggests the possibility of, not one, but numerous posthuman species:

> We will not opt for the same changes. We will not all choose the same direction of travel. Different men and women, different communities, different ideologies will all select different goals to work toward. Some of us will choose to stay as we are, while others will choose to transform. Humanity will expand, splinter and blossom.[35]

In addition to eliciting apprehension, the posthuman as such is absent—posthumanity remains a rhetorical invention, an imaginative projection. Narrative is thus critical to rendering this much anticipated new human species vivid or, in legal theorist Chaim Perelman's useful term, "present." Perelman explains the rhetorical strategy of presence:

> [O]ne of the preoccupations of a speaker is to make present, by verbal magic alone, what is actually absent but what he considers important to his argument or, by making them more present, to enhance the value of some of the elements of which one has actually been made conscious.[36]

Strategies of presence abound in posthuman narratives. Naam's capacious vision is captivating in its winsome, poetic optimism about the posthuman future. In an epiphany that aligns the worlds of present humans and future posthumans Naam allays audience fears—the posthuman is not an unknown, unpredictable and potentially dangerous "other":

> At some point, one hundred years or one thousand years or one million years from now, our world and perhaps this corner of our universe will be populated by descendants we might not recognize. Yet they will think, and love, and dream of better tomorrows, and strive to achieve them, just like us. They will have the traits most dear to us. They will be different in ways we cannot imagine.[37]

Bostrom has been more influential than perhaps any other writer in advancing the posthuman possibility. He forges connections between the "capacities" of the human being and the posthuman:

> I shall define a posthuman as a being that has at least one posthuman capacity. By a posthuman capacity, I mean a general central capacity greatly exceeding the maximum attainable by any current human being without recourse to new technological means.[38]

Posthuman capacities include "Healthspan—the capacity to remain fully healthy, active, and productive, both mentally and physically," and cognition. The latter includes "general intellectual capacities, such as memory, deductive and analogical reasoning, and attention, as well as special faculties such as the capacity to understand and appreciate music, humor, eroticism, narration, spirituality, mathematics, etc." Also on the list is emotion, or "the capacity to enjoy life and to respond with appropriate affect to life situations and other people."[39]

To establish posthuman presence Bostrom places the reader in the role of a newly augmented person: What does this new person experience? How does life feel to a posthuman? What is it like to inhabit a posthuman body? Bostrom's narrative focuses first on general considerations such as robust health, youthful appearance, and a clear mind:

> Let us suppose that you were to develop into a being that has posthuman healthspan and posthuman cognitive and emotional capacities. At the early steps of this process, you enjoy your enhanced capacities. You cherish your improved health: you feel stronger, more energetic, and more balanced. Your skin looks younger and is more elastic. A minor ailment in your knee is cured. You also discover a greater clarity of mind. You can concentrate on difficult material more easily and it begins making sense to you. You start seeing connections that eluded you before.[40]

In this description the posthuman "you" is a lone hero, an isolated entity enjoying new powers, albeit not within the context of community.[41] Such was the plight of Frankenstein's monster and other posthumans of literature.

Increased cognitive capacities lead to doubts about cherished convictions: "You are astounded to realize how many beliefs you had been holding without ever really thinking about them or considering whether the evidence supports them." Not surprisingly, the posthuman you is mentally sharper: "You can follow lines of thinking and intricate argumentation farther without losing your foothold. Your mind is able to recall facts, names, and concepts just when you need them."

Naam's narrative extends even to posthuman social skills: "You are able to sprinkle your conversation with witty remarks and poignant anecdotes. Your friends remark on how much more fun you are to be around." Despite the implied inevitability of this development, it is equally likely that a posthuman would intimidate original-version humans. Regardless of how posthumans might fare in social settings, they will enjoy richer sensory and artistic experiences. "Your experiences seem more vivid. When you listen to music you perceive layers of structure and a kind of musical logic to which you were previously oblivious; this gives you great joy." While there is no reason contained within the concept of posthumanity itself, Bostrom suggests that the posthuman's tastes become more refined: "You continue to find the gossip magazines you used to read amusing, albeit in a different way than before; but you discover that you can get more out of reading Proust and *Nature*."

Finally, Bostrom suggests for the posthuman a greater measure of emotional balance: "You begin to treasure almost every moment of life; you go about your business with zest; and you feel a deeper warmth and affection for those you love, but you can still be upset and even angry on occasions where being upset or angry is truly justified and constructive." Readers experience the posthuman vision as lived experience. Bostrom creates a vivid imaginative experience that renders the otherwise elusive posthuman tangibly present.

An undeniable confidence is evident in these expressions of the posthuman possibility, and for good reason. The posthuman is a logically necessary extension of three basic Transhumanist assumptions: First, human beings will take charge of their own evolution. Second, over time such technologically directed processes will produce beings that can no longer be said to be human. Third, posthumans will be vastly more intelligent than *Homo sapiens* and will thus one day supersede us as a species. This last development is not to be regretted; it is simply the working out of evolutionary and technological destiny because what might appear to be an ominous cloud comes with a silver lining: posthumans will solve persistent problems including poverty, disease, war, and climate destruction. We need them, though they may decide they don't need us. A few within the enhancement movement contend that some philosophical problems are so complex that they "will not yield at all until we can develop minds (posthuman or artificial) smart enough to handle them."[42]

Inevitability characterizes the posthuman myth as related by Naam, Bostrom, Kaku and others. In this respect it is like other myths. Warner notes that Roland Barthes exposed the timeless and necessary quality of mythography, pointing to the genre's contingency and rhetorical adaptability:

> Barthes's fundamental principle is that myths are not eternal veri-
> ties, but historical compounds which successfully conceal their own
> contingency and changes and transitoriness so that the story they
> tell looks as if it cannot be told otherwise, that things always were
> like that and always shall be.[43]

While the posthuman vision is a necessary extension of technofuturist
mythology, such imagining has at times generated more exotic narratives.
Bostrom is known for promoting the "simulation hypothesis": we exist in
a computer simulation run by future posthumans who are doing research
on their ancestors. He has suggested a theological quality to this idea. "It
is possible to draw some loose analogies" between the simulation hypothesis and "religious conceptions of the world." Bostrom's hypothesis parallels religious creation myths and, like other creation accounts, his narrative
operates simultaneously in two independent time frames. By bringing the
world of present lived experience into alignment with the posthuman future,
Bostrom's hypothesis reflects a mythic epiphany: "In some ways, the posthumans running a simulation are like gods in relation to the people inhabiting
the simulation." Specifically,

> the posthumans created the world we see; they are of superior intel-
> ligence; they are 'omnipotent' in the sense that they can interfere in
> the workings of our world even in ways that violate its laws; and they
> are 'omniscient' in the sense that they can monitor what happens.[44]

What began as a straightforward posthuman narrative—highly evolved
humanity assumes qualities so distinct as to render them a new species—
grows into an origin myth explaining the source of humans and their relationship to the supernatural world. We are the creations of advanced beings
interested in our responses to their constructions. If we place Bostrom in the
stream of Nikolai Federov, Teilhard de Chardin and even Julian Huxley, the
entrance of such a distinctly religious note is in keeping with a technofuturist mythic tradition.

RESPONSES

According to the enhancement *mythos*, human-machine merger, vastly improved techniques of genetic alteration, nanotechnology, and increasingly
sophisticated drugs will render enhancement inevitable. Enhancement technology, guided by narratives of a perfect human, will produce the posthuman. This vision is sacred in the enhancement movement, a spiritual epipha-

ny that depends for its realization upon our intentional cooperation. Biotech entrepreneur Gregory Stock, for instance, writes:

> In offering ourselves as vessels for potential transformation into we know not what, we are submitting to the shaping hand of a process that dwarfs us individually. . . . From a spiritual perspective, the project of humanity's self-evolution is the ultimate embodiment of our science and ourselves as a cosmic instrument in our ongoing emergence.[45]

While stories do not dictate outcomes, narratives play a crucial role in shaping such a vision, in suggesting "values and expectations." We might note that the myth of the posthuman challenges some rather powerful existing myths regarding the notions of essence and the fixity of species. As early as 1969 molecular biologist Robert Sinsheimer wrote:

> For the first time in all time, a living creature understands its origin and can undertake to design its future. Even in the ancient myths man was constrained by essence. He could not rise above his nature to chart his destiny. Today we can envision that chance—and its dark companion of choice and responsibility.[46]

Midgley comments that what is at risk in suggestions of altering the human genome so as to "perfect" the human race is "the concept of a species." She writes, "Our tradition has so far held that this concept should be taken pretty seriously, that the boundaries of a species should be respected. Even our mythology warns against the chimera, the mixed species such as the gorgons or minotaurs. "They are usually seen as alien and destructive forces."[47] It is, then, *mythos* vs. *mythos*—in order to propose the *logos* of a research regimen leading to the posthuman, a new grounding myth was necessary.

Posthumans are archetypical beings that represent an ideal model, a vision of what we can never become but what we might create. Kant wrote, "[W]e have no other standard for our actions than the conduct of this divine man within us, with which we compare and judge ourselves, and so reform ourselves, although we can never attain to the perfection thereby prescribed."[48] Something like this inner sense of a perfect human guides the posthuman myth. Proponents and critics alike recognize the centrality of this vision to Transhumanist rhetoric of the future; critics have been quick to point out ethical, metaphysical, and political problems associated with the vision.

Hava Tirosh-Samuelson notes that "humans are now able not only to redesign themselves, presumably in order to get rid of various limitations, but also to redesign future generations, thereby affecting the evolutionary process itself." The endpoint is "a new *posthuman* phase in the evolution of the human species . . . in which humans will live longer, will possess new physical and cognitive abilities, and will be liberated from suffering and pain due to aging and diseases." Thus, "what nature has placed out of reach science may make available to all—or so the contemporary argument for enhancement suggests."

> We need no longer wait and hope for the chance operations of nature to take their course; technology places before us the possibility of a heightened existence, a better life, perhaps a new human species. Human destiny is to take control of our own evolution, directing it toward ends of our own choosing.[49]

Physician and philosopher Jeffrey Bishop contends that the posthuman aspiration places technology in the role of divine creative force. Technological power, which Bishop terms an "ordering force," is "directed toward a new *telos*, the posthuman, the highest of beings, perhaps even Being itself in the singularity, pure mental power." The posthuman is not merely a re-ordered *Homo sapiens*, a better human, but a divine human. Such an entity would represent the culmination of directed evolution. Bishop writes that "the transhumanist metaphysical belief is that we human beings are on an evolutionary journey, from human to posthuman; those wise and smart enough to see and understand the transitory nature of human being are thus transitional humans." Transhumanism "seeks to order evolutionary becoming." This is a cardinal function of myth, "to impose structure and order."[50]

Despite their protestations to the contrary, "the god of these transhumanist philosophers is the god that orders the creative power toward a new being, a new god, that is to say toward the posthuman." Rather than assisting human, "they turn in the conscious moment toward control, toward mastery. Transhumanism seeks to differently embody the *Übermensch*." However, Bishop notes that

> to question the posthuman future is to question evolution and scientifically grounded ontology; to question the posthuman future is to question our liberty to become what we will. To question the posthuman future is to question all the good that has been produced from the Enlightenment, liberalism, and indeed humanism.[51]

Historian Francis Fukuyama has levelled a frequently cited criticism of the posthuman vision, calling it the most dangerous idea in the world today. Fukuyama's concern is principally political in nature, though he envisions a host of problems associated with the foundational concept. While he notes that Transhumanists "want nothing less than to liberate the human race from its biological constraints," he does not find the possibility implausible.

Fukuyama asks whether "the fundamental tenet of transhumanism—that we will someday use biotechnology to make ourselves stronger, smarter, less prone to violence, and longer-lived" is "really so outlandish?" Indeed, Fukuyama contends that "Transhumanism of a sort is implicit in much of the research agenda of contemporary biomedicine." He recognizes the inherent appeal in the Transhumanists' most basic aspiration: "If it were technologically possible, why wouldn't we want to transcend our current species?" Nevertheless, radical enhancements may "come at a frightful moral cost," and "the first victim of transhumanism might be equality." Specifically, visions of posthumanity raise the question of "who qualifies as fully human," a classification that has often been contested. "In effect, we have drawn a red line around the human being and said that it is sacrosanct."

The deeper assumption of human rights is "that we all possess a human essence that dwarfs manifest differences in skin color, beauty, and even intelligence. This essence, and the view that individuals therefore have inherent value," writes Fukuyama, "is at the heart of political liberalism." However, "modifying that essence is the core of the transhumanist project." Fukuyama is concerned about potential inequities. For instance, "if some move ahead, can anyone afford not to follow?" In the world's poorer countries "biotechnology's marvels likely will be out of reach—and the threat to the idea of equality becomes even more menacing."

Transhumanists "are happy to leave behind the limited, mortal, natural beings they see around them in favor of something better. But do they really comprehend ultimate human goods?" Fukuyama is concerned that "modifying any one of our key characteristics inevitably entails modifying a complex, interlinked package of traits, and we will never be able to anticipate the ultimate outcome. As we consider the posthuman vision, an earlier version comes to mind. Despite the confident narrative projections of writers like Bostrom and Naam, "nobody knows what technological possibilities will emerge for human self-modification. Fukuyama writes that we "can already see the stirrings of Promethean desires in how we prescribe drugs to alter the behavior and personalities of our children." Moreover:

> The environmental movement has taught us humility and respect for the integrity of nonhuman nature. We need a similar humility concerning our human nature. If we do not develop it soon, we may unwittingly invite the transhumanists to deface humanity with their genetic bulldozers and psychotropic shopping malls.[52]

The concerns of Tirosh-Samuelson, Fukuyama and Bishop raise strike at the heart of Transhumanist mythology. Without a vision of the posthuman, directed evolution, brain augmentation and lifespan extension remain mere enhancements, and claims about the transformative power of technology lose some of their force. The posthuman thus animates Transhumanist projections, a hero on the horizon beckoning us to pursue the transforming vision. However, the arrival of the posthuman means obsolescence for *Homo Sapiens*; the human era ends in a triumphant posthuman apocalypse. In the face of such possibilities—viewed as a welcome development by many in the Transhumanist community—it will be important to remind ourselves that the posthuman *mythos* remains, not an inevitable and transcendent prophecy, but a strategic rhetorical construction.

9 EXTENDING LIFE, ENDING DEATH

Even if it took a hundred years to create the requisite nano-robots, eventually the resurrection and repair of the frozen dead would be possible.

—James Hughes

For Kurzweil the uploading of ourselves into a human made machine is the spiritual goal of transhumanism, since it promises transcendence and even immortality.

—Hava Tirosh-Samuelson

O death, where is your victory? O death, where is your sting?

—St. Paul

The Terasem Movement, Inc., headed up by entrepreneur and AI researcher Martine Rothblatt, has the stated purpose of "preserving, evoking, reviving and downloading human consciousness."[1] Terasem is one of several increasingly prominent organizations, including Strategies for Engineered Negligible Senescence (SENS) and the Methuselah Foundation, cultivating public interest in radical life extension. In 2013 Google entered the life extension industry with the announcement of its Calico (California Life Company) initiative. The corporation's purpose is to invest in research and technologies that will address the processes of aging.[2] Terasem has changed its name to Terasem Faith; listed among its core beliefs are "Death is Optional." Other major technology concerns are also getting involved in anti-aging research.[3]

Historian Carole Haber notes that the formal discussion of methods of achieving long life dates from at least the sixteenth century. As early as the Renaissance there were advocates for systematic approaches to extreme longevity. "One of the most influential of these advocates was Luigi Cornaro, an Italian nobleman who in 1550 wrote *The Art of Living Long*." The work was "translated into English, French, Dutch, and German," and became "the bible of prolongevity advocates who asserted that a long and healthy life was a very real possibility." Cornaro's book was popular right through the nineteenth century. "In his study, the author argued that individuals were not destined to die at 60 or 70, but with care and a good constitution, could live extremely long lives." He outlined techniques for preserving the "vital energy" that allowed life to continue, and that slowly ebbed with age. In an age of short average life-spans Cornaro lived to be ninety-eight.[4]

In the eighteenth century the Marquis de Condorcet (1743–1794) affirmed that, despite the natural deterioration of living organisms over time, progress in nutrition, sanitation, medicine, and other sciences "must necessarily tend to prolong the common duration of man's existence, and secure him a more constant health and a more robust constitution." Condorcet's narrative of the future imagined the eradication of death itself. Writing near the end of the century he asked:

> Would it even be absurd to suppose this quality of melioration in the human species as susceptible of an indefinite advancement; to suppose that a period must one day arrive when death will be nothing more than the effect either of extraordinary accidents, or of the slow and gradual decay of the vital powers; and that the duration of the middle space, of the interval between the birth of man and this decay, will itself have no assignable limit[5]

A century later Russian Cosmist Nikolai Rozhkov (1868–1927) envisioned the immortality of future generations and predicted the scientific resurrection of the dead. His mentors, Nikolai Fedorov (1829–1903) and Konstantin Tsiolkovsky (1857–1935), had propagated the myth of mass resurrection of all past generations through a cooperative world-wide technological effort.[6] As his contribution to the project, Tsiolkovsky developed the first modern theory of rocketry. *Logos* followed *mythos*—in Fedorov's myth of universal resurrection, locating the molecular elements of the deceased would require exploration of space. Fedorov warranted this vision by reference to the Christian narrative of a general resurrection at the end of history. Cosmist-influenced Soviet belief in the technological resurrection vision led to the anticipatory preservation of Lenin's corpse.[7]

Science fiction writers were early proponents of a technological immortality *mythos*. Neil P. Jones, for instance, published "The Jameson Satellite" in 1931. Professor Jameson, learning of his impending death, creates a spacecraft for the purpose of having his body launched into space. Millions of years later aliens known as the Zorome discover Jameson's frozen remains still drifting through the cosmic abyss. Frederik Pohl and Hans Moravec pick up the story at that point:

> So they surgically removed the brain from the frozen corpse, thawed it out and implanted it in a robot machine that resembled a breadbox with tentacular metal arms and legs. Then, renamed 21MM392 by his new Zorome friends, the professor went on to have endless adventures in space.[8]

The myth of technological immortality is central to enhancement and Transhumanist rhetoric, evolving over time in response to scientific breakthroughs and changing social circumstances.[9] No longer is death humanity's "capital punishment," as Kenneth Burke termed it in his *Rhetoric of Religion*; in enhancement narratives death is not a spiritual but a technical problem.[10] In its exploration of the myth of the informational person, Chapter Six considered the prospect of digital immortality. This chapter considers narratives of technological immortality developing around the *biological* person and physical death. In direct contradiction of religious narratives that connect death, resurrection, and immortality to the spiritual life, narratives of technological immortality renders all such considerations solely material concerns to be resolved by transcendent methodologies.[11]

According to Northrop Frye, myth reveals a tension between timeless and inviolable essences, and temporal conditions of violation. The archetype of myth's ironic double-nature is Adam—"human nature under sentence of death."[12] Into this narrative tension steps the tragic hero, taking arms against the inexorable forces of nature and lifting human beings heavenward by his sacrifice.[13] In the *mythos* of technological immortality, enhancement activists are such tragic heroes seeking to bridge the gap between the natural law of death and the transcendent aspiration of humankind toward continued flourishing. Myth is, for Warner, a way of "making sense of universal matters . . ."[14] No matter is more universal than death, now rendered sensible in the expectant mythology of a deathless technological future. Without the promise of immortality, the radical enhancement vision acquires a fatal contingency, reduced to yet another attempt to make life a little longer and a little more pleasant. With its call to faith in everlasting conscious existence, however, the Transhumanist narrative takes on the positive urgency of a redemptve narrative, a gospel. The immortality *mythos* has developed along three distinct lines.

The Preservation/Restoration Myth

What can be termed the preservation/restoration narrative has attracted the most public attention and has perhaps the longest history of all myths of technological immortality. The story of freezing or otherwise preserving the deceased individual—or perhaps just her or his brain—is much discussed in enhancement circles, but is also a matter of caricature and ridicule by those outside the movement. The narrative's foundational premise is simple, and intersects with the myths of progress and the informational person: freeze or otherwise preserve the deceased and later generations applying the insights of inevitable technological progress will revive and restore her or him, or place her or his neural circuitry in a machine.

While head of PayPal, Peter Thiel, found this narrative so persuasive that—despite the conspicuous absence of a successful case of resuscitation and restoration—"proposed making cryogenic storage an employee perk."[15] In a remarkable interview with historian Francis Fukuyama, Thiel made technologically enhanced longevity the "culmination" of Western science's long saga. To turn our backs on longevity as a goal is to abandon progress:

> Take a step back: the entire longevity research program is the cul-mination of the Western scientific project. It was part of Francis Ba-con's *New Atlantis*, and has been a recurrent thread through much of the past 400 years of science. I don't think we can abandon it or carve it out without abandoning technological progress altogether. It's too closely linked to it.[16]

Thiel's statement reflects the centrality of an immortality *mythos* to contemporary technofuturist discourse.

The preservation narrative dates back to ancient mummification practices; the preserved body was important to a happy afterlife. As a means of restoring physical life, Cosmists suggested preservation in the nineteenth century. By the 1920s the idea had prominent proponents in the science and science fiction communities. As noted in Chapter Eight, Irish scientist J. D. Bernal affirmed in 1929 that the brain is the essence of the person.[17] Thus, a frozen and then resuscitated brain might be as good as preserving a full body, and presumably much less expensive to achieve. Jones's "The Jameson Satellite" reminds us that cryonics was among the early technological dreams of overcoming death. He had already anticipated the narrative line: freezing the deceased would make possible later resuscitation when advanced technology would allow physical repair or transferal of consciousness.

Cryonic practice can be traced to physicist Robert Ettinger (1918–2011), a childhood fan of Jones's story and founder of The Immortalist Society and the Cryonics Institute. In *The Prospect of Immortality (1962)*, Ettinger argued for a contradiction: death did not have to mean the end of life. Isaac Asimov endorsed the book, leading to considerable discussion of Ettinger's provocative ideas. Anticipating and shaping the *mythos* of transcendence through technological progress, Ettinger wrote: "If civilization endures, medical science should eventually be able to repair almost any damage to the human body, including freezing damage and senile debility or other cause of death."[18] Though his technique was primitive and legally ambiguous, he and members of his organization did freeze over one hundred deceased individuals. His 1972 book, *Man into Superman*, extended the immortality narrative and marked Ettinger as an early proponent of the futurist philosophy that would become Transhumanism.[19] His audacious myth "created an opening" into a new world that transcended "the established limits of our *actual* world."[20]

The *mythos* of technological immortality generated a *logos* of cryogenic practice. Today organizations such as Arizona-based Alcor Life Extension Foundation, headed by Transhumanism founding figure Max More, offer more sophisticated cryonics services to the public for a fee. Alcor views its cryogenically preserved clients as "legally dead, but biologically alive."[21] The cost of preservation stands at $200,000 for "whole body patient" and $80,000 for a "neuro-patient," an individual opting only for a cryopreserved head.

In a 2014 interview, More acknowledged the technological difficulties involved in the process, and public reservation about the basic idea:

> Cryonics is especially hard to convey because it's complicated. You've got to look at the evidence for it and you've got to think about death, which is very uncomfortable to many people. What's worse is that we don't give you a nice, comforting answer. We don't say, like a religion, "Oh, sign up with us and we guarantee we'll bring you back." That's dishonest, we can't guarantee that. It depends on how well preserved you were in the first place and we can't really guarantee the technology that will be developed.

More is also up front about the fact that the technology of restoration lags far behind that of preservation:

> In terms of the revival end of things, it's a long way off. [Alcor] isn't doing a whole lot of research there because it's too much of a cap on

what we can do. There is a startup company that I can't really talk about that that's doing that, trying to grow tissues, grow organs. The whole field of regenerative medicine is really relevant to what we're doing.[22]

Cryonic preservation remains a relatively rare practice—Alcor listed 123 patients as of 2014. Following a different path to preservation—and endorsing Bernal's notion that the brain is the person—Ken Hayworth and John Smart of the Brain Preservation Foundation advocate plastination—injecting the brain with resins at the moment of death. This technique, like other preservation approaches, assumes that personalities—understood as informational persons—can be retrieved from a preserved brain. This outcome requires that damage to the brain can be avoided in the preservation process. Hayworth and Smart exhibit such confidence: "Can a mind be extracted from a plasticized brain? The answer is almost certainly, yes."[23] Hayworth has written of "a surgical protocol that can reliably and demonstrably preserve a human brain's precise neural circuitry for long-term," by which he means more than a hundred years. This prospect would, if progress prevails, "give interested persons a means of avoiding death and reaching the distant future."[24] Thus, this variant of the *mythos* of technological immortality "introduces metaphysical significance"—the avoidance of death and the acquisition of the future. [25]

Smart and Hayworth have developed a protocol for plastic preservation of the brain as the individual is dying, an example of a narrative *mythos* yielding a practical *logos*. Despite Bernal's insistence that "it is the brain that counts," few in the general public consider a preserved brain a person. For Frye, myth renders such dreams "plausible" and thus "acceptable to a social waking consciousness."[26] Smart and Hayworth's proposal depends for its plausibility on the narratives of progress and the informational person: data preserved in the plasticized brain's neural networks would ultimately be uploaded into a computer or synthetic body. The plasticized brain is not itself revived; it is merely a means of preserving circuitry—i.e., information—which could be mimicked in a machine.

According to the Brain Preservation Foundation, the technologies necessary to brain preservation are straightforward:

> [F]rom a medical and technical standpoint all that is needed is the development of a surgical procedure for perfusing a patient's circulatory system with a series of fixatives and plastic resins capable of perfectly preserving their brain's neural circuitry in a plasticized block for long-term storage.

Suspended in mythic epiphany, preserved patients enter a realm between the worlds of the living and the dead. Transcending time in a "long dreamless sleep" they "wait out the decades or centuries necessary for the development of the more advanced technology required to revive them." If everything works as planned, "the patient awakes to a new dawn of unlimited potential."

The Foundation seeks "to make it every person's right to experience the future centuries from now, and to live without the constant fear that aging and crippling disease will take away their joy for life, make them a burden to their loved ones, and strip them of their dignity." In step with the Transhumanist vision, the Foundation affirms that "our scientific and medical communities have it within their power *today* to create that world." *Mythos* has yielded *logos*: the Brain Preservation Foundation has proposed a Bill of Rights to protect those who choose the preservation path. The preamble reflects a militant tone that suggests the myth's force:

> This is a list of demands of sort, or perhaps a call to arms. It is what I think people who believe in mind uploading should be pushing for—a society in which they and their loved ones have a reasonable chance at reaching the future, and where the main obstacles to achieving that goal are real technical ones, and not legal roadblocks imposed by the ignorant and superstitious.

The rights of the preserved include "quality long term storage and protection from harm with no removal from storage due to insufficient funds," and "revival rights." The right to "monetary and other assets" is also guaranteed, "so that they can be retrieved by the individual upon successful revival."[27] Smart and Hayworth suggest that such technology might be available within fifty years. Smart finds in technological immortality "a future very much worth fighting for."[28] This insistence on a particular mythic vision of the future, however, brings to mind "the dangers of the logic of 'perfectionism.'"[29]

AUBREY DE GREY AND THE WAR ON AGING

According to T. S. Eliot, James Joyce revealed how myth controlled, ordered and gave shape and significance to "the immense panorama of futility and anarchy" we encounter in "contemporary history."[30] Death is disorder for scientist Aubrey de Grey, a Transhumanist proponent who has declared biotechnological war on aging. De Grey has fashioned a new narrative of death and immortality, one designed to displace the disordered thinking that feeds a culture of aging. The side-show quality of preservation narratives attracts media attention; staid biotechnological approaches assume a lower profile, albeit one more in keeping with public expectations rooted in medical history.

Promising approaches to life extension buoy public expectations. These approaches include work at the University of California on genetically engineered yeast that lives ten times longer than normal. By deleting two genes in the yeast's genome and putting it on a calorie restricted diet, Dr. Valter Longo developed a strain of yeast fungus that can live for ten weeks instead of dying at its usual maximum age of one week. Translated into the human domain such an increase would have people living for eight hundred years or more. "We're setting the foundation for reprogramming healthy life," says Longo, adding, "I don't think there is an upper limit to the life of any organism."[31]

One promising approach to extreme longevity includes bolstering the protein telomerase, a binding agent that secures the ends of chromosomes. As we age telomerase breaks down, leading to the chromosome deterioration, the death of cells, and thus eventually death. One theory of extending life involves increasing the body's levels of telomerase. A research team at Spanish National Cancer Centre in Madrid "tested the theory on mice and found that those genetically engineered to produce 10 times the normal levels of telomerase lived 50 percent longer than normal." Team leader Maria Blasco claims that telomerase is capable of transforming "a normal, mortal cell into an immortal cell." She added that she was "optimistic that a similar approach may eventually lead to extended human lifespans—though she urged caution. 'You can delay the aging of mice and increase their lifespan, [But] I think it is very hard to extrapolate data from mouse aging to human aging.'"[32]

Another biotechnological approach reinforcing narratives of technological immortality involves gene manipulation. Researchers have "partially reversed age-related degeneration in mice, an achievement that suggests a new approach for tackling similar disorders in people." Researchers at the Dana-Farber Cancer Institute in Boston augmented a gene that in turn "reversed brain disease and restored the sense of smell and fertility in prematurely aged mice." This experiment demonstrated that "some age-related problems in animals have actually been reversed." Researcher Ronald DePinho explained, "These mice were equivalent to 80-year-old humans and were about to pass away." Following the procedure, "they were the physiological equivalent of young adults."[33] Other anti-aging biotechnologies also show promise, such as pharmaceuticals that improve cellular vibrancy, genetic interventions that slow the aging process, and even the use of nanobots to repair damaged cells and deliver anti-cancer drugs directly to tumors.

De Grey is the leading proponent of biotechnological approaches to radical longevity. Best-known as the founder of Strategies for Engineered Negligible Senescence (SENS), de Grey promotes a vision of radically longer life-spans in his many publications and public appearances.[34] A computer scientist by training, and a self-taught biologist, de Grey is the editor of the journal *Rejuvenation Research*, an adviser to the Singularity Institute and author of *The Mitochondrial Free Radical Theory of Aging* (1999) and *Ending Aging* (2007). In de Grey's rendition of the life-extension *mythos*, the first 1,000-year-old person is probably only twenty years younger than the first 150-year-old person, who is already among us.[35] Myths "define enemies and aliens. . . ." [36] In de Grey's narrative death is alien, an enemy that attacks mind and body and one we will defeat with biotechnology.

Under the SENS protocol, de Grey identifies seven biological causes of aging. These include chromosome mutation, harmful aggregates accumulating inside and outside of cells, cell loss and cell aging, and the depletion of stem cell pools.[37] As de Grey tells the story of aging, biological death occurs not because of genetically encoded aging mechanisms or a divine judgment, but as a consequence of accumulated age-related damage to cells. He thus advocates deploying specific "strategies" to prevent and repair cellular damage. Death also results from psychological and cultural resistance to facing the aging process rationally, a condition de Grey dubs the "pro-aging trance," a durable cultural myth of inevitable death.

Ending Aging is conversational in tone, the narrative developing around a series of vivid metaphors and simple scenarios. De Grey's storytelling is straightforward and engaging, involving vivid metaphors, striking phrases, and clearly drawn protagonists and antagonists. Dead cells that remain in the body are "zombies," removing accumulated detritus in cells is "breaking the shackles" of aging, the "pro-aging trance" is a "rational irrationality" to be overcome in a "War on Aging." De Grey is a self-conscious mythographer, his War as much a rhetorical as a scientific battle, the public mind the real battleground. The mental grip of the pro-aging trance "will end only when its claim to rationality becomes unable to withstand even simple assaults, the sort that most people can understand." Something akin to a vast religious conversion must take place, for "science is in a very real sense the new religion: what individual scientists say can be doubted, but the public scientific consensus is gospel."[38]

As noted, progress narratives undergird preservation narratives; cryonic and plastination approaches assume massive and inexorable advances in medical research. Following de Grey's narrative, however, breaking the pro-aging trance's grip and embracing death-prevention strategies, which he contends are readily at hand, will eliminate the need for such precarious procedures as freezing the deceased. Despite the fact that his views have been denounced by high-profile biologists and gerontologists, de Grey enjoys considerable support among enhancement proponents and is a frequent speaker at Transhumanist events. His name is now equated with the biotechnological approach to ending aging.

THE CLONING NARRATIVE

Replication by cloning represents a third strand of the myth of technological immortality. Like the other narrative branches, the cloning narrative projects a future in which technological progress overcomes the limits of the body. The practice of direct cellular replication of a mammal not involving gamete cells captured the public imagination with the cloning of Dolly the sheep by Ian Wilmut and Keith Campbell at the Roslin Institute in Scotland in 1996. Cloning had been successfully demonstrated using frogs as much as thirty years earlier. Nicholas Agar notes that the procedure was quickly appropriated by progressive scientists such as J. B. S. Haldane, albeit as an approach to eugenics rather than immortality. Adding a eugenic turn to the narrative, Haldane suggested creating copies of the most gifted among us:

> In the wake of the first successful cloning of frogs in the early 1960s, the distinguished British biologist J. B. S. Haldane suggested that we select the most talented human beings for cloning. He thought it wise in most cases to wait until candidates were in their fifties so as to be sure that their genomes really warranted repetition.

For Haldane, cloning might "raise the possibilities of human achievement dramatically."[39] Cloning's apocalyptic vision promised endless life without sexual reproduction, that is, "another mode of existence entirely, to be realized just beyond the present time and place."[40]

With its intimately personal, disturbingly uncanny and inherently moral components, the cloning narrative carries an intrigue that has made it a frequent theme of science fiction. The technique has taken on a mythic life of its own, as reflected in a wide range of utopian and dystopian movies and novels. *The Boys from Brazil* (novel 1976, movie 1978), *The Island* (movie 2005), *Blueprint* (novel 2002, movie 2002), *Moon* (movie 2009), *Never Let Me Go* (novel 2005, movie 2010) and many other popular narratives have addressed the question of cloning. Such artifacts have familiarized the public with the idea of cloning, but may also cloud the issue of whether cloning represents a path to immortality.

The cloning narrative is embraced by some as pointing the way to immortality. The strangest and most influential of cloning narratives was propagated by Frenchman Claude Vorilhon, known as Rael to his followers. Rael claims that on the morning of December 13, 1973 he was driving near Clermont-Ferrand, France and ended up at a local extinct volcano in Auvergne. Here he saw a saucer shaped space vehicle hovering overhead and met the diminutive humanoid aliens on board. They entrusted Rael with the secrets of human origin, which had a lot to do with cloning; the human race resulted from a cloning experiment by visiting alien scientists.

Cloning remains central to the Raelian immortality narrative, as evidenced in Raelian alignment with human cloning research organization, Clonaid. Future human beings will download their personalities from one body to another throughout eternity, a sacred reenactment of the original story of alien creation. While this theory also involves the extremely difficult question of transferring consciousness from one brain to another, with 50,000 adherents the Raelian cloning myth stands as perhaps the most widely embraced of all technological immortality tales. Cloning as the key to immortality is not much discussed in Transhumanist circles, however, where preservation and biotechnological approaches are embraced.

RESPONSES

For Vico, myth anticipated all "human actions and institutions," including our vast cultural system for addressing aging, death, and life beyond death.[41] By myth we create this part of the world we inhabit. For Coupe, myth functions like magic in primitive societies, rendering possible a cohesive culture capable of addressing "intolerable problems such as scarcity and the threat of death."[42] In traditional sacred narratives death belongs to the present world, immortality to a world to come. The enhancement and Transhumanist writers examined in this chapter challenge the "imaginative patterns" of earlier mythic systems, proposing a new *mythos* of this-worldly immortality through preservation, a war on aging, and cloning. In these new myths we encounter Ricoeur's "disclosure of unprecedented worlds" and "an opening on to other *possible* worlds which transcend the established limits of our *actual* world."[43]

Ray Kurzweil predicts that as soon as the 2040s we will "live indefinitely without aging." He embraces the idea that we will transfer "a person's entire personality, memory, skills and history."[44] Like the Russian Cosmists writing more than a century ago, Kurzweil's vision is cosmic in scope and mythic in nature. Journalist Mike Hodgkinson captures Kurzweil's vision: "Humans and non-biological machines will . . . merge so effectively that the differences between them will no longer matter; and, after that, human intelligence, transformed for the better, will start to expand outward into the universe, around about 2045." For Kurzweil this "inevitable move towards non-biological intelligence is 'an essentially spiritual undertaking.'"[45]

Some in the technology world are concerned over a rising mythos of the technological conquest of death, and the legal and practical *logos* it may generate. Computer scientist Jaron Lanier, for instance, raises one of the leading ethical questions associated with the technological eradication of aging—

the just distribution of the technologies. "Medicine is on the verge of mastering some of the fundamental mechanisms of aging," he writes. "Drastic differences in people's wealth will translate into drastic differences in life expectancy."[46]

Leading Transhumanist critic and religion scholar Tirosh-Samuelson expresses a different concern about myths of technological immortality. She contends that the dream of eliminating pain and death "ignores the value of insecurity, anxiety, and uncertainty, which are very much part of being human." For Tirosh-Samuelson, "human culture (especially art and philosophy) could not have been possible without these allegedly negative aspects of being human." If suffering, contingency and death are eradicated, "what will be the source of creativity?" The Transhuman quest for perfection is "not a prescription for cultural depth and creativity; it is a prescription for childish shallowness. . . ."[47]

Philosopher Michael Hauskeller finds the Transhumanist narrative of immortality to be rooted in teleological narratives that see humans as the kinds of beings who are destined to become immortal. Such thinking follows a classic Aristotelian narrative. "[T]he acorn strives to grow into an oak," and we can be sure "the same holds true for the expected transformation of the human from a mortal into an immortal being. It is simply a matter of learning to be the kind of being that we were always meant to be."[48] Major moral and practical questions attend the technological pursuit of immortality, but the existence of these questions has not dampened enthusiasm for the project. Whether or not our nature destines us to it, a powerful myth of technological immortality will ensure that the goal of immortality will be aggressively pursued.

10 Artificial Intelligence, Superintelligence and Emergent Gods

Perhaps our role on this planet is not to worship God—but to create Him.

—Sir Arthur C. Clarke

[T]he first ultraintelligent machine is the last invention that man need ever make.[1]

—I. J. Good

I find it hard to believe that we could manufacture robots that actually worked and not have them disturb our ideas of religion and God. Someday we will make other minds, and they will surprise us. . . . if we give these minds their full embodiment, they will call themselves children of God, and what will we say?

—Kevin Kelly

Coined in the mid-1950s, the term *artificial intelligence* came into wide use among scientists after MIT researcher John McCarthy imagined in 1960 the possibility of computers not simply managing data, but thinking like human beings. The development of AI owes a great deal to one of McCarthy's students, Marvin Minsky (1927–2016). Minsky has influenced the field of AI more than any other single figure. Several noteworthy enhancement proponents, including Kurzweil, call Minsky their mentor. Author of *The Society of Mind* (1988) and among the first important scientific voices to suggest machine-based intelligence, he remained throughout his life a leading proponent of downloading human consciousness into machines. Minsky advanced a theory of mind as consisting of a large number of "agents," responsible for particular tasks and not themselves thinking entities. However, taken together, the individual agents produce mind. Thus, the summary of his case has been presented as: minds are what brains do.[2] Presumably, a sufficiently sophisticated computer could possess such a mind.

In 1989 eminent mathematician Roger Penrose defined the "objectives" of AI as "to imitate, by means of machines, normally electronic ones, as much of human mental activity as possible, and perhaps to improve upon human abilities in these respects."[3] In *The Emperor's New Mind: Concerning Computers, Minds and the Laws of Physics*, Penrose rejected the possibility of Strong AI, the idea that, as the brain operates like a computational machine, any machine capable of complex computation was also capable of experiencing consciousness. Toward the end of the twentieth century, Penrose did not believe that much progress had yet been made toward the creation of an intelligent machine, though he was not willing to rule out the possibility given rapid advances in computer technology. On the possibility of Strong AI he remained a skeptic.[4]

Many of those anticipated advances in AI research have now arrived, while high profile scientists and digital technology leaders have expressed concern over the direction of AI. Bill Gates states that he "does not understand" why there is little concern expressed on the part of the well informed. Similar sentiments have been expressed by physicist Stephen Hawking and entrepreneur Elon Musk, the latter having contributed ten million dollars to the Future of Humanity Institute to fund research into AI risks. AI is occasionally presented to the public as a force so powerful and uncontrollable that the "further development of artificial intelligence could endanger our civilization." Gates subscribes to a cautionary AI narrative:

> I am in the camp that is concerned about super intelligence. First the machines will do a lot of jobs for us and not be super intelligent. That should be positive if we manage it well. A few decades after that, though, the intelligence is strong enough to be a concern.[5]

This chapter explores narratives that have developed around efforts to create computer-based intelligence at the human level and beyond. These tales envision artificial intelligence (AI)—alternately referred to as superintelligence or artificial general intelligence (AGI)—as an inevitable outcome of continued progress in computer technology. A persistent theme in these accounts is the potential to create machine-gods so powerful that they would threaten the future of the human race. The AI *mythos* has acquired an apocalyptic quality—the arrival of AI will reveal a new order that will change us and our machines forever. Limitless power would be in the hands of the first humans to create such machine-based demigods.

The first part of the chapter explores some of the important early statements regarding artificial intelligence. We will consider early dreams of machine intelligence proposed by visionaries such as Alan Turing and I. J. Good. The focus of these narratives was whether a machine could be made that would imitate human thinking. The chapter then takes up efforts to simulate a human brain using highly complex circuitry in a vast computer. This vision of a machine simulation of the human brain raises the possibility of a machine person, a development that would challenge existing "imaginative patterns" and current discursive practices regarding personhood.

We will then consider AI expert Hugo de Garis's *mythos* of divine artificial intelligence possessing virtually limitless power, which de Garis treats as a real possibility. The chapter then moves to a more recent account of extraordinarily powerful "superintelligence" in the work of philosopher and Transhumanist Nick Bostrom. Bostrom's narrative of a coming superintelligence imagines unassailable AI power in a single entity; he urges caution lest we find ourselves at the mercy of our machines. The chapter thus traces a narrative arc from the possibility of thinking machines to humanly created, superintelligent deities.

The myth of human-level AI is of particular interest to the enhancement and Transhumanist communities. AI is presented as a goal in directed evolution, the basis of human merger with machines, the key to exponential technological growth, and a harbinger of the superintelligent future. As such, narratives of artificial intelligence play a crucial role in the rhetoric of the future, and in imagining technological culture generally.

We have noted that *mythos* "precedes and informs *logos*," that narrative provides the foundation for the superstructure of propositional claims.[6] Donald Philip Verene has taken note of Vico's interest in the *vera narratio* or *true narration*, a term referring to myth as a story with power to create the world.[7] Such stories arise from *fantasia*, the imaginative force through which the human world is "felt and formed."[8] Myth as true narration, operating through *fantasia*, shapes culture. Narratives surrounding AI are shaping the cultural future through a comprehensive strategic reimagining of machine, person, intelligence, and deity. Crafting this new *mythos* is crucial to advancing the *logos* of research agendas surrounding computer intelligence, and to shaping public expectations of the technological future.

ALAN TURING

Alan M. Turing (1912–1954) is famed for his role in breaking the Nazi Enigma code during World War II. His name and story are increasingly well known due to movies such as *The Imitation Game* (2014). His Turing Machine is considered one of the first computers following a contemporary understanding of such devices. Turing is also credited with the first theory of a data-storing computer, the ACE or Automatic Computing Engine. He is famed for a proposal for determining when a computer has achieved true artificial intelligence.

In his classic essay, "Computing Machinery and Intelligence," Turing addressed the highly nuanced question of whether a machine might think. He suggested substituting a question more clearly capable of an answer: whether a machine could imitate the functioning of a human mind. This is the question he proposed assessing in his famed Imitation Game, which has since come to be termed the *Turing Test*. "It was suggested tentatively that the question, 'Can machines think?' should be replaced by 'Are there imaginable digital computers which would do well in the imitation game?'" In other words, if one modified a computer called C so that it had "adequate storage," sufficient speed and "an appropriate programme," that our modified computer "can be made to play satisfactorily the part of A in the imitation game . . .?"[9]

Turing did express some reservations about moving too quickly to a direct analogy between a human brain and an electrical computing machine. He wrote, "The fact that Babbage's Analytical Engine was to be entirely mechanical will help us to rid ourselves of a superstition."

> Importance is often attached to the fact that modern digital computers are electrical, and that the nervous system also is electrical. Since Babbage's machine was not electrical, and since all digital computers are in a sense equivalent, we see that this use of electricity cannot be of theoretical importance. Of course electricity usually comes in where fast signaling is concerned, so that it is not surprising that we find it in both these connections. In the nervous system chemical phenomena are at least as important as electrical. In certain computers the storage system is mainly acoustic. The feature of using electricity is thus seen to be only a very superficial similarity.

Turing thus appears to reject the idea, already current in 1950, of a direct analogy between human minds and "thinking machines." In this respect he does not represent the dominant narrative of artificial intelligence, which rests on a direct analogy between human and machine minds. Indeed, the dream of downloading requires such an analogy.

Turing ends this observation with his typical emphasis on function: "If we wish to find such similarities we should look rather for mathematical analogies of function." Turing is more interested in functional than in metaphysical similarities between computers and the human mind. The question of whether machines can be made to think was, for Turing, misdirected:

> The original question, 'Can machines think?' I believe to be too meaningless to deserve discussion. Nevertheless I believe that at the end of the century the use of words and general educated opinion will have altered so much that one will be able to speak of machines thinking without expecting to be contradicted. I believe further that no useful purpose is served by concealing these beliefs.

Turing brought the question of divinity into the discussion of AI, where it found a permanent residence. In a section on objections to constructing thinking machines he first addressed what he termed *The Theological Objection*. Turing puts the objection as follows: "Thinking is a function of man's immortal soul. God has given an immortal soul to every man and woman, but not to any other animal or to machines. Hence no animal or machine can think." He responds, "I am unable to accept any part of this, but will attempt to reply in theological terms . . ." The objection was "arbitrary" when considering "how it might appear to a member of some other religious community. How do Christians regard the Moslem view that women have no souls?" Turing adds that the theological objection "implies a serious restriction of the omnipotence of the Almighty." He asks the religious advocate, "Should we not believe that He has freedom to confer a soul on an elephant if He sees fit?" The case of a thinking machine would be analogous to that of a thinking elephant.

Turing then advances a critical analogy that would mark subsequent discussions of AI: "In attempting to construct such machines we should not be irreverently usurping His power of creating souls, any more than we are in the procreation of children: rather we are, in either case, instruments of His will providing mansions for the souls that He creates."[10] In Turing's AI narrative, creating thinking machines—computers with artificial intelligence—is no different than creating children. Turing contributed to the developing narrative of AI the crucial notion that a thinking machine might constitute a person.

I. J. GOOD

I. J. Good (1916–2009) was a British mathematician and cryptologist known for having been part of Alan Turing's team during the second world war. He is credited with the idea of a technological singularity in its contemporary Transhumanist sense. Good also served as an advisor to Stanley Kubrick in the production of the movie, *2001: A Space Odyssey.*

In 1965, Good published, "Speculations Concerning the First Ultraintelligent Machine," a widely cited essay in which he set out the social implications of what would later be termed artificial intelligence. Particularly provocative was his claim—now central to the artificial intelligence *mythos*—that superintelligent machines would be capable of increasing their own intelligence, creating ever more superintelligent machines, and eventually leaving human beings in the technological dust:

> Let an ultraintelligent machine be defined as a machine that can far surpass all the intellectual activities of any man however clever. Since the design of machines is one of these intellectual activities, an ultraintelligent machine could design even better machines; there would then unquestionably be an 'intelligence explosion,' and the intelligence of man would be left far behind. Thus the first ultraintelligent machine is the last invention that man need ever make, *provided that the machine is docile enough to tell us how to keep it under control.*[11]

Here Good anticipates or invents the concept of the technological singularity. He also constructs the critical analogy between machine intelligence and human intelligence; each is a variation on the same theme. Consequently, a machine intelligence explosion might pose a threat to the human race. This concern was explored a few years later in the famed HAL 9000 AI of *2001: A Space Odyssey* and is now a regular feature of discussions of artificial intelligence.

Documentary filmmaker James Barrat has recently summarized Good's position as follows:

> To paraphrase Good, if you make a superintelligent machine, it will be better than humans at everything we use our brains for, and that includes making superintelligent machines. The first machine would then set off an intelligence explosion, a rapid increase in intelligence, as it repeatedly self-improved, or simply made smarter machines. This machine or machines would leave man's brainpower in the dust.

Barrat adds, hopefully: "After the intelligence explosion, man wouldn't have to invent anything else—all his needs would be met by machines."[12]

THE AI NARRATIVE IN ENHANCEMENT DISCOURSE

In 1997 an IBM computer dubbed Deep Blue defeated chess champion Gary Kasparov. In 2011, another IBM supercomputer dubbed Watson competed with two champions from the game show *Jeopardy*. Watson won, bringing practical AI into American living rooms. A computer-industry insider claimed that Watson represents a significant step in AI because the computer "can answer verbal questions posed by humans." Richard Doherty of Envisioneering Group stated, "to reach [a computer] conversationally and have it respond with knowledgeable answers is a sea change in computing."[13] In 2016, the AI AlphaGo again challenged the assumed boundaries of machine intelligence by defeating champion go player Lee Sedol.[14]

Transhumanist author James Hughes has written, "Even if it takes another decade or two to make hardware as flexible as neurons and software as robust and complex as human consciousness, we will create human-level artificial intelligence before the middle of this century."[15] Hughes's confident prediction rests on observations of exponential technological advances that have led to the formulation of "laws" of progress such as Moore's Law and Ray Kurzweil's Law of Accelerating Returns. His comment, however, also reflects what Northrop Frye has termed "an epiphany of law," meaning a vision of "that which is and must be."[16] A law, like a bridge or a mountain, may connect disparate realms such as the realm of machines and the human realm. Thus, even such a mundane prediction may suggest the presence of a myth. The following sections explore various examples of an emerging *mythos* of AI in the work and writing of three prominent AI researchers.

HENRY MARKRAM AND BRAIN SIMULATION

Engineers and psychologists are coming together in a bid to create an entirely new computing architecture that can simulate the brain's capacities for perception, interaction, and cognition. New nanomaterials will "create logic gates and transistor-based equivalents of neurons and synapses," resulting in "a hardware-based, brain-like system." A major challenge facing such research is the fact that the human brain processes information on several levels at the same time, and with connections running among the various levels. It goes without saying that the brain's complexity is stunning. As just one example, every neuron "receives input from eight thousand other neurons and sends an output to another eight thousand."[17]

Henry Markram of the Ecole Polytechnique Federale de Lausanne heads up an enormous international project aimed at the creation of a virtual human brain. The Human Brain Project seeks to imitate the brain's circuitry in a computer. Markram's narrative emphasizes the therapeutic necessity of such a machine: A synthetic brain will allow researchers to address the growing problem of brain diseases and resulting dementias. "The virtual brain will be an exceptional tool giving neuroscientists a new understanding of the brain and a better understanding of neurological diseases." [18]

The Human Brain Project is a collaborative effort involving 126 universities, businesses, and independent laboratories; twenty six countries; and thousands of research scientists and graduate students. The sheer computing force required for such an undertaking is nearly incomprehensible—each simulated neuron requires computational power equivalent to a laptop computer. One science reporter adds that "a model of the whole brain would have billions of such neurons." Regardless of such enormous complexity, "supercomputing technology is rapidly approaching a level where simulating the whole brain becomes a concrete possibility." Markram says that he "realized already in the early 1990s that if we ever want to understand the brain and its diseases, we will need to develop a functional computer model of a working brain." Eventually this synthetic brain "should be able to almost exactly mimic the activity of a human brain," and could then "be used for basic brain research, for analysis and treatment of brain diseases, and development of new pharmaceutical treatments for brain diseases."[19]

This phrase, "to almost exactly mimic the activities of the human brain," might indicate that Markram's vision is not mythic but commonsensical. *Mythos* appears to yield *logos*: if the brain is a series of electrical circuits (as the narrative of a synthetic brain suggests), then it will be capable of imitation in a computer. However, the imitation is not exact, for a human brain is an integral part of an organic human body and interacts with that body in ways not yet well understood. Any computer brain must, therefore, be limited to imitating or mimicking aspects of a human brain. We might, then, set the mimetic brain in a mythic frame. Frye noted Aristotle's treatment of mimetic heroes in narrative:

> If [the hero] is superior neither to other men nor to his environment, the hero is one of us: we respond to a sense of common humanity, and demand from the poet the same canons of probability that we find in our own experience. This gives us the hero of the *low mimetic* mode. . . .[20]

Under Aristotle's analysis, Markram's envisioned electronic human brain would constitute, not so much a sophisticated machine as an unsophisticated mythic hero—a low mimetic reflection of its creators.

As a mimetic person this hero may, nevertheless, be aware of its existence. Markram has created controversy by suggesting that an electronic brain could potentially achieve consciousness. His confident assertion that "the brain model we develop will have most, if not all, human cognitive capabilities" gives ethicists and scientists alike pause.[21] In "only a few years" he anticipates a sentient machine with which researchers can interact intelligently to address research questions more efficiently than is possible with human dementia patients—*Anthropos ex machina*.[22]

Markram's futuristic narrative takes us well beyond current technological possibilities. An electronic duplication of the human brain would require twenty thousand times the computing power currently available to researchers, and memory capacity five hundred times that of the Internet. IBM's "cat brain simulation involves one billion spiking neurons and ten trillion individual learning synapses, and was accomplished on an IBM Blue Gene/P supercomputer with 147,456 processors and 144TB of main memory."[23] IBM announced that research using light pulses rather than electrons running through wires and chips would result in computers that operate one hundred times faster than the human brain by 2018. The new technology would increase the speed of a super-computer by one thousand times, allowing for a quintillion operations per second.

Markram's narrative of a mimetic brain envisions a future in which customized brain simulation eliminates much social and therapeutic guesswork. "By 2020, genetics and brain simulation will be giving us personalized prescriptions for marriage, lifestyle, and healthcare." Following the *mythos* of the mimetic brain, the Human Brain Project introduces a new world and the beginning of a cultural revolution that eliminates psychiatry, pharmaceuticals, dementia, mental illness, and chronic pain. We will "log into a simulation of our own brain, navigate around in this virtual copy and find out the origins of our quirks. . . ." A computer "will look at a virtual copy of our brains and work out exactly what we need to stop our headaches, quiet the voices talking in our heads and climb out of the valley of depression to a world of color and beauty."[24] Markram's myth adjusts transcendent ideas of health and well-being to contemporary audiences, rendering dreams "plausible" and in this way, as Frye argues, "acceptable to a social waking consciousness."[25]

Markram dismisses claims that he is playing God: from a religious perspective his experiments assist us to probe the divine mind and advance the work of healing. "I don't think it goes against any religion to find out how God built us and to help heal people who are suffering from diseases of the brain."[26] Markram, who did much of his groundbreaking work at the Weisman Institute in Israel, notes that Judaism "has never been afraid of science and discovering the truth of who we are and what reality is."[27] Nevertheless, accurately simulating the brain would constitute a major step toward machines more powerful than the human brain itself, supercomputers that could be networked into a cloud computing architecture to amplify their processing capabilities. The *mythos* of brain simulation would have produced the *logos* of machines rivaling and even exceeding human intelligence.

Hugo de Garis and Computer Gods

Celebrity physicist Michio Kaku has argued that "the gods of mythology, with their divine power, could animate the inanimate." He also notes that, "according to the Bible, in Genesis, Chapter 2, God created man out of the dust, and 'breathed into his nostrils the breath of life, and man became a living soul.'" Given the extraordinary "advances in robotics and artificial intelligence, we now give life to inanimate matter: Today, we are . . . forging in our laboratories machines that breathe life not into clay but into steel and silicon."[28] Discussions of AI reveal a myth of god-like machines: a sufficiently powerful AI would be a deity. Transhumanist AI expert Ben Goertzel rehearses a persistent trope of Transhumanist discourse: "Whether or not transhuman minds now exist in the universe, or have ever existed in the universe in the past, current evidence suggests it will be possible to create them—in effect to build 'gods.'"[29]

While Transhumanist author Zoltan Istvan admits, "I dislike the idea of mixing religion with transhumanism," he acknowledges that such mixing may be inevitable. "The two viewpoints may be inextricably joined more than either side cares to admit." Zoltan himself can sound quite religious in describing the technofuture: "It's likely within a few months of AGI arriving it will independently upgrade itself into something monumentally more intelligent and complex than humans." Civilization may be "heading for a Jesus Singularity," suggesting that "perhaps the first AGI will become the Second Coming of Christ, as detailed in Revelations in the bible." The first successful AGI might be programmed to resemble a "Judeo-Christian minded God." On the other hand, the first AGI might "become the Antichrist, setting off a terrible chain of events for civilization that will end with Armageddon." All of this speculating leads Istvan to the conclusion that "transhumanists and atheists remain more open to working with formal religion. . . ."[30]

A *mythos* of god-like computers is ubiquitous in AI quarters. Austrian computer scientist and AI expert Hugo de Garis develops a creation narrative from the basic mythic materials available to him. Since human scientists "have got the modeling of how to build baby universes," it is possible that an artificial intelligence of sufficient power might actually "build universes." He adds, "Now if it can do that, then by definition it's a god, right? It's a creator."[31] "Artilect" is de Garis' term for AI that has achieved omnipotence and omniscience, and he is one of several AI theorists who predict such limitless machine intelligence will soon be present on the scene. In the movie *Transcendent Man*, Ray Kurzweil muses, "There may not be a god now, but there will be someday."[32]

De Garis' projections are startling, even in the context of futurist discourse: "Can you sort of sense a kind . . . almost like a religious awe almost? We could build gods. I mean . . . you cannot stop it." The story of technology rides the wave of inevitability. For those harboring reservations about future-tech, the fear that "you cannot stop it" looms large. But, for de Garis and like-minded technofuturists, following technology wherever it leads and asking the big questions later is just an outworking of our natural inquisitiveness. Curiosity is a force not to be denied, and curiosity eventually expresses itself as technology.

But there is more than curiosity at work here. De Garis feels constrained by a religious quality in his work:

> I'm not traditionally religious, but I feel a need, if you see what I mean. So my something, gut level, is pushing it, and my head—my scientific knowledge—is rejecting it. But the impulse is still there. So if you could invent something that would satisfy the impulse *and* satisfy the criteria from your intellect, from your knowledge, from your science—a kind of scientifically-based belief system that energizes, that creates a vision, that excites . . . the idea of god building.

De Garis' call for a "scientifically based belief-system" reflects his recognition that technofuturism requires a warranting *mythos* that links AI research to the transcendent. De Garis recognizes that while *logos* observes and deduces, myth introduces "metaphysical significance . . . into the world."[33] A foundation in myth will embolden human beings to cross the threshold of the gods.[34]

Nick Bostrom and the Superintelligence Singleton

Philosopher Nick Bostrom is the head of the Future of Humanity Institute at Oxford University. He is also the co-founder with David Pearce of the World Transhumanist Association (WTA), now referred to as Humanity+. Bostrom has been one of the leading voices on the philosophy and ethics of radical human enhancement. Recently he has devoted his attention to risk assessment—evaluating the existential threats to the human race posed by dramatic technological developments, particularly in the field of artificial intelligence. His book, *Superintelligence: Paths, Dangers, Strategies* (2014) offers a thorough review of approaches to AI and risks associated with the development of powerful AIs that he refers to as superintelligence. Bostrom reviews at length what he takes to be the major risks associated with machines or other entities acquiring intelligence that vastly exceeds human intelligence.[35]

Bostrom writes of what he terms "a superintelligence": "We can tentatively define a superintelligence as any intellect that greatly exceeds the cognitive performance of humans in virtually all domains if interest."[36] A superintelligence may arise in a powerful computer, but might also be achieved with an augmented human, an interface between a human and a machine, organizations, or a large network of humans and machines. Warner notes that "myths define enemies and aliens, and in conjuring them up they say who we are and what we want, they tell stories to impose structure and order."[37] Bostrom's cautionary myth renders the concentration of power in a single, monolithic superintelligence, a monster that threatens the human future. His solutions to this possibility constitute an effort to "impose structure and order" on the burgeoning world of AI.

Following Bostrom's narrative, evolution has already produced one source of intelligence, and so it stands to reason that directed evolution is capable of producing others:

> . . . an artificial intelligence need not much resemble a human mind. AIs could be—indeed, it is likely that most will be—extremely alien. Their "cognitive architectures" and their "cognitive strengths and weaknesses" will differ from our own.[38]

There is also no reason to assume that AIs would share our values or moral orientation—a matter of great concern to Bostrom in *Superintelligence*. Moreover, it would require great investment of resources to teach our values to a superintelligence.

As Bostrom narrates the future of AI, competition among nations becomes a concern. Advanced AI and cognitive enhancement would trigger an intelligence gap between have and have-not nations. Governments with less computing power would find themselves marginalized in the global AI race.

> Once the example has been set, and the results start to show, holdouts will have strong incentive to follow suit. Nations would face the prospect of becoming cognitive backwaters and losing out in

economic, scientific, military and prestige contests with competitors that embrace the new human enhancement technologies.[39]

Bostrom notes that there are several possible paths to superintelligence in addition to powerful computers. These include whole brain emulation, biological enhancement of the human brain, human-machine interface, and organizations and networked intelligences. Rehearsing a familiar theme from enhancement mythology, he describes what sounds like the noosphere: "If we gradually increase the level of integration of a collective intelligence, it may eventually become a unified *intellect*—a single large 'mind' as opposed to a mere assemblage of loosely interacting smaller human minds."[40] Noting the force of narrative he warns that we must avoid "the tendency toward anthropomorphizing" that can "lead us to underestimate the extent to which a machine superintelligence could exceed the human level of performance."[41] We must also be cautious of conceptions such as "smart" and "stupid," human categories that might lead us to misjudge superintelligences.

At the center of Bostrom's AI *mythos* is the looming threat of an apocalyptic superintelligence resulting in a "singleton," or a "world order in which there is at the global level a single decision-making agency."[42] This myth of a dominant and dangerous regime in possession of a superintelligence capable of unified control requires a plausible presentation lest it be dismissed as science fiction. As Frye reminds us, myth renders imaginings "plausible." To this end Bostrom develops a vivid and detailed "AI Takeover Scenario" involving extraordinary and irreversible risk. Research aimed at developing such superintelligence is termed "a project": "We thus find that a project that controls a superintelligence has access to a great source of power. A project that controls the first superintelligence in the world would probably have great strategic advantage." A superintelligent computer might become a monstrous agent. "A machine superintelligence might itself be an extremely powerful agent, one that could successfully assert itself against the project that brought it into existence as well as against the rest of the world." He adds, "This is a point of paramount importance," and one that necessitates the construction of an alternative *mythos*.[43] Bostrom proposes just such an alternative narrative—a story of a "wise singleton," a political entity in charge of a singleton, but also "sufficiently patient and savvy about existential risks to ensure a substantial amount of well-directed concern for the very long-term consequences of the system's actions."[44] In this way we might manage the AI monster.

Bostrom's myth takes on characteristics of a creation account with the addition of a "cosmic endowment." Just as Adam and Eve were given an earthly paradise for their own purposes, the cosmic endowment is that portion of the universe available for human colonization and resource collection. The endowment renders the expansion of the human race—and thus of human happiness—essentially limitless.[45] It is important to beware of cunning serpents in this garden as well:

> An unfriendly AI of sufficient intelligence realizes that its unfriendly final goals will be best realized if it behaves in a friendly manner initially, so that it will be let out of the box. It will only start behaving in a way that reveals its unfriendly nature when it no longer matters whether we find out; that is, when the AI is strong enough that human opposition is ineffectual.[46]

Nick Bostrom's AI myth places readers on the cusp of a dramatic transition for which they are unprepared. We are like children playing with a bomb:

> Before the prospect of an intelligence explosion, we humans are like small children playing with a bomb. Such is the mismatch between the power of our plaything and the immaturity of our conduct. Superintelligence is a challenge for which we are not ready now and will not be ready for a long time. We have little idea when the detonation will occur, though if we hold the device to our ear we can hear a faint ticking sound.[47]

As the narrative *mythos* of superintelligence grounds the *logos* of policy, Bostrom writes that we must not ignore "the essential task of our age." The present generation's "principal moral priority (at least from an impersonal and secular perspective)" is "the reduction of existential risk" associated with superintelligence, and "the attainment of a civilizational trajectory that leads to a compassionate and jubilant use of humanity's cosmic endowment."[48] Nick Bostrom's myth of superintelligence is a warning about the serpent in the AI garden, and an imaginative pattern for achieving the blessed order of the latter.

RESPONSES

Toward the end of his life artificial intelligence pioneer Joseph Weizenbaum (1923–2008) registered concern about the direction of AI research, especially the possibility that it would imitate every human rational function. Weizenbaum expressed his reservations about AI in his 1976 book, *Computer Power and Human Reason: From Judgment to Calculation*.[49] Weizenbaum argued for the preservation of what he termed "judgment" as a uniquely human capacity that could not and should not be turned over to machines.[50] As Katherine Hayles summarizes Weizenbaum's position, "The issue is an ethical imperative that humans keep control; to do otherwise is to abdicate their responsibilities as autonomous independent beings."[51]

Advocating for human exceptionalism in the arena of human problem solving, Weizenbaum reasoned as follows:

> No other organism, and certainly no computer, can be made to confront genuine human problems in human terms. And, since the domain of human intelligence is, except for a small set of formal problems, determined by man's humanity, every other intelligence, however great, must necessarily be alien to the human domain.[52]

Weizenbaum suggested that in our over-reliance on computers we might be seeking an escape from agency.

Computer scientist Jaron Lanier foresees a battle shaping up around varied narratives of an AI future.[53] Lanier identifies an AI *mythos* evident any time a proponent "preaches a story that goes like this:"

> [O]ne day in the not-so-distant future, the Internet will suddenly coalesce into a super-intelligent A.I., infinitely smarter than any of us individually and all of us combined; it will become alive in the blink of an eye, and take over the world before humans even realize what's happening.[54]

Accustomed to a narrative of progress, we assume technological advances equate to improvements in the human condition.

The stories we tell may determine which alternative we face in the future. Lanier is wary of a "constant stream of stories" suggesting that smart machines are "a new form of life, and that we should think of them as fellow creatures instead of as tools." Such a mythology is "reshaping the basic assumptions of our lives in misguided and ultimately damaging ways." Even our foundational conception of personhood is shifting in response to AI. "What bothers me most about this trend," writes Lanier, "is that by allowing artificial intelligence to reshape our concept of personhood, we are leaving ourselves open to the flipside: we think of people more and more as computers, just as we think of computers as people." However, Lanier notes that "the news is no longer about us but about the big new computational object that is greater than us." This new thing may turn out to be a friend of "a rough best, its hour come around at last."[55]

One of the sites of rhetorical battle will be the ethics of how we treat AIs. Concerns of this type will center on whether an AI can ever be considered a person. Studying dementia by afflicting a whole brain simulation with Alzheimer's disease would raise profound ethical considerations if we accepted that the machine was a self-aware intelligence. A growing body of opinion and research addresses the morality of torturing or terminating machine intelligences.[56] The closely related issue of AI rights has predictably arisen and is being hotly debated. Resolving such debates will depend in part on which narratives of the future prevail in the scientific community and in the arena of public opinion.

One such narrative envisions a future in which AIs are afforded legal rights. Physician Hutan Ashrafian has recently presented the case for AI rights—including the rights of intelligent robots—in *Nature*. Ashrafian transports his readers into that future:

> There is a strong possibility that in the not-too-distant future, artificial intelligences (AIs), perhaps in the form of robots, will become capable of sentient thought. Whatever form it takes, this dawning of machine consciousness is likely to have a substantial impact on human society.

A declaration of AI rights would prevent AI abuse that "would be detrimental to humankind's moral, ethical and psychological well-being." Ashrafian's narrative of the AI future envisions "scientists, philosophers, funders and policy-makers" working together to "develop a proposal for an international charter for AIs, equivalent to that of the United Nations' Universal Declaration of Human Rights." Though human level AI is not yet a reality, Ashrafian cautions his readers not to "underestimate the likelihood of artificial thinking machines." We are entering a new era, "arriving at the horizon of the birth of a new intelligent race." The language of race would appear to bring AIs within the category of persons, even human beings, as does Ashrafian's political language. In this new world, a "new digital populace will deserve moral dignity and rights, and a new law to protect them."[57]

Attorney and Transhumanism critic Wesley J. Smith hopes a different narrative will prevail, one which embraces human exceptionalism. In Smith's future, "machines have no dignity and no rights" because such "properly belong exclusively to the human realm." As Smith tells the story, machine intelligence "would only *mimic* sentience," remaining mere "inanimate objects" that could not be "harmed" any more than one could harm a household appliance. According to Smith, "machine rights advocacy is subversively reductionist," tending only to diminish "the meaning and unique value of human life." At the same time, those who reason that the human brain is merely a complex machine can make little case for why such an entity should be afforded rights:

> If the brain is a really machine, then any thinking machine deserves the same rights that a working brain possesses. But the human

brain—and, more importantly, the mind—is much more than a complex organic computer. ... [H]uman thought arises from a complex interaction of reason, emotion, abstract analysis, experience, memories, education, unconscious motivation, body chemistry, and so on. That can never be true of AI robots."

As for the AI rights movement, "let's hope it goes nowhere," because "there is a proper hierarchy of moral worth, and humans are at the apex." All that is accomplished in a push for AI rights "is the diminishment of the fundamental importance of being human." At the point that AI rights are embraced, "human entities would be just like other entities that possess a touch of processing capacity." Smith concludes, "This is not an act of respect and ennobling lesser beings. It is disrespect of human beings."[58] Other observers as well fear that a prevailing digital narrative reduces everything to computational mechanisms. Katherine Hayles, for instance, is concerned with a steady trend toward understanding the brain, the earth, and even the universe as computational machines.[59] Such computation reductionism leads to the view that "the most prized functionality is the ability to process information . . ."[60]

It seems clear that as intelligent machines come to more closely reflect human capabilities, questions of AI rights will continue to be debated. Whether AIs achieve divine powers—as Hugo de Garis and others have suggested—may depend on which myths of the AI future, which 'imaginative patterns," guide the *logos* of research agendas and legislation. For Bostrom as for Lanier, the question of which AI future we face is an urgent matter, and one pregnant with the greatest consequence—the future of the human race. The AI myths we select will in large measure determine the shape of that future.

11 Posthumans in Space

Let us create vessels and sails adjusted to the heavenly ether, and there will be plenty of people unafraid of the empty wastes. In the meantime, we shall prepare, for the brave sky-travelers, maps of the celestial bodies.

—Johannes Kepler, in a letter to Galileo

The Earth is the cradle of mankind, but one cannot live in the cradle forever.

—K. E. Tsiolkovsky

For transhumanists, not only is their flight from the body we now possess and know, there is a flight from the earth, from terra firma itself, into the realms of space.

—Jean Bethke Elshtain

Space exploration and colonization were early and prominent components of the Transhumanist vision. In one early statement on Transhumanist philosophy, philosopher Max More listed "space habitation" along with artificial intelligence, life extension, and several other research arenas as distinguishing interests of the movement.[1] The Transhumanist Declaration of 1998 also incorporated space exploration and colonization: "We envision the possibility of broadening human potential by overcoming aging, cognitive shortcomings, involuntary suffering, and our confinement to planet Earth."[2] After listing immortality and several oft-encountered Transhumanist goals, World Transhumanist Association co-founder Nick Bostrom wrote in "Transhumanist Values," "Other transhumanist themes include space colonization and the possibility of creating superintelligent machines . . ."[3] Nowhere is the mythic more evident than in imaginative tales of space, the "alternative world" we can see and have begun to enter.

In addition to NASA, a growing number of private organizations actively promote space exploration and colonization. Among the largest and most successful of these is the 100 Year Starship, a private foundation established in 2010 and funded by grants from the Defense Advanced Research Projects Agency (DARPA) and NASA. The organization, which sponsors conferences open to the public and actively enlists public input, exists "to make the capability of human travel beyond our solar system a reality within the next 100 years." Toward that end, they write:

> We unreservedly dedicate ourselves to identifying and pushing the radical leaps in knowledge and technology needed to achieve interstellar flight, while pioneering and transforming breakthrough applications that enhance the quality of life for all on Earth.

There is also a public outreach mission: "We actively seek to include the broadest swath of people and human experience in understanding, shaping and implementing this global aspiration."

The 100 Year Starship's myth is apocalyptic—interstellar flight promises transformative technological breakthroughs:

> When we explore space, we garner the greatest benefits here at home. The challenge of traveling to another star system could generate transformative activities, knowledge, and technologies that would dramatically benefit every nation on Earth in the near term and years to come.

The *mythos* of space colonization undergirds a *logos* of necessary technological developments. Among the breakthroughs required to make "travel to the stars" a reality are ways to generate and store "enormous quantities of energy safely" as well as advances in "sustainable habitats." Intentional "programs to establish a human presence on the Moon, Mars, or elsewhere in our solar system will be stepping-stones to the stars." The *mythos* connects space and human survival, for "all the capabilities needed to accomplish human interstellar travel are the same ones required for successful human survival." While the leap to an interstellar vision strikes many as "fantastical," it is "no more so than the fantasy of reaching the Moon was" when H.G. Wells was writing. "The truth is that the best ideas sound crazy at first. And then there comes a time when we can't imagine a world without them."[4]

Paul Ricoeur spoke of the "'symbolic function'" of myth, its "power of discovery and revelation."[5] Myths disclose "unprecedented worlds," providing "an opening on to other *possible* worlds which transcend the established limits of our *actual* world."[6] Myth thus promises "another mode of existence entirely, to be realized just beyond the present time and place."[7] 100 Year Starship backer and NASA Ames Research Center director, Pete Worden, explains that "the human space program is now really aimed at settling other worlds." Worden comments, "I think we'll be on the moons of Mars by 2030 or so," adding this intriguing statement suggesting corporate interest in the prediction:

> Larry [Page, of Google] asked me a couple weeks ago how much it would cost to send people one way to Mars and I told him $10 billion, and his response was, 'Can you get it down to 1 or 2 billion?' So now we're starting to get a little argument over the price.[8]

The turn toward space is evident even in Nick Bostrom's notion of a "cosmic endowment." Bostrom re-imagines the universe, not as a vast emptiness, but as a limitless resource for the expansion of human happiness.[9] The term "endowment" suggests more than mere access to resources—it suggests a sacred trust, a timeless reserve placed just out of our reach but belonging, nonetheless, to us.

New myths are required to get us within reach of this endless endowment. Sociologist William Sims Bainbridge argues for a new religious *mythos* to prepare us for space. "I have suggested that only a transcendent, impractical, radical religion can take us to the stars," he writes. "We need a spaceflight movement capable of giving us a sense of transcendent purpose to dominant sectors of the society. . . ." Bainbridge adds, "The heavens are a sacred realm that we should enter in order to transcend death."[10] The connection between overcoming death and space exploration, though not clearly explained, suggests the metaphysical significance of space for humanity and posthumanity. Space is our evolutionary destiny, a location for dramatic technological advances, the repository of limitless resources, a new home should Earth expire, a frontier to satisfy human curiosity and thirst for adventure, and the setting in which we will encounter other intelligent species.

This chapter examines a mythology of space colonization that has developed in technofuturist discourse. We will begin with late nineteenth and early twentieth-century discussions of space in the works of Nikolai Federov and the Russian Cosmists. We will then explore the rising private space industry and the narrative by means of which space exploration is rhetorically justified. The chapter concludes by considering space narratives that develop around continued human evolution and the need to ensure our survival.

DREAMS OF SPACE

The link between space and modern theories of human enhancement can be traced back to the latter's very origins in the nineteenth century. Michael Hagemeister notes that the Russian Cosmists, who provided the foundation for technofuturism and Transhumanism, were captivated by the idea of space flight. Cosmist influence on Soviet ideas about space was substantial. Space was associated with a worldview that found technology redemptive and sought immortality among the stars. Historian George Young notes that for Nikolai Fedorov, space exploration "should not be undertaken simply for itself, out of curiosity or as an adventure or conquest, but for a specific purpose: life over death for all humanity."[11]

Space exploration and a transformed human race can occasionally be found as complementary elements in visions of the technological future. Even in the secular Soviet Union space held a spiritual appeal. Hagemeister writes that rediscovering rocket scientist Konstantin Tsiolkovsky's philosophy sheds "new light on the Soviet space program—a program that was supposed to open the cosmic way to the transfiguration and perfection of humanity, and finally to eternal salvation." He adds:

> The advancement into space was intended not merely to expand human powers and capabilities but also to rebuild the human body in order to accommodate it to the conditions of life in the cosmos.

According to the Cosmist *mythos*, space was the proving ground for a new kind of human being:

> This development, in turn was supposed to bring forth a generation of superhumans who would be to us what we are to a unicellular organism. Ultimately, the human race would lose its corporeality and individuality and turn into a kind of radiation, 'immortal in time and infinite in space.'[12]

Following Fedorov's technofuturist narrative, science and art would explode the barriers of "space and time." He thus developed "plans for expansion into outer space and for the regulation of geological, meteorological, and cosmic processes, all leading to the bold vision of a complete restructuring and domination of the universe, the creation of an all-powerful 'new man,' the abolition of death, and the resurrection of the dead."[13] The "search for the dispersed particles of [our] ancestors" would cause us to "expand out into space" where "the resurrected will take up residence, inhabiting the universe with reason and transforming it into a work of art." As a result, "resurrection and the conquest of the universe are dependent on each other . . ."

Future generations will witness "the transformation and colonization of the universe," goals intimately related to Fedorov's "Common Task"—"the resurrection of the dead." In the Cosmist *mythos* the "struggle against death" and the "conquest of space" were joint projects.[14] The Petrograd Biocosmists-Immortalists took as their motto: Immortalism and Interplanetarianism. "In effect," writes Hagemeister, the Cosmists "put the abolition of death, the colonization of the universe, and the resurrection of the dead on the agenda."[15]

The idea of space and its transformative promise animated other writers as well in the early twentieth century. Futurist and scientist J. D. Bernal anticipated other elements of the space mythology in the late 1920s:

> [O]nce acclimatized to space living, it is unlikely that man will stop until he has roamed over and colonized most of the sidereal universe, or that even this will be the end. Man will not ultimately be content to be parasitic on the stars but will invade them and organize them for his own purposes.

Through the power of myth, "we originally make the human world." Bernal's narrative reflects Vico's notion of *fantasia* at work, the "power fully and completely to order the world," or in this case, the universe.[16] Myth, operating through *fantasia*, shapes the humanized cosmos we will inhabit. Stars "will be turned into efficient heat-engines," while we employ technology to achieve "intelligent organization" of the cosmos, an intervention that would mean "the life of the universe could probably be prolonged to many millions of times what it would be without organization."[17] Bernal suggested a spherical space habitat for long-term stays and as a foundation for space colonies. Space exploration would provide humanity with the sense of limitlessness necessary to dramatic technological advances. Human space colonization would transform the universe.

While Teilhard de Chardin did not show a consistent interest in space exploration, he did write in the 1930s of escape from earth as a catalyst for spiritual evolution:

> [W]e may begin by asking seriously whether life will not perhaps one day succeed in ingeniously forcing the bars of its earthly prison, either by finding the means to invade other planets or . . . by getting into psychical touch with other focal points of consciousness across the abysses of space.

Teilhard associated the sanctuary of space with his trademark future vision of the noosphere. The myth of a global mental network is augmented by the possibility of joining planetary noospheres:

> The meeting and mutual fecundation of two noospheres is a supposition which . . . is merely extending to psychical phenomena a scope no one would think of denying to material phenomena. Consciousness would thus finally construct itself by a synthesis of planetary units.[18]

Interplanetary noospheric communion would enhance humanity's spiritual evolution and assist the cosmos in the achieving of Christ Consciousness.

SPACE AS LIMITLESS RESOURCE

Private space exploration ventures have flourished in recent years, lending credibility to the narrative of a human future in space. In early 2011, Bigelow Aerospace of Las Vegas, Nevada—founded by real estate magnate Robert Bigelow—announced that seven nations intended to lease room on one of its inflatable orbiting space habitats. Other private spaceflight firms including Virgin Galactic offer customers the opportunity to "Book your Place in Space."[19] Another example of private enterprise entering the space race is the successful launch, orbit, and reentry of the Dragon space capsule developed by Elon Musk's Space Exploration Technologies (SpaceX) in December 2010. The ship also docked with the International Space Station in 2012. "There's so much that can go wrong and it all went right," said Musk following the capsule's successful splash-down in the Pacific Ocean.[20] A competing private space flight organization congratulated SpaceX by writing, "The Dragon's mission has been one small step for SpaceX, but is one giant leap for commercial space."[21]

> Other successful entrepreneurs are backing space technologies of interest to Transhumanists and enhancement advocates. Peter Diamandis MD, president and co-founder with Ray Kurzweil of Singularity University, is the co-author with Steven Kotler of, *Abundance: The Future is Better than You Think* (2012). Diamandis is associated with several efforts to privatize space exploration. Among his many honors, the government of Russia has presented Diamandis the Konstantin E. Tsiolkovsky Award for his work in establishing the International Space University. In *Abundance*, Diamandis and Kotler tell the story of Burt Rutan and his efforts to take space flight private. The narrative persuasively illustrates that private entrepreneurial efforts are more effective and efficient than is big government involvement in space exploration.[22]

Inspired about space colonization as a child absorbing the *Star Trek* and NASA narratives, Diamandis eventually became frustrated with the slow progress of government-funded space exploration. "He built his first companies—12 of them—as social and technological thrusters designed to clear the way for human space colonies."[23] Diamandis is the founder and chair of the XPrize Foundation, which offers large cash prizes to the first individuals or groups to accomplish various goals associated with practical spaceflight. His Ansari X Prize was offered to the first private company both to send a human being into space and see to that person's safe return to Earth. Space-ShipOne, a joint effort of Burt Rutan and Microsoft co-founder Paul Allen, won the prize in 2004.

Diamandis' narrative incorporates a moral obligation to colonize space, an accomplishment that will have a transformative effect on humans—we will become "a multiplanetary species:"

> My first ambition was to get off the world. My childhood dreams were focused on being part of the effort to make humanity a multi-planetary species. I believe we have a moral obligation to back up the biosphere, take it off-planet, and give ourselves the safety of ubiquity. Ultimately it's what we do. We have the exploration gene.[24]

Diamandis recognizes the power of skillfully deployed rhetorical strategies such as narrative and visualization in efforts to alter public perceptions. "Getting the public to change its beliefs is the underpinning of an X Prize: demonstration leading to paradigm change."[25]

Diamandis' latest venture, Planetary Resources, will mine asteroids for water and metals. Diamandis explains:

> We're working with the US government to define regulations that allow commercial exploitation of asteroids. Unlike oil reserves or even the oceans, which are limited, resources in space are infinite. Anyone who wants will have access to them, so everyone benefits when a company like this succeeds.[26]

Whereas Diamandis' reference to the infinite is specifically focused on vast new fields of industrial resources, the vision of limitlessness fuels space narratives more generally. Bostrom's "cosmic endowment" represents a similar limitless construct. Implicit in Diamandis' space narrative is the notion that space offers human beings ownership of anything they can reach. Space is an infinite treasure store of resources available to fuel humanity's limitless expansion as a multi-planetary species.

SPACE AS SURVIVAL NARRATIVE

Actor Lloyd Bridges, the beleaguered mission director in *Rocketship XM* (1950), announces in the movie's closing lines that in space exploration will be "humankind's salvation." Many today rehearse a *mythos* of space as means of ensuring humanity's survival and eventual interplanetary flourishing. The 2014 Christopher Nolan movie, *Interstellar*, develops around essentially the same theme: planets in deep space will provide humanity's next home as earth's environment declines, provided we are bold enough to venture out. The narrative had been deployed a few years earlier in a less successful film, *Knowing* (2009), directed by Alex Proyas. In this version of the narrative of space as survival, an alien race selects certain human children and transports them to an edenic planet as earth is destroyed in a massive solar flare.

The space-as-survival narrative is not a theme for fiction only, however. The Transhumanist-aligned Lifeboat Foundation lists space colonization among the ten technologies of greatest interest to Transhumanists. Overpopulation of the earth is mentioned as a concern. "Space colonies will become necessary to house the many billions of individuals that will be born in the future as our population continues to expand at a lazy exponential." But, our corporate human destiny to populate the cosmos and extend biodiversity in the process is also important to the Foundation's interest in space colonization. "[B]y expanding outwards into the cosmos in all directions, we'll be able to seed every star system with every species of plant and animal imaginable. The genetic diversity of the embryonic home planet will seem tiny by comparison." Brute nature will thus be humanized.

A Lifeboat Foundation Science Advisory board member affirms that the foundational *mythos* of Transhumanism is crucial to visions of space colonization: "Space colonization is closely related to transhumanism through the mutual association of futurist philosophy, but also more directly because *the embrace of transhumanism will be necessary to colonize space.*" (emphasis added) Radical human enhancement and space colonization are connected in visions of the technological future. Because of the harsh conditions in space, "the only reasonable solution is to upgrade our bodies. Not terraform the cosmos, but cosmosform ourselves."[27] The *mythos* of enhancement drives the *logos* of practical preparations to enter space.

Myth gives rise to ritual, and Northrop Frye has written about ritual's impetus to humanize "stupid and indifferent nature" so that it is "no longer the container of human society, but is contained by that society, and must rain or shine at the pleasure of man. . . ."[28] Similarly, poetry can reveal an "omnipotent human society that contains all the powers of nature within itself."[29] For Ricoeur, myth discloses "possible worlds."[30] Nowhere in the mythology of Transhumanism and technofuturism are these anagogic and apocalyptic qualities more evident than in narratives of space and space colonization.

There are risks associated with this myth. The story of space as a refuge for humans in crisis does not—cannot—involve the entire human race; even the most optimistic technofuturist would recognize that transporting all living human beings into space is unachievable. Rather, survival narratives emphasize the survival of the human *species*, albeit perhaps shaped anew by the forces of space. In a 2006 speech in Hong Kong, eminent physicist Stephen Hawking urged that "it is important for the human race to spread out into space for the survival of the species." Extinction his principal concern. "Life on earth is at the ever-increasing risk of being wiped out by a disaster, such as sudden global warming, nuclear power, a genetically engineered virus or other dangers we have not yet thought of."[31]

Hawking has continued to promote the idea of species survival in space. "Once we spread out into space and establish independent colonies," Hawking told a BBC interviewer, "our future should be safe." On his seventieth birthday in 2012 he again affirmed the concept. The near certainty of a wide-spread catastrophe formed his narrative's foundation: "It is possible that the human race could become extinct but it is not inevitable. I think it is almost certain that a disaster, such as nuclear war or global warming, will befall the Earth within a thousand years."[32] This mythic quest for salvation in space drives visions of human survival away from Earth, and away from the vast majority of the human race. While "the human race" may survive, any particular human being may not.

Sir Martin Rees (b. 1942), a leading astrophysicist and Astronomer Royal of Great Britain, also promotes the myth of space as sanctuary. Because of "the ever-present slight risk of a global catastrophe," humans ought to establish colonies in space. "Humankind will remain vulnerable so long as it stays confined here on Earth," he writes. "Once self-sustaining communities exist away from Earth—on the Moon, on Mars, or freely floating in space—our species would be invulnerable to even the worst global disasters."[33] Rees, like Hawking, appears concerned with human beings as a species rather than with the survival of individual members of the human race. As myths are "the matrix of thought, the background that shapes our mental habits," this turn away from the individual could encourage expectations that compromise personal rights. Myths suggest "imaginative patterns" that exert considerable power over expectations of science and interpretations of facts.[34] In Rees's narrative "our species" may supersede any particular member of that species.

Our species may give rise to other species in space. In Rees's mythology, living machines or cyborgs "unconstrained by any restrictions" will likely "exploit the full range of genetic techniques and diverge into new species."[35] Such an eventuality would require a lengthy presence in space: "Once the threshold is crossed when there is a self-sustaining level of life in space, then life's long-range future will be secure. . . ." Galactic manifest destiny prevails in this narrative; as in Bostrom's vision of cosmic endowment, space is ours for the taking. Rees predicts that genetic duplication of humans will occur "on promising planets," thus guaranteeing "a diffusion through the entire Galaxy."[36] Rees's quest myth envisions a new human or posthuman era on a vast new stage, or perhaps just the long-range persistence of "life."

Myth implies "a drive towards completion, an insistence on seeing things through to as near their full development as is practicable."[37] The notion of a human *telos* or perfection in space is evident in Rees's rendition of the myth; a permanent human presence in space "would be as epochal an evolutionary transition as that which led to land-based life on Earth." Be this as it may, "it could still be just the beginning of cosmic evolution."[38] In this narrative, the human species is assured "a near-infinite future" which will "open up speculative scenarios that could transform our entire universe eventually into a 'living cosmos.'" Rees's myth takes an apocalyptic turn as he looks toward a "post-human potential . . . so immense that not even the most misanthropic amongst us would countenance its being foreclosed by human actions."[39] One transgresses the promise of perfection in space at one's own peril.

Physicist Freeman Dyson (b. 1923) is another prominent proponent of the space colonization *mythos*. From 1957 to 1961 he was associated with the Orion Project that proposed space flight using nuclear engines. Dyson also served for a period as president of the Space Studies Institute, an organization founded in the 1970s by Princeton University physicist and space colonization advocate, Gerard K. O'Neill (1927–1992). O'Neill's 1977 book, *The High Frontier: Human Colonies in Space*, was a groundbreaking treatment of the promise and perils of space colonization.[40] O'Neill provided a blueprint for the next step in space exploration following NASA's Apollo program.

Dyson's narrative, like those of Hawking and Rees, develops around metaphors of escape and sanctuary. "If life succeeds in escaping from Earth and spreading out into the universe," he writes, "the next thousand years might be a golden age of science."[41] Permanent space communities are a stage in our evolutionary progress, the destined expansion of the human species into new territory. New human and posthuman worlds will emerge as limitless sanctuary yields diversity: "There is no reason why a variety of intelligent species should not fill a variety of ecological niches in different physical environments. . . ." In space "our one species will become many."[42]

In Dyson's version of the myth, diversity and boundless territory generate cosmic segregation of "deviant populations": "Genetic differences which would be socially divisive and politically intolerable on Earth may be harmless when the deviant populations are living on distant asteroids."[43] In the *mythos* of limitless evolutionary expansion, humanity colonizes the solar system, the galaxy and the universe. "Small-scale emigration may continue for a few hundred years before life is thoroughly adapted and growing wild on the multitude of worlds that are orbiting around the sun."[44]

Dyson envisions transporting large numbers of people to large numbers of space colonies, resulting in a significant reduction in earth's population. Earth becomes a memorial park: "If it were possible to export surplus populations of people and industries into space habitats scattered over the solar system, then the earth might be preserved as an unspoiled wilderness or as an ecological park."[45] The *mythos* of space colonization again shapes the *logos* of future population policy away from earth and toward space. *Everything* in the universe is available for human appropriation, something like Bostrom's cosmic endowment, but earth is rendered a vast museum of the organic past.

J. Richard Gott III (b. 1947) of Princeton University has also endorsed the myth of space as human sanctuary. He has written that "self-sustaining colonies in space would provide us with a life insurance policy against any catastrophes that might occur on Earth, a planet covered with the fossils of extinct species." Gott adds, "The goal of the human spaceflight program should be to increase our survival prospects by colonizing space."[46] However, "our" again refers to the human species and not to human individuals:

> [S]ince time is short, we should concentrate on establishing the first self-supporting colony in space as soon as possible. . . . Existence of even one self-supporting colony in space might as much as double the long-term survival prospects of our species—by giving us two independent chances instead of one.

Mars would be a likely place to begin. In the Mars Direct program proposed by Professor Robert Zubrin, "rather than bring astronauts back from Mars, we might choose to leave them there to multiply, living off indigenous materials. We want them on Mars. That's where they benefit human survivability."[47]

In other versions of the myth of space colonization, permanent colonies will have to wait for the advent of practical machine-human cyborgs. For Roger Launius (b. 1954), senior curator at the Smithsonian National Air and Space Museum, colonies in space will require cyborg technology. Following the quest myth formula and its pursuit of perfection, the purpose of space colonization is closely tied to the development of the human species. Our goal becomes "to get off this planet and become a multi-planetary species."

Space is apocalypse, a new order, the "next state of human evolution." The cyborg, a step toward apocalypse, is at hand:

> There are cyborgs walking about us. There are individuals who have been technologically enhanced with things such as pacemakers and cochlea ear implants that allow those people to have fuller lives. I would not be alive without technological advances.

Cyborgs are central to some versions of the narrative of space as sanctuary. Rather than transporting an earth-like environment into space, "humans should be willing to partially adapt to the environment to which they would be traveling."[48] Becoming interplanetary posthumans is "going to force you to reconsider how to reengineer humans."[49]

RESPONSES

Carl Sagan (1934–1996) wrote early in his career of a "time in our future history when the Solar System will be explored and inhabited. . . ." Himself deeply involved with the Voyager project, Sagan was convinced that "the present moment will be a pivotal instant in the history of mankind. There are not many generations given an opportunity as historically significant as this one." For Sagan, the Cosmist rocket scientist Tsiolkovsky was a source of vision and hope. "To paraphrase K. E. Tsiolkovsky, the founder of astronautics: The Earth is the cradle of mankind, but one cannot live in the cradle forever."[50] Such mythologizing about a human quest for perfection in space has shaped "values and expectations" that are evident in the discussion of space exploration right up to the present.[51]

Myths of space build on myths of inevitable progress and the posthuman. Space mythographers from the Cosmists to Sagan have imagined distant planets and the great reaches of the cosmos as our posthuman, evolutionary destiny, spiritual sanctuary and limitless resource. The space *mythos* reveals realms unknown, opening the public imagination to "other *possible* worlds which transcend the established limits of our *actual* world."[52] Rather than a harsh and foreign territory, space is filled with promise for the daring colonizer and the courageous entrepreneur. The myth assures us that perennial problems will find their solutions once we break the chains binding us to earth and realize our place among the stars. Evolutionary destiny and inevitable progress lend urgency to space colonization; we must seize the moment.

For figures like Hawking, Rees, Gott and Launius, narratives of space colonization provide a matrix of survival scenarios as earth is depleted or humanity decimated by disease and warfare. Space is the everlasting and inexhaustible heaven of enhanced humans, posthumans, and cyborgs. According to the myth, colonizers will extend the reach of our highly evolved descendants to every corner of the galaxy, one step in the process of awakening the cosmos to consciousness and thus "humanizing brute nature." In the narrative of space, a new heaven awaits earth-dwellers equipped with the requisite technology and willing to have their own bodies and minds transformed by additional technology.

The ethical implications of such a vision are freighted with apocalyptic despair for this tired planet. Narratives of imminent environmental collapse, devastating wars, and a resulting exodus leave little incentive for environmental action, let alone large scale and coordinated worldwide environmental and political action; planets unspoiled and numberless await our arrival. Old earth becomes a destination for a new generation of eco-tourists interested in their ancestors. Moreover, the sheer vastness of space and its limitless planets can tempt the imagination with scenarios of separation rather than narratives of increasingly diverse but interdependent cultures. As new human species develop and competition occurs, planetary separation is a possible solution.

Our dreams of space have been transformed from ventures of discovery into a quest myth of evolutionary destiny and posthuman perfection. What we seek in space, writes Mary Midgley, is "not just science, but omniscience."[53] Though earth is our home and place of origin, space is relentlessly presented as the location of human survival, a sanctuary for our redemption and transformation. The realities of an aging earth and a morally challenged human race require a new vision of sanctuary, redemption and heaven.

12 CONCLUSION

There's nothing that we cannot do.

—Peter Diamandis

We want to become posthuman.

—Lincoln Cannon

We could build gods.

—Hugo de Garis

In any case, whatever the faults of religion, science cannot sensibly be put in its place.

—Mary Midgley

I have argued that an interconnected set of myths present in enhancement, Transhumanist, and technofuturist discourse propagate a vision of inevitable technological transcendence. In this way these sacred narratives constitute a rhetoric of the future, a discourse about technology's role in shaping the human future and the future human. The writers and thinkers considered here—Ray Kurzweil, Nick Bostrom, Ben Goertzel, Ramez Naam, Anders Sandberg, Max More, James Hughes, Martine Rothblatt, and others—have appeared on the scene at a time of extraordinary technological breakthroughs that promise to deliver dramatic social, cultural, and commercial change. Despite the enormous impact of these technologies, the public often misunderstands their nature and potential cultural impact. Moreover, there is no widely embraced vision as regards their uses or even their regulation. Our technological future, that is, must be invented. The mythologies explored here are the closest thing we have to such a comprehensive vision of the technological future. Consequently, these narratives provide an ideal set of texts for exploring one aspect of the rhetoric of science and technology— its potential to cast a mythic vision of the future.

Following the lead of writers such as Giambattista Vico, Mary Midgley, Jonathan Gottschall, Marina Warner, Northrop Frye, Kenneth Burke, Laurence Coupe, Brent Waters, and other theorists of myth, I have sought a framework for discussing myth that takes in a wider range of narrative concerns than occupied earlier scholars of myth such as Eliade, Fraser, and Levi-Strauss. This conceptual framework affords possibilities for evaluating Transhumanist and enhancement discourse, thus allowing insights into the strategic potential—the rhetoric—of myth. My particular concern has been to render an account of myth deployed to shape a vision of the future, hitherto a relatively unexplored potential of the genre. Employing concepts such as apocalypse epiphany, *fantasia*, imaginative pattern, perfection, and quest, I have assessed the discursive force of dominant narratives in shaping our lives, ways of thinking, and dreams of the future.

Mary Midgley opened the way to such analysis with her idea of myth as imaginative pattern. As creators of such patterns, the narratives discussed in the preceding chapters constitute not simply a set of predictions, but a persuasive vision of the future. Stories that once resided on the margins of public and scientific discourse and in the pages of adolescent fiction have assumed cultural center-stage. Their mythic force as visionary patterns is now sufficient to challenge the hegemony of major Western ideological systems including capitalism, Christianity, and Darwinism. Moreover, as these myths provide the only comprehensive blueprint for thought, action, and regulation of the greatest commercial force in the world today—technology—they are acquiring an unprecedented rhetorical power. To the mythographers discussed here belongs the future.

Nevertheless, these narratives have to this point largely flown under the cultural radar as themes in TED talks, fiction movies and novels, trade books appealing to the technologically educated, as the topics of academic conferences, and as the subject of seminars for the initiated. Only Ray Kurzweil and his construct of the Singularity have gained sufficient cultural capital to be widely recognized beyond the boundaries of the technofuturist world. For this reason the narratives of technological transcendence explored here might be dismissed as reflecting the concerns of an idealistic minority or even as a projection of science fiction fantasies. However, as Brent Waters writes, "posthuman ideas and rhetoric are already shaping the expectations and imaginations of late moderns." Specifically, "individuals increasingly regard themselves as self-constructed projects, projections, and artifacts of their own will, and they are turning to technology to overcome the bodily limitations that impede them from satisfying their desires."[1] Writers from Vico to Midgley remind us that myth exerts a powerful influence over thought and action. With this force comes the risk posed by an excessive realism that ignores the symbolic nature of myth, or an unyielding vision of perfection that might ignore personal rights that impede the myth's fulfillment.

In the following pages I want to consider several recurring issues in critical reaction to the human enhancement vision as advanced in the myths examined here. It is common for a mythic vision to be venerated within a discourse community, to create group identity, to encourage certain attitudes and actions. However, when such a transcendent vision is tested against the realities of the world in which we live our lives—a world of limited resources, the ambiguities of embodied experience, the uncertainties of political systems, clashing religious faiths and failures of justice—how does it stand up? Responsible criticism of the technofuturist narratives have tended to cluster around several high-order concerns. These include control, human nature, justice, ethics and religion.

CONTROL

Control is a theme that marks critical reaction to Transhumanism and related narratives. The myths of technological transcendence envision, not simply radical enhancements to the body and mind, but rational, moral, and physical control over the future. No longer will humanity be subject to the dictates of nature, religion, or economic disparity. Political control is less frequently addressed, but does represent an implicit topic of concern. If technological enhancement follows the Transhumanist *mythos*, then the *logos* of policy might come to the fore as a means of ensuring enhancement. Such a prioritizing of a particular agenda could eventuate in curtailed personal rights.

From the days of J. D. Bernal and Julian Huxley, directed evolution has been a crucial component of the broader enhancement *mythos*—we will take technological control of our evolution. By means of technology we will shape ourselves into an imagined ideal form, physically and mentally, eventually rendering our descendants posthuman. Francis Fukuyama writes that Transhumanists "want nothing less than to liberate the human race from its biological constraints." In apocalyptic Transhumanist mythology, "humans must wrest their biological destiny from evolution's blind process of random variation and adaptation and move to the next stage as a species."[2]

Enhancement proponents understand narratives of control over human nature as courageous opposition to conventionality, conservatism, and outdated religious ideology. Philosopher Robert Sparrow has noted that "there is a tendency for advocates of human enhancement" to see themselves as "bravely defying the forces of irrationality and conservatism in order to reach the difficult conclusions that others dare not."[3] Political scientist Michael Sandel sounds a similar concern about the prospect of radical enhancement at the genetic level. The project may be "the ultimate expression of our resolve to see ourselves astride the world, the masters of our nature."[4]

Physician and philosopher Jeffrey Bishop also finds in the Transhumanist vision a "will to power" producing a "power ontology, where power circulates in the stops and starts of evolutionary biology." The posthuman vision takes hold of this "natural circulation of power," this "coming into being," and harnesses "these creative evolutionary forces" as a means of "ordering . . . the chaotic forces." For Bishop, "This ordering force—this human will set to order the powers of creation—is transhumanism's theology." In this theology "the human will to power" is focused on "a new telos, the posthuman, the highest of beings, perhaps even Being itself in the singularity, pure mental power." In this new theology "the god of these transhumanist philosophers is the god that orders the creative power toward a new being, a new god, that is to say toward the posthuman." Bishop wonders whether "transhumanism is already wedded to a power theology, a subtle theology of the *Ubermensch*?"

Bishop contends that technology is not neutral, not simply a kind of tool. Rather, "in the contemporary epoch, technology has fundamentally shifted our metaphysical thinking." Technology is "a stance struck toward the world, a way of challenging the world to produce things for us." The Transhumanist power ontology renders things valuable only as they are "things that are useful." Thus, to borrow an example from our chapter on space, an asteroid is not a thing to be appreciated in itself, but a new territory to be mined for materials that will contribute to human advancement.

Science is never free of political influence for "there is always a political directionality toward which the scientific question is asked. . . ." Nor can science ever be cut free of rhetoric, for there is always a public and funding agencies that need convincing. For Bishop, Francis Bacon "demonstrates the instrumentality of both scientific process and justification." The association of power with science leads Bishop to suggest that "bad politics can come to affect good science, and bad science often accompanies bad politics." This is a rhetorical result, for "It is never the case that science and technology are already political." As part of his critique of Transhumanist ideology, Bishop invokes historical precedents for turning "medical science" into a means of "political power." Under the regime of a new biopolitics of enhancement, humans may be cast in the role of means to an end—the inevitable and omnibenevolent posthuman future.[5]

Sociologist Michael Hauskeller is also concerned with the power dynamics inherent in the Transhumanist *mythos*, particularly as he takes the enhancement narrative to be a species of utopian thinking.[6] "There is nothing very unusual about the utopian outlook that [Nick] Bostrom endorses so unabashedly," he writes. "On the contrary, it is rather common and apparently shared by many who see humanity's salvation in emerging and converging technologies and technological growth in general."[7] The technofuturist vision of utopia owes much to H. G. Wells, "who also distinguished the 'modern' utopia by its inherent commitment to constant progress."[8] Hauskeller argues that Transhumanism focuses its efforts on overcoming nature, "not only the nature that surrounds us, but also the nature that we are ourselves." Only from "this vision of complete control that pervades transhumanist writings" is the potential for "the *ultimate utopia*" realized. Signs of a longing for control show up "in the unconcealed desire for personal immortality and the acquisition of god-like qualities such as omnipotence, omniscience, and even omnibenevolence."[9] Thus, Hauskeller shares Kenneth Burke's concern about the totalitarian potential in an ideology of perfection.

For Hauskeller, understanding "what exactly the function of utopian ideas and images in transhumanist writings is" is the key to understanding the movement. Recognizing the close relationship between *mythos* and *logos*, he notes that utopian narratives "provide considerable motivation for the development and endorsement of enhancement technologies . . ." Just as Midgley affirms that myth supplies imaginative patterns that guide actions, it is "very likely that without a prominent display of such utopian fantasies, there would be far less willingness to fund research into, and development of, enhancement technologies. Those ideas thus function as a call to arms to prospective followers and investors."[10]

The "ideas and images" that characterize the Transhumanist narrative are not simply "motivational aids to get people to support the radical enhancement agenda, they also affect the very arguments that are proposed in favor of human self-transformation, and in particular in support of the claim that it is our moral duty to develop and use technologies to make the transformation happen."[11] This dual potential—to set an agenda and to infuse that agenda with moral urgency—accounts for much of the force of Transhumanist and enhancement mythology. Such utopian discourse seeks "a life not limited by things that we cannot control."

Something new has been added to the old equation, however:

> What has changed is that for the first time in history, mainly due to the rapid development of the biosciences and related technologies, it actually seems possible that we will very soon achieve all this:

that we will be free of sickness and disease, free of the necessity to die, know everything that there is to know, enjoy pleasures without restraint or remorse, and live in complete harmony with others and with ourselves.[12]

The "ideal order" of utopia feels as if it is within reach, which suggests that intimations of control informed by the "logic of perfectionism" may characterize the rhetoric of the future. [13] While myth's vision of perfection is "inseparable from the idea of totality," myth "has only ever been a gesture towards it." Myth "may posit a perfect beginning, or paradise, or it may posit a perfect ending, a Messianic kingdom," but it "always does so 'in the midst,' between the two."[14] When that kingdom seems at hand, the equation may change and epistemic humility be lost.

HUMAN NATURE

The late theologian Jean Bethke Elshtain also detects a control impulse in technofuturist ideology. She writes,

> The totalitarian impulse lies behind utopian visions—this impulse does not exhaust what utopian dreams are all about, but we dare not ignore that an impulse to achieve total control is a major part of the legacy of utopian dreams.[15]

Bethke Elshtain discerns a link between control in enhancement discourse and the question of whether human beings possess a fixed nature:

> [T]here are those who see human bodies as raw material to be ma-nipulated every which way. We do not really have a "nature," so there is no problem with this ethically. The only frustration is a practical one: how do we get as quickly as possible to full control over what sorts of entities we wish to be?[16]

Referring to the ancient gnostic *mythos* that elevated spirit and denigrat-ed the physical, Bethke Elshtain writes: "When I note some of the bizarre scenarios," advocated by enhancement proponents, "it puts me in mind of Gnosticism, an earlier flight from the messiness of human embodiment into the realm of pure spirit."[17] She specifically notes the cryopreservation op-tion of just having one's head frozen. With reference to one variation on the myth of technological immortality, Bethke Elshtain writes, "Evidently this form of what I will call 'Cartesian decapitation' is entirely fine for trans-humanist publicists, as future science will surely produce nonhuman bod-ies in the future." The body is expendable and replaceable—it is, as Bernal said in 1929, the brain that counts. Bethke Elshtain refers to this demotion of the body as "modern excarnation," calling it "a perfect monument to latent Gnosticism."[18]

Human nature stands at the center of the human enhancement debate. Proponents of enhancement reject the notion of a defining nature in human beings, and thus find no obstacle in the way of shaping new humans. They have adopted a narrative of the human in which our nature is always changing, a story in which nothing about human beings is fixed, constant, or sacrosanct. Enhancement critics, on the other hand, fear the loss of human nature—whether as a gift from God, evolution, or both—as we gradually change ourselves into posthumans, download ourselves into computers, or otherwise radically modify ourselves. The debate over human nature has taken on urgency due to new tools that facilitate the profound changes in genetic structure considered by some to carry the potential for altering human nature. Technology known as CRISPR/Cas9 is currently electrifying the biotech world due to the ease and accuracy it brings to genetic treatments.[19] Recent genetic interventions have moved beyond trait selection and therapy toward the alteration of heritable genetic traits, a development that has implications for the genetic code of the entire human race.

Harvard's Life Sciences Project founder Juan Enriquez anticipates genetic omnipotence. "Now we are beginning to be able to rewrite life, not just gene by gene, but entire genomes at a time." Enriquez explains:

> This is the difference between inserting a single word or paragraph into a Tolstoy novel (which is what biotechnology does) and writing the entire book from scratch (which is what synthetic biology does). It is far easier to fundamentally change the meaning and outcome of a novel, seed, animal or human organ if you write the entire thing.[20]

Such potential is already present in biotech labs. In late 2012 a research team headed up by Dr. Shoukrat Mitalipov at the Oregon Health and Science University announced that they had replaced disease-bearing genes in the mitochondrial DNA of a human egg cell. These alterations were "germ line" in nature, that is, capable of transmission from one generation to the next. Ethicist Marci Darnovsky commented, "That kind of genetic engineering has been ruled off-limits," adding, "it's a very bright line that has been observed by scientists around the world." With new genetic techniques, however, "we would be moving toward a world in which some people—and it would be people who could afford these procedures—would have either real or perceived genetic advantage." Despite the concerns, researchers say the real benefits of preventing genetic diseases outweigh hypothetical risks.[21] A similar research result was reported in China in 2015, raising similar ethical concerns.[22] Francis Fukuyama believes we can already feel "the stirrings of Promethean desires" is already evident "in how we prescribe drugs to alter the behavior and personalities of our children." He adds, "The environmental movement has taught us humility and respect for the integrity of nonhuman nature."

JUSTICE

Questions of human nature are intricately connected with research that might affect the structure of human DNA, and with it bring visions of a posthuman species. However, human nature in the radical human enhancement debate has also been tied to a concern for justice. Fukuyama also harbors deep concerns about efforts to alter fundamental *human* qualities. While it may be tempting "to dismiss transhumanists as some sort of odd cult, nothing more than science fiction taken too seriously," Fukuyama believes, however, that Transhumanism is a movement to be taken seriously. In particular, he is concerned for the impact of Transhumanist ideology and goals on structures of justice. Moreover, Fukuyama finds that "the seeming reasonableness of the project, particularly when considered in small increments, is part of its danger." He writes:

> Society is unlikely to fall suddenly under the spell of the transhumanist worldview. But it is very possible that we will nibble at biotechnology's tempting offerings without realizing that they come at a frightful moral cost.

These costs may be high: "The first victim of transhumanism might be equality." Historically, the question of who counts as a human being has been associated with serious human rights abuses:

> The U.S. Declaration of Independence says that "all men are created equal," and the most serious political fights in the history of the United States have been over who qualifies as fully human. Women and blacks did not make the cut in 1776 when Thomas Jefferson penned the declaration. Slowly and painfully, advanced societies have realized that simply being human entitles a person to political and legal equality. In effect, we have drawn a red line around the human being and said that it is sacrosanct.

The belief that all individuals possess a human essence, and that this essence dwarfs manifest differences among people—undergirds the very idea of human rights and political liberalism generally. "This essence, and the view that individuals therefore have inherent value, is at the heart of political liberalism. But modifying that essence is the core of the transhumanist project." Even the idea of "transforming ourselves into something superior" raises the question of "what rights will these enhanced creatures claim, and what rights will they possess when compared to those left behind? If some move ahead, can anyone afford not to follow?" This set of issues is particularly troubling when considering "the world's poorest countries—for whom biotechnology's marvels likely will be out of reach . . ."

At the heart of the problem is the Transhumanists' belief that "they understand what constitutes a good human being" and the corresponding potentiality that "they are happy to leave behind the limited, mortal, natural beings they see around them in favor of something better." Because "humans are miraculously complex products of a long evolutionary process," to tamper with the basic building blocks of humans is to tempt fate. Even to eliminate an apparent weakness is to affect the complementary strength. For instance, "if we never felt jealousy, we would also never feel love." Thus, "modifying any one of our key characteristics inevitably entails modifying a complex, interlinked package of traits, and we will never be able to anticipate the ultimate outcome."[23]

Another challenge that the enhancement vision poses is the potential for new elites to arise that will control both access to enhancement technologies and the mechanisms of regulation. Hava Tirosh-Samuelson raises this concern in writing, "technology is the means by which humans have expressed their will to power, and the rate of technological change is accelerating dramatically and extends the gaps between elites and those who have no access to technological advances."[24] Along similar lines, Bethke Elshtain has expressed concern over what she perceives as a disdain for women in the Transhumanist vision. A dream of escaping the body incorporates a rejection of the feminine, according to Bethke Elshtain. "A tiny minority, overwhelmingly male . . . wants to eliminate the body as we now recognize it altogether. We will, according to the posthumanist Princeton biologist Lee Silver, 'change the nature of our species.'"[25]

Elshtain finds in such visions a rejection of the familiar, the private, and what she calls "evocations of nature and transcendence." And, the proponents of such aversions are, for the most part, male:

> It is interesting that "women" always emerge as a bit of a problem in such visions; they are too defined by embodiment, too wedded to particular ties and attachments, especially to their own children, and so on. So it is not surprising that the contemporary advocates of excarnation should be demographically male (overwhelmingly so) and relatively privileged.[26]

The exclusivity of technofuturist narratives is evident in their inattentiveness to issues of class, race, and gender, oversights that may reflect the predominance of white, male and highly educated leaders.

ETHICS

The narratives of technological transcendence may appear as simple future projection; however, based on responses already explored in this chapter they are more than that. Implicit in these stories is an ethic of the future, an ethic of technological progress, and an ethic of the person. Mary Midgley has noted:

> The prophets of this scientistic movement expected from the thing they called "science" nothing less than a new and better ethic, a direct basis for morals, a distinctive set of secular values which would replace the earlier ones supplied by religion. They hoped that it would supersede and replace the corruption and confusion of traditional moral thinking.[27]

Futurist myths may subtly shift the focus of technological discourse from the *is* of description to the *ought* of moral prescription; mythographers offer the astonishing speed and complexity of technological progress as assurance of its inevitability, and inevitability as evidence of its moral trustworthiness. In the rhetoric of the future, the *rate* of technological change can be equated with the *rightness* of that change. Here is another reason to be careful in the selection of our myths, for as Midgley and Burke have noted, we may choose our myths but "we do not have a choice of understanding [the world we inhabit] without using any myths or visions at all."[28] *Mythos* provides narrative grounding for the propositional *logos* of doctrine and policy, but also for the didactic *logos* of ethics.

The urgency and force of the myths explored here pose the risk of apocalyptic distraction—the tendency to focus on the imminent end of the present order to the exclusion of present moral concerns. Thus, Lanier expresses reservation about discussing the Singularity myth in a totalizing, anticipatory future-tense that distracts attention from present problems. "The difference between sanity and fanaticism is found in how well the believer can avoid confusing consequential differences in timing." He explains:

> If you believe the Rapture is imminent, fixing the problems of this life might not be your greatest priority. You might even be eager to embrace wars and tolerate poverty and disease in order to bring about the conditions that could prod the Rapture into being. In the

same way, if you believe the Singularity is coming soon, you might cease to design technology to serve humans, and prepare instead for the grand events it will bring.[29]

Another ethical concern of the futurist discourse we have examined is its tendency toward reductive metaphors of the person. The machine and information metaphors lurk in the background, insisting that we are machines awaiting the perfection of merging with actual machines, or as information to be downloaded into a computer. With their intimations of hybridity and immortality, the machine and information metaphors challenge traditional conceptions of human nature, and ethics based on these conceptions. Asked about the tendency to compare humans with machines, Midgley suggests that the metaphor leads us to "think of *people* as machines," and thus to the conclusion that we "have only to engineer the machine a little bit differently and society will be greatly improved."[30] Such thinking props up strategies of utopian control and encourages the moral error of seeing human beings as imperfect means to perfect ends.

Also of ethical consideration are reductionist tendencies in describing the body. Enhancement mythology from Bernal to the present views the body as less important than the brain, or as a mortal prison to be escaped. Transhumanist myths venerate *leaving* the body and its contingent limitations. In the works of fiction writers such as Clarke and Stapledon, and in the vision of contemporary AI experts such as Goertzel and de Garis, a highly evolved posthumanity eventually jettisons the physical as a rudimentary relic of the biological past. Transformation as a species involves our translation into immortal electrons pulsing through silicon. This narrative reduction to electrons, information or intellect subtly undermines concern for bodies at all, and particularly for hungry bodies, tortured bodies, disabled bodies and diseased bodies.

Bethke Elshtain fears that myths of technological transcendence return us to a Gnostic perspective that understood the body as a prison and physical embodiment as a debased and rudimentary existence. The spiritual goal of the Gnostic was, therefore, escape from the physical realm. While the myths of technological transcendence envision a radically enhanced human race, the vision of enhancement rests on the assumption that *some* human qualities are worth refining while others can be ignored or even discarded. The ones most valued tend to be located in the brain.

Such a conception may reflect a dangerously incomplete understanding of a perfected human being and of a desirable human community. Phrases such as "the best and the brightest" can obscure the fact that "the worst and the dumbest" are also human, also bear instructive traits, and also live lives that deserve protection. We are again reminded of Kenneth Burke's warning about totalitarian visions of perfection. A society's capacity to recognize and protect its weakest members may be the true test of its moral stature. Given the choice between being unusually unattractive or unusually attractive, most people would choose the latter. Given the choice between being intelligent or dull, most would choose the former. This preponderance of preference on the "better than average" side of the ledger does not alter the fact that most of us are not extraordinarily beautiful or intelligent, and that even those of us who are naturally gifted do not possess those gifts for a lifetime. History is replete with warnings about the dangers of visions of human perfection; nevertheless, there is a growing literature arguing for genetic interventions and other technologies aimed at perfection.[31]

Jaron Lanier has written that the first failure of technofuturist thinking may be a "spiritual failure" that encourages "narrow philosophies that deny the mystery of the existence of experience." As a consequence, "we become vulnerable to redirecting the leap of faith we call 'hope' away from people and toward gadgets."[32] In the name of improvement, enhancement reduces the human to the observable, perhaps nothing more than the currently fashionable. Ideas about progress and improvement notwithstanding, how many of us would want to have been genetically shaped according to contemporary values or scientific insights circa 1860, or even 1960? And yet some advocates of a posthuman vision of the future assume that we are now somehow less limited by the assumptions of our time than were our ancestors. Will the conception of a perfect person circa 2060 suffice for all time? We don't know everything, we will always face weakness and our decision-making is fallible. Nevertheless, the discourse of technofuturism and the human enhancement movement suggest with unaccountable confidence that immortality, omniscience, and omnipotence may, and ought to be, manufactured technologically.

Religion

Myths of technological transcendence envision a future marked by immortality, machine gods, and posthumans, arriving on a wave of exponential technological growth. The parallels to, or parodies of, religion are inescapable in technofuturist texts. The nineteenth-century Cosmist Fedorov prophesied a technological resurrection of the entire human race, while German biologist Ernst Haeckel founded a religion on evolution and sun worship. Jesuit paleontologist Teilhard de Chardin experienced visions of an evolving Cosmic Christ in the 1920s, while his admirer and friend Julian S. Huxley preached a religion of evolution in the 1940s and 1950s.

More recently journalist Joel Garreau has suggested that religious rituals might be developed to assist with the emotional adjustment to enhancement procedures, filmmaker Jim Gilliam has asserted that online communities working toward a common goal become "the Creator," and physicist Michio Kaku has predicted that our descendants might appear to us as gods. Computer scientist Ben Goertzel is confident of the emergence of machine gods, while philosopher Nick Bostrom presents his simulation hypothesis as a contemporary creation myth with posthumans in the role of gods, while sociologist William Sims Bainbridge calls for a new religion that will make straight the path into space. Immortality and resurrection are imagined by a wide range of technofuturists from Max More of Alcor to Martine Rothblatt of Terasem. Religious categories such as miracle, resurrection, eternal life, and God are now contested territory, with old-style spiritual religionists pitted against new-style technological ones. It is no longer a question of science vs. religion, but of new scientific religions vs. old traditional ones.

A number of observers have suggested that we are currently witnessing the emergence of a powerful new technological religion. Some embrace the possibility while others detect in it serious dangers. As narratives that mingle an aggressive technological agenda with spiritual aspiration, technofuturist myths address the longing expressed by artificial intelligence specialist Hugo de Garis to "invent something" that would satisfy spiritual longing "*and* satisfy the criteria from your intellect, from your knowledge, from your science." For de Garis this dream of wedding spiritual longing to technological realities constitutes "a kind of scientifically-based belief system that energizes, that creates a vision, that excites." De Garis labels this hope, "the idea of god building."[33] Neuroscientist Sebastian Seung, a critic of Transhumanism, secures the point in writing, "The Bible said that God made man in his own image. The German philosopher Ludwig Feuerbach said that man made God in his own image. The transhumanists say that humanity will make itself into God."[34] Yet, the ethical details of this new technological religion are conspicuously absent from the discussion. De Garis, Seung, and many others raise the question: How should we think about the religious aspirations present in the Transhumanist vision?

Lanier has been a leading critic of the emerging techno-religion. He detects a risky religious fervor in the "constant stream of stories" suggesting that smart machines are "a new form of life, and that we should think of them as fellow creatures instead of as tools." Such narratives are "reshaping the basic assumptions of our lives in misguided and ultimately damaging ways." To true believers who think "that we can live forever as algorithms inside the global brain," Lanier replies:

Yes, this sounds like many different science fiction movies. Yes, it sounds nutty when stated so bluntly. But these are ideas with tremendous currency in Silicon Valley; these are guiding principles, not just amusements, for many of the most influential technologists.

This narrative is "bound up equally in faith, which suggests something remarkable: What we are seeing is a new religion, expressed through an engineering culture."

Lanier cautions that the religious rhetoric about technology needs to be toned down before the associated tensions overwhelm us:

> If technologists are creating their own ultramodern religion, and it is one in which people are told to wait politely as their very souls are made obsolete, we might expect further and worsening tensions. But if technology were presented without metaphysical baggage, is it possible that modernity would not make people as uncomfortable?

Lanier is a skeptic of the new religious vision. Scientists, he writes, "serve people best when we keep our religious ideas out of our work."[35]

Despite such concerns, some technofuturist movements are beginning to identify themselves as religions. Narrative *mythos* is spawning doctrinal *logos*. Sandberg notes that "deliberately constructed transhumanist religious systems also exist. For example, the Terasem movement claims to be a 'transreligion': 'a movement which can be combined with any existing religion, without having to leave a previous religion.'"[36] Transhumanist author Giulio Prisco has also advanced a technofuturist faith he terms Cosmism, promoting the system as "an emerging 'religion 2.0' that is part of a radical futurist conception of the future development of humanity." Cosmism will provide the "positive optimism" needed "to overcome our current problems and embark on our cosmic journey." The "future magic" of Cosmist religion reaches "beyond our current understanding and imagination." The ideas constituting this futurist faith "were first developed in the late 19th century by Russian Cosmism." Konstantin Tsiolkovsky and Nikolai Fedorov "considered science as a tool given to us by God to enable us to resurrect the dead and, as promised, enjoy immortal life."

Prisco anticipates "that God-like beings will exist in the future, and they may be able to affect their past—our present—by means of space-time engineering." Moreover, it is likely that "civilizations out there have already attained God-like powers." Future technologies, which Prisco refers to as future magic, "will permit achieving, by scientific means, most of the promises of religions—and many amazing things that no human religion ever dreamed of."[37] He sometimes refers to his project as the Turing Church—in honor of mathematician Alan Turing (1912–1954) and philosopher Alonzo Church (1903–1995). Prisco sees his initial efforts as "a proposal for a religion 2.0 based on mind uploading, synthetic realities and technological resurrection." The Turing Church is "a closed working group at the intersection of science and religion."

At the center of this techno-religion is the Turing-Church conjecture in keeping with the myth of the informational person: the human mind is a computational machine that may be transferred to any other computational machine such as a computer, resulting in immortality for a personality. The Turing-Church "will be a meta-religion: a community without a central doctrine, and a loose framework of ideas, concepts, hopes, feelings and sensibilities at the intersection of science and religion, compatible with many existing and new frameworks." The new religion will provide followers "meaning and sense of wonder, and hope in personal immortality and resurrection, based on science."[38]

There are certainly external challenges, internal accommodations and inter-group controversies in the offing as Transhumanist and enhancement religions take shape, and as their supporting narratives become more familiar to the general public. In addition to organizations such as Terasem Faith and the Turing-Church there is already a Christian Transhumanist Association, while the Mormon Transhumanist Association is the largest Transhumanist chapter in the world.[39] There can be no doubt that we are entering a period in which visions of technological transcendence will vie for loyalty with sacred myths associated with traditional religions, stories that have provided a moral structure and a sense of hope for the billions of people.

Critics detect risks inherent in theologies based on technological inevitability; among these risks is the very tendency to close off critical assessment of the vision itself. Jeffrey Bishop, a physician and philosopher, has written that to question technological religion "is to question our liberty to become what we will" as well as "all the good that has been produced from the Enlightenment, liberalism, and indeed humanism." When we turn radical enhancement ideology into a totalizing theology, then "to question the posthuman future is to question the posthuman god, a contemporary sacrilege."[40]

Technological advancement is a fact of modern existence, one inextricably bound to financial systems, scientific enterprises, medical practices, educational curricula, social structures, and even the forms of government under which we will live. Technological progress is also connected to deep moral questions including what it means to be human, the value of the human and the limits of technological intervention in our own structure.

The environments in which we work, our educational settings and aspirations, the medical treatments to which we submit, the homes in which we live, the relationships we value most, and our systems of defense and of justice—all will be dramatically transformed by rapidly arriving technologies. Moreover, each new transformative technological breakthrough will need to be founded on reliable and tested narratives in order to withstand the moral strain of visions of an imminent technological utopia. Comprehensive and urgent theorizing about an idealized future "soon presents its own eschatology and its own revelations about what is really going on—portentous events that no one but the initiated can appreciate."[41] The present calls for caution as we look back to excesses that scarred the past, and ahead to potent forces that will shape us and with which we are not yet familiar. Tested myths that have already guided and shaped the communities we inhabit ought not to be traded in for new myths without careful consideration by a broad cross-section of citizens. The technological future is unavoidable; what may be avoided are damaging excesses resulting from an inviolable mythic vision of our technologically transformed selves. As Midgley and Burke would remind us, while we may choose our myths, "we do not have a choice of understanding [the world we inhabit] without using any myths or visions at all."[42]

NOTES

CHAPTER 1

1. 2045 Initiative, "About Us," 2045: Strategic Social Initiative, last modified July 17, 2012, http://2045.com/dialogue/29819.html.

2. The Mission Statement reads as follows: "Humanity+ is an international nonprofit membership organization which advocates the ethical use of technology to expand human capacities. In other words, we want people to be better than well." Humanity+ adds in a philosophy statement that, "Transhumanism is a loosely defined movement that has developed gradually over the past two decades." The webpage cites an early theorist, Max More, to the effect that: "Transhumanism is a class of philosophies of life that seek the continuation and acceleration of the evolution of intelligent life beyond its currently human form and human limitations by means of science and technology, guided by life-promoting principles and values." (1990) Humanity+, "Mission," Humanity+, accessed June 22, 2015, http://humanityplus.org/about/mission; Humanity+, "Philosophy," Humanity+, accessed June 22, 2015, http://humanityplus.org/philosophy.

3. Conversation with the author, Cambridge MA, June 12, 2010.

4. James Hughes, *Citizen Cyborg: Why Democratic Societies Must Respond to the Redesigned Human of the Future* (Cambridge, MA: Westview Press, 2004), 176.

5. FM-2030, *Are You a Transhuman? Monitoring and Stimulating Your Personal Rate of Growth in a Rapidly Changing World* (New York: Warner Books: 1989).

6. Nick Bostrom, "Transhumanist Values." World Transhumanist Association, accessed May 29, 2012, http://www.transhumanism.org/index.php/WTA/more/transhumanist-values/.

7. Anders Sandberg, "Transhumanism and the Meaning of Life," in *Religion and Transhumanism*: *The Unknown Future of Human Enhancement Religion*, ed. Calvin Mercer and Tracy J. Trothen (Santa Barbara CA: Praeger, 2015), 3.

8. See, for example, Jürgen Habermas, *The Future of Human Nature* (Cambridge, UK: Polity Press, 2004); Allen E. Buchanan, *Beyond Humanity? The Ethics of Biomedical Enhancement* (Oxford: Oxford University Press, 2011); *Human Enhancement*, ed. Julian Savulescu and Nick Bostrom (Oxford: Oxford University Press, 2011); Michael Sandel, *The Case Against Perfection: Ethics in the Age of Genetic Engineering* (Cambridge MA: Harvard University Press, 2009); Nicholas Agar, *Humanity's End: Why We Should Reject Radical Enhancement* (Cambridge, MA: MIT Press, 2010); Michael Hauskeller, "Reinventing Cockaigne: Utopian Themes in Transhumanist Thought," *The Hastings Center Report* (42:2), April 2012, pp. 39–47.

9. Lincoln Cannon, "Trust in Posthumanity and the New God Argument" (speech presented at the *Transhumanism and Spirituality Conference*, Salt Lake City, October 1, 2010), transcript on *Lincoln Cannon* (blog), accessed May 23, 2012, http://lincoln.metacannon.net/2010/10/transcript-of-presentation-at.html.

10.Hava Tirosh-Samuelson, "Engaging Transhumanism," in *Transhumanism and Its Critics*, ed. Gregory R. Hansell and William Grassie (Philadelphia PA: Metanexus Institute, 2011), 19–20.

11. Hugo de Garis, "Globa: Accelerating Technologies Will Create a Global State by 2050," *Kurzweil Accelerating Intelligence*, (January 19, 2011) http://www.kurzweilai.net/globa-global-state-by-2050.

12. Nick Bostrom, "Human Genetic Enhancements: A Transhumanist Perspective," *The Journal of Value Inquiry* 37 (2003): 493–506.

13. The 2010 Humanity+ Summit convened at Harvard University was subtitled, *Rise of the Citizen Scientist* (June 12–13, 2010).

14. Thiel Fellowship, accessed May 31, 2012,http://www.thielfoundation.org/index.php?option=com_content&view=article&id=15&Itemid=19.

15. See the organization's webpage: www.singularityu.org, accessed-January 24, 2017.

16. For a good overview of the basic principles, procedures and language of regenerative medicine, see: Tristan Keys, Nancy M. P. King and Anthony Atala, "Faith in Science: Professional and Public Discourse on Regenerative Medicine," in *After the Genome: A Language for our Biotechnology Future,*

ed. Michael J. Hyde and James A. Herrick (Waco, TX: Baylor University Press, 2013).

17. David Plotz, "Total Recall: The Future of Memory," *Slate*, March 11, 2003, http://www.slate.com/articles/health_and_science/super-man/2003/03/total_recall.single.html. See also: Lewis D. Solomon, *The Quest for Human Longevity: Science, Business, and Public Policy* (New Brunswick, NJ: Transaction Press, 2006).

18. E. S. Boyden, "In Pursuit of Human Augmentation," *Ed Boyden's Blog, MIT Technology Review*, September 17, 2007, http://www technologyreview.com/blog/boyden/21839/.

CHAPTER 2

1. The fact that theories of myth arise from so many different academic disciplines supports Robert A. Segal's contention that, "Strictly, theories of myth are theories of some much larger domain, with myth a mere subset. . . . There are no theories of myth itself, for there is no discipline of myth in itself. . . . There is no study of myth as myth." *Myth: A Very Short Introduction* (Oxford, UK: Oxford University Press, 2004), 2.

2. Joseph Campbell, *The Hero With a Thousand Faces* (New York: MJF Books, 1949), 3.

3. Laurence Coupe, *Myth* (New York: Routledge, 1997), 74.

4. Jonathan Gottschall, *The Storytelling Animal: How Stories Make us Human* (New York: Houghton Mifflin, 2012), 102.

5. Gottschall, 119.

6. Gottschall, 55.

7. Gottschall, 120.

8. Gottschall, 121–22.

9. Brent Waters, "Flesh Made Data: The Posthuman Project in Light of the Incarnation," in *Religion and Transhumanism: The Unknown Future of Human Enhancement*, ed. Calvin Mercer and Tracy J. Trothen (Santa Barbara CA: Praeger, 2015), 294.

10. Don Cupitt, *The World to Come* (London UK: SCM Press 1982), 29. Quoted in Coupe, 5.

11. Marina Warner, *Six Myths of Our Time* (New York: Random House, 1995), xx.

12. Warner, xx.

13. Paul Ricoeur, *A Ricoeur Reader: Reflection and Imagination*, ed. M. J. Valdes (New York: Harvester/Wheatsheaf, 1991), 485.

14. Coupe, *Myth*, 9.

15. Ricoeur, *Reader*, 486.

16. Claude Mangion, "Nietzsche's Philosophy of Myth," *Humanitas* 2 (2003): 1–11, p 3.

17. Cupitt, 29.

18. Waters, 294.

19. Karen Armstrong, *A Short History of Myth* (New York: Canongate Books, 2005), 6.

20. Armstrong, 2.

21. Mircea Eliade, "Cosmogonic Myth and 'Sacred History,'" in *Sacred Narrative: Readings in the Theory of Myth*, ed. Alan Dundes (Berkeley, CA: University of California Press, 1984), 138.

22. Eric Dardel, "The Mythic," *Sacred Narrative: Readings in the Theory of Myth*, ed. Alan Dundes(Berkeley, CA: University of California Press, 1984), 230.

23. Dardel, 226.

24. Warner, 19.

25. On the question of myth's relationship to science and modern de-mythologizing efforts, see: Segal, especially chapters 1 and 2. "Myth is a victim of the process of secularization that constitutes modernity." (13)

26. See: *The New Science of Giambattista Vico*, trans. Thomas Goddard Bergin and Max Harold Fisch (Ithaca: Cornell University Press, 1984).

27. Joseph Mali, *The Rehabilitation of Myth: Vico's* New Science (Cambridge, UK: Cambridge University Press, 1992), 7.

28. Mangion, 1. Mangion adds, "The negative evaluation of myth by modernity correlated by Nietzsche to modernity's over-valorization of reason." (ibid., 2)

29. Coupe, 119.

30. Mali, 3.

31. Mali, 150. Benjamin Bennett writes that in *The Birth of Tragedy*, Nietzsche asserts that myth is "unconscious metaphysics." "Nietzsche's Idea of Myth: The Birth of Tragedy from the Spirit of Eighteenth-Century Aesthetics," *Proceedings of the Modern Language Association* 91, no.3 (May, 1979): 420–422, p. 421.

32. Mali, 9.

33. Mali, 13. Nietzsche also considered myth to reflect the poetic nature of ancient thought. Claude Mangion writes of Nietzsche's interest in ancient myth, "Mythical communication touches the inner life of humanity because of its poetic genius" (Mangion3).

34. Donald Phillip Verene, *Vico's* New Science: *A Philosophical Commentary* (Ithaca: Cornell University Press, 2015), 77.

35. Verene 83.

36. Claude Levi-Strauss, "The Structural Study of Myth," *The Journal of American Folklore* 68, no. 270 (1955): 429.

37. Levi-Strauss, 430.

38. Levi-Strauss, 430.

39. Levi-Strauss, 430.

40. Claude Levi-Strauss, *Myth and Meaning* (1978; rpt. Oxford, UK: Routledge), 1.

41. Levi-Strauss, "Study," 431.

42. Levi-Strauss, Ibid., 431.

43. Northrop Frye, *Anatomy of Criticism: Four Essays* (Princeton, NJ: Princeton University Press, 1957), 116.

44. Frye, 42.

45. Mary Midgley, *Science as Salvation: A Modern Myth and Its Meaning* (New York: Routledge, 1992), 13.

46. Frye, 118.

47. Frye, 119.

48. Frye, 119–120.

49. Frye, 120.

50. Frye, 127.

51. Frye, 145.

52. Armstrong, 4.

53. Frye, 203.

54. Frye, 208.

55. Paul Ricoeur, *The Symbolism of Evil*, trans. Emerson Buchanan, (Boston MA: Beacon Press, 1967), 5.

56. Ricoeur, *Reader*, 490.

57. Mary Midgley, *The Myths We Live By* (New York: Routledge, 2011), ix.

58. Midgley, Ibid., xii-xiii.

59. See, for example, Midgley, *Myths*, Ch.3: Progress, Science and Modernity.

60. Midgley, *Myths*, xii. Segal notes Karl Popper's related idea: "Popper even maintains that scientific theories *remain* myth-like, for theories, like myths, can never be proved, only disproved, and therefore 'remain essentially uncertain or hypothetical" (34).

61. Midgley, xii.

62. Warner, 7.

63. Midgley, *Myths*, 5.

64. Midgley, *Ibid.*, 5.

65. Midgley, *Science*, 57.

66. Midgley, Ibid., 13.

67. Ricoeur, *Symbolism*, 348.

68. Coupe, 7.

69. Kenneth Burke, "Revolutionary Symbolism in America," unpublished paper, 1935. Reprinted in *The Legacy of Kenneth Burke*, ed. Herbert Simons and Trevor Melia (Madison WI: University of Wisconsin Press, 1989) 267–268. See also: Kenneth Burke, "Myth and Ideology," *Accent: A Quarterly of New Literature*, 7 (Summer, 1947): 195–205.

70. Coupe, 88. Coupe quotes Kenneth Burke, *Language as Symbolic Action: Essays on Life, Literature and Method* (Berkeley, CA: University of California Press, 1966), 16.

71. Coupe, 170.

72. Coupe, 73.

73. Coupe, 98, 99.

74. Ricoeur, *Reader*, 484.

75. Coupe, 195. Coupe quotes Gianni Vattimo, *The Transparent Society* (Cambridge, UK: Polity Press, 1992), 40.

76. See: Kenneth Burke, *The Philosophy of Literary Form* 3rd ed. (Berkeley, CA: University of California Press, 1973), pp. 3–4.

77. Gottschall, 102.

78. Gottschall, 55.

79. Warner, 19.

80. Mali, 3.

81. Warner, 19.

82. Warner, 28.

83. Verene, 83.

84. Frye, 118.

85. Burke, "Symbolism," 267–268.

86. Ricoeur, *Reader*, 490.

87. Mangion, 9. Mangion adds, "This is why it is not important to judge myths on logical grounds: the question is not whether they are true or false, but whether they can reveal different modes of existence."

88. Frye, 119.

89. Frye, 119–120.

90. Coupe, 8–9.

91. Frye, 203.

92. Frye, 208.

93. Midgley, *Myths*, ix.

94. Midgley, Ibid., 5; *Science*, 57.

95. Midgley, *Science*, 13.

96. The phrase "myths are linguistic constructs" comes from Mangion, 10.

CHAPTER 3

1. Joel Garreau, *Radical Evolution: The Promise and Peril of Enhancing Our Minds, Our Bodies—and What It Means to Be Human* (New York: Doubleday, 2005), 264.

2. Garreau, 265.

3. Garreau, 265.

4. George Young, *The Russian Cosmists: The Esoteric Futurism of Nikolai Fedorov and His Followers* (Oxford, UK: Oxford University Press, 2012), 14.

5. Quoted in: Valerii A. Kuvakin, *A History of Russian Philosophy: From the Tenth through the Twentieth Centuries* v. 1 (New York: Prometheus Books, 1994), 114.

6. The work, *The Philosophy of the Common Task* (*Filosofia Obshago Dela*), advances Fedorov's elaborate and exotic theories. Following his request, his associates did not publish the book until 1906, three years after his death, and distributed it without cost. Fedorov also requested that the work be published anonymously, a request his friends did not honor.

7. Stephen Lukashevich, *N. F. Fedorov (1828-1903): A Study in Russian Eupsychian and Utopian Thought* (Cranbury, NJ: Associated University Presses, 1977), 13.

8. Michael Hagemeister, "Russian Cosmism in the 1920s and Today," in *The Occult in Russian and Soviet Culture*, ed. Bernice Glatzer Rosenthal (Ithaca: Cornell University Press, 1997),185. See also, Young.

9. Hagemeister, 186.

10. Hagemeister, 185. For a contemporary rendition of the same concern see: Julian Savulescu, "Genetically Enhance Humanity or Face Extinction," *Festival of Dangerous Ideas*, Sydney, Australia (2009) http://www.themonthly.com.au/genetically-enhance-humanity-or-face-extinction-julian-savulescu-2065

11. Hagemeister, 186.

12. Lukashevich, 43.

13. Lukashevich, 195.

14. George M. Young, Jr., "Federov's Transformations of the Occult," in Rosenthal, ed., 172.

15. Young, "Federov's Transformation," 175.

16. Hagemeister, 185-186.

17. Hagemeister, 187.

18. Young suggests that Teilhard and his colleague Edouard le Roy heard Vernadsky's lectures at the Sorbonne in which he set out the theory that became the basis of the noosphere. They supplied the term. Young, *Cosmists*, 156.

19. Bernice Glatzer Rosenthal, "Introduction," *The Occult in Russian and Soviet Culture*, ed. Bernice Glatzer Rosenthal (Ithaca: Cornell University Press, 1997), 27. Hans Jonas's, *The Gnostic Religion: The Message of the Alien God and the Origins of Christianity* (Boston, MA: Beacon Press, 1958) remains a good introduction to the topic.

20. Lukashevich, 15.

21. Hagemeister, 188.

22. Ben Goertzel, *A Cosmist Manifesto* blog, http://cosmistmanifesto. blogspot.com/ (January 21, 2011).

23. On Teilhard, see: Robert Speaight, *Teilhard de Chardin: A Biography* (New York, Collins and World, 1968; Ursula King, *Spirit of Fire: The Life and Vision of Teilhard de Chardin* (Maryknoll: Orbis Books, 1998); Kathleen Duffy, *Teilhard's Mysticism: Seeing the Inner Face of Evolution* (Maryknoll: Orbis Books, 2014).

24. Frye, 119.

25. Frye, 145.

26. Teilhard de Chardin, *The Phenomenon of Man*, trans. Bernard Wall (New York: Harper and Brothers: 1959), 270.

27. Teilhard *Phenomenon*, 252.

28. Teilhard de Chardin, *The Future of Man*, trans. Norman Denny (New York: Harper and Row, 1964), 190–191. See also, Teilhard de Chardin *The Divine Milieu* (New York: Harper Perennial Classics, 2001).

29. Teilhard, *Future*, 161–62.

30. Teilhard, *Phenomenon*, 282.

31. See: Tim Radford, "Arthur C. Clarke's *Profiles of the Future*—A Review," *The Guardian* (March 4, 2011). http://www.theguardian.com/science/2011/mar/04/profiles-future-arthur-clarke-review.

32. Arthur C. Clarke, *Profiles of the Future: An Inquiry into the Limits of the Possible* (New York: Harper & Row, 1962). The book was revised and updated in 1983 and again in 1999.

33. Clarke, 208.

34. Clarke, 209.

35. Clarke, 209.

36. Clarke, 210.

37. Arthur C. Clarke, *The City and the Stars* (1956, rpt. London UK: Orion Publishing, 2001), 21.

38. Clarke, *Profiles*, 213.

39. Clarke, Ibid., 222.

40. Clarke, Ibid., 223.

41. Clarke, Ibid., 226.

42. Frye, 145.

43. Clarke, *Profiles*, 227.

44. Clarke, ibid. 227, 228.

45. Clarke, ibid. 229–230.

46. Nikolai Fedorov, *The Common Task*, v. 2: 239. Quoted in Lukashevich, 49.

47. Lukashevich, 15.

48. Teilhard, *Phenomenon*, 250.

CHAPTER 4

1. Hugo de Garis, "GLOBA: Accelerating Technologies will Create a Global State by 2050" (January 19, 2011).
http://www.kurzweilai.net/globa-accelerating-technologies-will-create-a-global-state-by-2050. (August 17, 2015).

2. On conceptions of progress, see: Ronald Wright, *A Short History of Progress* (Boston MA: De Capo Press, 2005); Daniel Sarewitz, "The Idea of Progress," in *A Companion to the Philosophy of Technology*, ed. Jan-Kyrre Berg Olsen (Oxford, UK: Wiley-Blackwell, 2009).

3. Russell, *Has Man a Future?* (New York: Simon and Schuster, 1961).

4. Freeman Dyson, *Imagined Worlds* (Oxford: Oxford University Press, 1997), 123.

5. Kevin Kelly provides an extended treatment of the progress myth in *What Technology Wants* (New York: Penguin, 2011), Ch. 5, "Deep Progress." See also, Michael S. Burdett, "The Religion of Technology: Transhumanism and the Myth of Progress," in *Religion and Transhumanism: The Unknown Future of Human Enhancement,* ed. Calvin Trencher and Tracy J. Trothen (Santa Barbara CA: Praeger, 2015), 131-148.

6. Max More, *The Principles of Extropy*, Version 3.11, 2003, accessed June 6, 2012. http://www.extropy.org/principles.htm.

7. Oliver Bennett, *Cultural Pessimism: Narratives of Decline in the Postmodern World* (Edinburgh UK: Edinburgh University Press, 2001).

8. Burdett, 144.

9. Joel Garreau, "Environmentalism as Religion," *The New Atlantis* (28, Summer 2010), 61–74. Some writers argue for an even earlier origin of ideas about progress. See: Ludwig Edelstein, *The Idea of Progress in Classical Antiquity* (Baltimore MD: Johns Hopkins University Press, 1967).

10. Coupe, 98.

11. Mary Pickering, *August Comte: An Intellectual Biography* 3 vols. (Cambridge, UK: Cambridge University Press, 2006–2009).

12. Edward S. Reed, *From Soul to Mind: The Emergence of Psychology from Erasmus Darwin to William James* (New Haven, CT: Yale University Press, 1997), 158.

13. C. Maurice Davies, *Heterodox London: Phases of Free Thought in the Metropolis* (1874; New York: A. M. Kelley, 1969), 2: 254.

14. J. B. S. Haldane, *Possible Worlds* (London: Chatto and Windus, 1937), 263.

15. Haldane, 301.

16. Ricouer, *Reader*, 490.

17. Haldane, 304.

18. John C. Green, "The Interaction of Science and Worldview in Sir Julian Huxley's Evolutionary Biology," *Journal of the History of Ideas* 23 (1990): 51. Quoted in Paul Philips, "One World, One Faith: The Quest for Unity in Julian Huxley's Religion of Evolutionary Humanism," *Journal of the History of Ideas* 68, no. 4 (October 2007): 618.

19. George Bernard Shaw, "The New Theology," *The Christian Commonwealth* (May, 1907). http://en.wikisource.org/wiki/The_New_Theology_%28Shaw%29 (March 15, 2014).

20. Teilhard, *Future*, 137–39.

21. On the fair, see: James Mauro, *Twilight at the World of Tomorrow* (New York: Ballantine Books, 2010).

22. Peter Diamandis, Steven Kotler, *Abundance: The Future is Better than You Think* (New York: Free Press, 2012), 304.

23. For a critique of the precautionary principle by a technofuturist writer, see: Ronald Bailey, "Precautionary Tale," *Reason* (April 1999). Bailey writes of the principle as applied by environmentalists. He paraphrases environmentalist Jeff Howard—the precautionary principle "calls for precaution in the face of any actions that may affect people or the environment, no matter what science is able—or unable—to say about that action." http://reason.com/archives/1999/04/01/precautionary-tale. For a statement on finding appropriate limits to technological development, see: Bill McKibben, *Enough: Staying Human in an Engineered Age* (New York: St. Martins, 2004).

24. See Ray Kurzweil's critique of the precautionary principle in *The Singularity Is Near: When Humans Transcend Biology* (New York: Viking 2005), 403. Kurzweil calls for a new and opposite principle to obtain—the proactionary principle—following the lead of Max More.

25. Quoted in: Lee M. Silver, "Reprogenetics: How Reproductive and Genetic Technologies Will be Combined to Provide new Opportunities for People to Reach their Reproductive Goals," in *Engineering the Human Germline*, ed. Gregory Stock and John Campbell (New York: Oxford University Press, 2000), 59.

26. Nicholas Agar, *Liberal Eugenics: In Defense of Human Enhancement* (Hoboken NJ: Wiley-Blackwell, 2004), 175. Agar advances a more skeptical view in: *Humanity's End: Why We Should Reject Radical Enhancement (Life and Mind: Philosophical Issues in Biology and Psychology* (Cambridge MA: Bradford, 2013).

27. Kevin Kelly, *What Technology Wants* (New York: Penguin, 2011). While Kevin Kelly is a technofuturist writer, he is not associated with the human enhancement or Transhumanist movements.

28. Kelly, 9.

29. Kelly, 10.

30. Kelly, 12.

31. Kelly, 15.

32. Kelly, 17.

33. Kelly, 45.

34. Kelly, 67.

35. Kelly, 41.

36. Kelly, 60.

37. Kelly, 66.

38. Kelly, 69.

39. Kelly, 89.

40. Kelly, 98.

41. Kelly, 97.

42. Kelly, 103.

43. Mali, 150

44. Kelly, 110.

45. Kelly, 118.

46. Kelly, 118.

47. Gianni Vattimo, *The Transparent Society* (Baltimore, MD: Johns Hopkins University Press, 1992), 40.

48. Kelly, 351.

49. Kelly, 352.

50. Kelly, 359.

51. Kelly, 357.

52. Kelly, 358.

53. Kelly, 358.

54. Kelly, 354.

55. T. S. Eliot, "Ulysses, Order, and Myth," in *Selected Prose*, ed. F. Kermode (London: Faber and Faber, 1975), 177–8. Originally published in *The Dial*, 1923.

56. Movies include: *Transcendent Man,* directed by Barry Ptolemy (2009); *The Singularity Is Near,* directed by R. Kurzweil, A. Waller, and T. Hoo (2010).

57. Jaron Lanier, *You Are Not a Gadget: A Manifesto* (New York: Knopf, 2010), 25.

58. Mali, 150

59. Kurzweil, 7.

60. Kurzweil, 5.

61. Waters, 294.

62. Kurzweil, 24.

63. Frye, 208.

64. Kurzweil, 35.

65. Kurzweil, 361–2. Kurzweil is quoting his, *The Age of Spiritual Machines: When Computers Exceed Human Intelligence* (New York: Penguin Books, 2000).

66. Kurzweil, 364.

67. Ricoeur: *Reader* 490.

68. Frye, 119.

69. Frye, 119–20.

70. I. J. Good, "Speculations Concerning the First Ultraintelligent Machine" in *Advances in Computers,* ed. F. Alt and M. Rubinoff (6: 1965), 31–88 (New York: Academic Press). http://www.acceleratingfuture.com/pages/ultraintelligentmachine.html (May 29, 2012).

71. Lanier, 24.

72. Lev Grossman, "Singularity," *Time,* February 21, 2011, 45.

73. Lanier, 27.

74. Lanier, 25.

75. Gottschall, 102.

76. Mali, 150.

77. Coupe, 110.

78. Michael Hauskeller, "Reinventing Cockaigne: Utopian Themes in Transhumanist Thought," *Hastings Center Report* 42, no. 2 (March-April 2012): 44.

Chapter 5

1. Marvin Minsky, "Will Robots Inherit the Earth? *Scientific American,* October 1994. http://www.scientificamerican.com/article/will-robots-inherit-the-earth/.

2. Frye, 119–20.

3. Edward S. Reed, *From Soul to Mind: The Emergence of Psychology from Erasmus Darwin to William James* (New Haven, CT: Yale University Press, 1997), 14.

4. Midgley, *Myths*, xii.

5. Quoted in *Classics of Free Thought*, ed. Paul Blanchard (Buffalo: Prometheus Books, 1978), 46–47.

6. T. H. Huxley, "Evolution and Ethics," Romanes Lectures 1893, in *Collected Essays IX: Evolution and Ethics and other Essays* (London: 1893). http://aleph0.clarku.edu/huxley/CE9/E-E.html#cite20.

7. Coupe, 88. Coupe quotes Kenneth Burke, *Language as Symbolic Action: Essays on Life, Literature and Method* (Berkeley CA: University of California Press, 1966), 16. See also: Laurence Coupe, *Kenneth Burke on Myth* (London: Routledge, 2004).

8. Sam Moskowitz, *Explorers of the Infinite: Shapers of Science Fiction* (Westport, CT: Hyperion Press, 1963).

9. Olaf Stapledon, "The Splendid Race," in *An Olaf Stapledon Reader* (Syracuse New York: Syracuse University Press, 1997).

10. Stapledon, 145.

11. Stapledon, 147.

12. Stapledon, *Last and First Men* (1930, rpt. Los Angeles, CA: Jeremy Tarcher, 1988), xiv.

13. Moskowitz, 273.

14. Moskowitz, 274.

15. For a review of the debate over Darwin's views on biological progress, see Robert Richard's response to Richard Lewontin's, *The Wars over Evolution* in *The New York Review of Books* (October 20, 2005), http://www.nybooks.com/articles/archives/2005/dec/15/darwin-progress/?pagination=false. Richards contends that Darwin himself eventually came to embrace the view that evolution was progressive.

16. Sander Gliboff, H. G. Bronn, *Ernst Haeckel, and the Origins of German Darwinism: A Study in Translation and Transformation* (Cambridge, MA: MIT Press, 2008). For a cinematic treatment of Haeckel, see: David Lebrun, *Proteus*, documentary film (Los Angeles CA: Night Fire Films, 2004).

17. Ernst Haeckel, *The Riddle of the Universe at the Close of the Nineteenth Century*, trans. Joseph McCabe (New York: Harper and Brothers, 1900), 80.

18. Mario A. Di Gregorio, *From Here to Eternity: Ernst Haeckel and Scientific Faith* (Amsterdam: Vandenhoeck and Ruprecht, 2005). Haeckel's, *The Riddle of the Universe*, sold an astonishing 100,000 copies in one month following its publication in 1899.

19. Haeckel, 337. *The Riddle of the Universe* sold an astonishing 100,000 copies in the month following its publication in 1899.

20. Julian Huxley, *New Bottles for New Wine* (New York: Harper, 1957), 17.

21. Julian S. Huxley, *Evolution: The Modern Synthesis* (1942, rpt. London: Allan and Unwin, 1942), 573–574.

22. Coupe, 8.

23. Coupe, 8–9.

24. Kenneth Burke, "Myth and Ideology," *Accent: A Quarterly of New Literature*, 7 (Summer 1947), 195.

25. Huxley, *Evolution*, 575.

26. Julian S. Huxley, "The Evolutionary Vision," in *Evolution After Darwin: Issues in Evolution* v.2 (Chicago IL: University of Chicago Press 1960), pp.249-251, 251.

27. Huxley, "Vision," 251.

28. Huxley, "Vision," 251.

29. Paul Philips, "One World, One Faith: The Quest for Unity in Julian Huxley's Religion of Evolutionary Humanism," *Journal of the History of Ideas* 68, no. 4 (October 2007): 620.

30. Huxley, "Vision," 252.

31. Philips, 618. Philips adds that Huxley had learned that "the method of presentation was the key to the success of the message itself" (619). Huxley's capacities as a mythographer were honed through his association with H.G. Wells.

32. Huxley, "Vision," 249.

33. Huxley, Ibid., 259.

34. Huxley, Ibid., 251.

35. Huxley, Ibid., 252.

36. Huxley, Ibid., 253.

37. Huxley, Ibid., 258.

38. Huxley, Ibid., 260.

39. Huxley, Ibid., 260.

40. Hans Moravec, *Mind Children: The Future of Robot and Human Intelligence* (Cambridge, MA: Harvard University Press, 1990), 158.

41. Moravec, 158.

42. Hans Moravec, *Robot: Mere Machine to Transcendent Mind* (New York: Oxford University Press, 2000).

43. Moravec, *Robot*, 77–78.

44. Warner, 28.

45. Moravec, *Robot*, 168.

46. John Harris, *Enhancing Evolution: The Ethical Case for Making Better People* (Princeton, NJ: Princeton University Press, 2009), 11. See Also:

Simon Young, *Designer Evolution: A Transhumanist Manifesto* (Amherst: Prometheus Books, 2006).

47. Harris, 11.

48. Harris, 25.

49. Harris, 16.

50. Harris, 34.

51. Ray Kurzweil, *How to Create a Mind: The Secret of Human Thought Revealed* (New York: Viking, 2012), 2.

52. Kurzweil, *Singularity*, 390.

53. Kurzweil, *How to Create*, 4.

54. Kurzweil, *Singularity*, 389.

55. Kurzweil, Ibid., 389.

56. Frye, 120.

57. Mali, 150.

58. Donald J. McKay, *The Clock Work Image: A Christian Perspective on Science* (Downers Grove, IL: Intervarsity Press, 1974), 52.

59. Mary Midgley, *Evolution as a Religion: Strange Dreams, Stranger Fears* (London: Methuen, 1985; rpt. London: Routledge Classics, 2002), 33.

60. Jeffrey Bishop, "Transhumanism, Metaphysics, and the Posthuman God," *Journal of Medicine and Philosophy* 35 (2010): 706.

61. Bishop, 706.

62. Bishop, 706.

CHAPTER 6

1. See: James Watson, *The Double-Helix: A Personal Account of the Discovery of the Structure of DNA* (New York: Touchstone, 2001).

2. Richard Dawkins, *The Selfish Gene* (New York: Oxford University Press, 1976), 35.

3. Dawkins, 2.

4. Midgley famously objected to Dawkins' notion of a selfish gene. See: Mary Midgley, "Gene-Juggling," *Philosophy* 54 (October 1979). See also Dawkins' response: "In Defense of Selfish Genes," *Philosophy* 56 (October, 1981).

5. Lisa Nakamura, *Cybertypes: Race, Ethnicity and Identity on the Internet* (London: Routledge, 2002), 4.

6. Waters, 294.

7. See: *Cybernetics: The Macy-Conferences 1946-1953*, ed. Claus Pias (Zurich: Diaphanes, 2003).

8. Steve J. Heims, *Constructing a Social Science for Postwar America: The Cybernetics Group, 1946-1953* (Cambridge MA: MIT Press, 1999), 12.

9. On the development of machine metaphors of the mind, see: Jean-Pierre Dupuy, *On the Origins of Cognitive Science: The Mechanization of the Mind* (Cambridge, MA: MIT Press, 2009).

10. N. Katherine Hayles, *How We Became Posthuman: Virtual Bodies in Cybernetics, Literature, and Informatics* (Chicago, IL: The University of Chicago Press: 1999), 50.

11. Warren McCullough, "*Mysterium Iniquitiatus* of Sinful Man Aspiring into the Place of God (1955), in *Embodiments of Mind* (Cambridge, MA: MIT Press, 1965), 163. Quoted in Dupuy, 50.

12. McCullough, 163. Quoted in Dupuy, 51.

13. Dupuy, 54.

14. Dupuy, 7.

15. Dupuy,7.

16. Heims 37

17. Hayles, 53.

18. Hayles, 54.

19. Heims, 179.

20. Giulio Prisco, "The Cosmic Visions of the Turing Church," *Transhumanism and Spirituality Conference*, University of Utah (October 1, 2010). http://www.slideshare.net/giulioprisco/transpirit2010.

21. Hans Moravec, *Mind Children; The Future of Robot and Human Intelligence* (Cambridge, MA: Harvard University Press, 1988), 109–110.

22. Moravec, *Children*, 4.

23. Moravec, Ibid., 116–117.

24. On ethical concerns associated with separating the brain from the body, see: Jean Bethke Elshtain, "Is there a Human Nature? An Argument against Modern Excarnation," in *After the Genome: A Language for our Biotechnological Future*, ed. Michael J. Hyde and James A. Herrick, (Waco, TX: Baylor University Press, 2013).

25. Moravec, *Children*, 123–124.

26. Waters, 293.

27. J. Craig Venter Institute, "First Self-Replicating Synthetic Bacterial Cell," J. Craig Venter Institute, May 20, 2010, http://www.jcvi.org/cms/press/press-releases/full-text/article/first-self-replicating-synthetic-bacterial-cell-constructed-by-j-craig-venter-institute-researcher/home/. See also: http://www.jcvi.org/cms/press/press-releases/full-text/article/first-self-replicating-synthetic-bacterial-cell-constructed-by-j-craig-venter-institute-researcher/home/#sthash.OJ9iYTVT.dpuf

28. J. Craig Venter, "A DNA Driven World," *BBC Richard Dimbley Lecture* (December 4, (2007) http://video.google.com/videoplay?doc id=4893602463025557866; "Life: A Gene-centric View," *Edge: The Third*

Culture (January 2008) http://www.edge.org/documents/dawkins_venter_index.html.

29. J. Craig Venter, *Life at the Speed of Light: From the Double Helix to the Dawn of Digital Life* (New York: Viking, 2013), 5.

30. Venter, *Speed of Light*, 5.

31. Venter, Ibid., 17.

32. Frye, 203.

33. Venter, *Speed of Light*, 6.

34. Venter, Ibid., 7.

35. Venter, Ibid., 179.

36. "The Truths of Terasem," Terasem Faith, http://terasemfaith.net/beliefs, quoted in Anders Sandberg, "Transhumanism and the Meaning of Life," in *Religion and Transhumanism: The Unknown Future of Human Enhancement*, ed. C. Mercer and T. J. Trothen (Santa Barbara, CA: ABC Clio, 2014), 6.

37. Martine Rothblatt, *Virtually Human: The Promise and Peril of Virtual Immortality* (New York: St. Martins, 2014), 11.

38. Rothblatt, 11.

39. Rothblatt, 3.

40. Rothblatt, 98.

41. Verene, 83.

42. Rothblatt, 6.

43. Waters, 294.

44. Robert Herritt, "Google's Philosopher," *Pacific Standard*, December 30, 2014. http://www.psmag.com/navigation/nature-and-technology/googles-philosopher-technology-nature-identity-court-legal-policy-95456/.

45. Midgley, *Myths*, 96.

46. Hayles, 5.

47. Hayles, 12.

48. Hayles, 50.

49. Antonio Damasio, *Descartes' Error: Emotion, Reason, and the Human Brain* (New York: Penguin, 2005), xv. Quoted in Hayles, 245.

50. Juron Lanier, *You Are Not a Gadget: A Manifesto* (New York: Knopf, 2010), 29.

51. Lanier, Ibid., 69.

52. Lanier, Ibid., 50.

53. Ben Goertzel, *A Cosmist Manifesto* blog, accessed January 21, 2011, http://cosmistmanifesto.blogspot.com/.

54. Zygmunt Bauman, *Liquid Modernity* (New York: Polity Press, 2000).

CHAPTER 7

1. Teilhard, *Future,* 161–162.

2. John R. Shook, "Can We Make More Moral Brains?" *Free Inquiry* 32, no. 1 (December 2011/January 2012), 38.

3. Shook, 45.

4. E. S. Boyden, "In Pursuit of Human Augemtation," Ed Boyden's Blog, *MIT Technology Review,*September 17, 2007, http://www.technologyreview.com/blog/boyden/21839/.

5. Human Brain Project, accessed July 25, 2015, https://www.humanbrainproject.eu/discover/the-project/overview;jsessionid=1oye5kwj09qfwl38 cmh8cp4osx.

6. National Institutes for Health BRAIN Initiative, accessed July 25, 2015, http://braininitiative.nih.gov/about.htm.

7. Tirosh-Samuelson, 21.

8. Midgley, *Science,* 13.

9. J. D. Bernal, *The World, the Flesh and the Devil: An Enquiry into the Future of the Three Enemies of the Rational Soul* (1929, rpt. Bloomington, IN: Indiana University Press, 1969). http://cscs.umich.edu/~crshalizi/Bernal/.

10. The phrasing "ensouled bodies and embodied souls" was suggested by Professor Todd Daily in a presentation at Trinity International University, Deerfield, Illinois, July 15, 2010.

11. Gottschall, 55.

12. See Mary Midgley's discussion of Bernal's ideas about the body and the mind in, *Myths,* Chapter 7: "Motives, Materialism and Megalomania."

13. Allen Institute for Brain Science, accessed June 18, 2012, http://www.alleninstitute.org/.

14. Naam, *Human,* 175.

15. Anne Trafton, "Neuroscientists Plant False Memories in the Brain," *MIT News,* Massachusetts Institute of Technology, July 25, 2013,
http://www.kurzweilai.net/neuroscientists-plant-false-memories-in-the-brain.

16. Kerry Sheridan, "Coming Soon: A Brain Implant to Restore Memory," *Medical Xpress,* Science X, May 1, 2014, http://medicalxpress.com/news/2014-05-brain-implant-memory.html.

17. Emily Singer, "Watching a Single Thought Form in the Brain," *MIT Technology Review,* September 6, 2006, http://www.technologyreview.com/biomedicine/17458/?mod=related. On consciousness, see: Christof Koch, *Consciousness: Confessions of a Romantic Reductionist* (Boston MA: MIT Press, 2012).

18. See, for example, S. Kellim, K. Miller, K. Thomson, R. Brown, P. House, and B. Greger, "Decoding Spoken Words using Local Field Potentials Recorded from the Cortical Surface, *The Journal of Neural Engineering* v. 5: October 7, 2010).

19. "New genes linked to brain size, intelligence," Kurzweil Accelerating Intelligence, Kurzweil Network, April 16, 2012, http://www.kurzweilai. net/new-genes-linked-to-brain-size-intelligence.

20. Helen Thomson, "Electrical brain stimulation improves math skills," *New Scientist*, November 4, 2010, http://www.newscientist.com/article/dn19679-electrical-brain-stimulation-improves-math-skills.html.

21. Duncan Graham-Rowe, "World's first Brain Prosthesis Revealed," *The New Scientist*,March 12, 2003.
   http://www.newscientist.com/article/dn3488-worlds-first-brain-prosthesis-revealed.html\.

22. Agar, *Eugenics*, 95.

23. Naam, *Human*, 205.

24. Naam, Ibid., 205–206.

25. Naam, Ibid., 176.

26. Jim Gilliam, "The Internet is My Religion" YouTube video, 12:26, from the Personal Democracy Forum, 2011, posted by Pdf YouTube, June 9, 2011, http://www.youtube.com/watch?v=-4WKle-GQwk.

27. Michael Hagemeister, "Russian Cosmism in the 1920s and Today," in *The Occult in Russian and Soviet Culture*, ed. Bernice G. Rosenthal (Ithaca New York: Cornell University Press, 1997), 195. For a more recent treatment of the idea that mind is not a strictly natural phenomenon, see: Thomas Nagel, *Mind and Cosmos: Why the Materialist Neo-Darwinian Conception of Nature is Almost Certainly False* (New York: Oxford University Press, 2012).

28. Hagemeister, 198.

29. Hagemeister, 200–201. Some Russian occultists refer to themselves as *Noosfera*.

30. Teilhard, *Phenomenon*, 252.

31. Teilhard, Ibid., 264.

32. Teilhard, Ibid., 288.

33. Julian S. Huxley, "The Evolutionary Vision," in *Evolution after Darwin: Issues in Evolution* v.2 (Chicago, IL: University of Chicago Press 1960) 253.

34. Arthur C. Clarke, *Childhood's End* (New York: Ballantine Books, 1953).

35. Ramez Naam, *Nexus* (New York: Angry Robot Books, 2013).

36. Bryan Bishop, "Emotiv EPOC EEG Headset Hacked," *Humanity+*, September 13, 2010, http://hplusmagazine.com/2010/09/13/emotiv-epoc-eeg-headset-hacked/ (June 16, 2012).

37. Shan Li, "Mind Reading is on the Market," *LA Times*, August 8, 2010. http://articles.latimes.com/2010/aug/08/business/la-fi-mind-reader-20100808.

38. Leo King, "Mind-Controlled Drone Scientists Work On Ground-breaking Flight," Forbes Tech Online, Forbes, February 25, 2015, http://www.forbes.com/sites/leoking/2015/02/25/mind-controlled-drone-scientists-work-on-groundbreaking-flight/.

39. Duncan Graham-Rowe, "Wheelchair Makes the Most of Brain Control," *MIT Technology Review*, September 13, 2010, http://www.technologyreview.com/news/420756/wheelchair-makes-the-most-of-brain-control/.

40. Jonathan Moreno, *Mind Wars: Brain Research and National Defense* (2006; rpt. New York: Bellevue Literary Press, 2012).

41. William J. Tyler, "Remote Control of Brain Activity Using Ultrasound," *Armed with Science*, US Department of Defense, September 1, 2010, http://science.dodlive.mil/2010/09/01/remote-control-of-brain-activity-using-ultrasound/.

42. Walter Hickey, "These twenty Advanced Military Projects Will Change Your Life," *Business Insider*, July 27, 2012, http://www.businessinsider.com/darpa-military-projects-that-will-change-your-life-2012-7?op=1#ixzz224l6TypT (August 17, 2015).

43. Noah Shactman, "Air Force wants Neuroweapons to Overwhelm Enemy," *Wired: Danger Room*, Wired, November 2, 2010. http://www.wired.com/dangerroom/2010/11/air-force-looks-to-artificially-overwhelm-enemy-cognitive-capabilities/. For a cinematic portrayal of military interest in enhanced mental powers, see: *The Men Who Stare at Goats* (2009).

44. *Kurzweil Accelerating Intelligence*, "'Neural Dust' Brain Implants could Revolutionize Brain-machine Interfaces," July 17, 2013, http://www.kurzweilai.net/neural-dust-brain-implants-could-revolutionize-brain-machine-interfaces-and-large-scale-data-recording.

45. Dongjin Seo, et al., "Neural Dust: An Ultrasonic, Low Power Solution for Chronic Brain-Machine Interfaces," *Cornell University Library*, *arXiv*, July 8, 2013, accessed July 25, 2015, http://arxiv.org/abs/1307.2196.

46. Warner, 19.

47. All material on Miguel Nicoleli's experiments derived from Jen Whyntie, "One Rat Brain 'Talks' to Another Using Electronic Link," BBC Radio, February 28, 2013, http://www.bbc.co.uk/news/science-environment-21604005.

48. Nicole Kraft, "Brain-To-Brain Communication Achieved, Telepathy A Reality," *SourceFed*, Discovery Communications, November 10, 2014, http://sourcefed.com/brain-to-brain-communication-achieved-telepathy-a-reality/.

49. Quoted in Garreau, *Evolution,* 256.

50. George Dvorsky, "The Most Significant Tech of the Next 20 Years," IEET online, November 4, 2010, http://ieet.org/index.php/IEET/more/dvorsky20101104.

51. Quoted in Garreau, *Evolution,* 256.

52. Robert Wright, "Building One Big Brain," *New York Times Opinionator, New York Times,* July 6, 2010, http://opinionator.blogs.nytimes.com/2010/07/06/the-web-we-weave/.

53. Kurzweil, *Create,* 5.

54. Midgley, *Myths,* 43.

55. Diamandis and Kotler, *Abundance,* 303.

56. George Dvorsky, *Sentient Developments,* "The Most Significant Technological Developments of the Next Twenty Years," November 3, 2010, http://www.sentientdevelopments.com/2010/11/most-significant-technological.html.

57. Kurzweil, *Spiritual Machines,* 153.

58. See, for example: Peter V. Milo, "Scientists Successfully 'Hack' Brain to Obtain Information," CBS News (Seattle), August 25, 2012. http://seattle.cbslocal.com/2012/08/25/scientists-successfully-hack-brain-to-obtain-private-data/; Kerri Smith, "Mind-reading Technology Speeds Ahead," *Scientific American,* October 23, 2013, http://www.scientificamerican.com/article/mind-reading-technology-speeds-ahead/.

CHAPTER 8

1. Olaf Stapledon, "The Splendid Race," in *An Olaf Stapledon Reader* (Syracuse New York: Syracuse University Pres, 1997), 147–48.

2. Cupitt, 29.

3. See: Christopher M. Hutton, *Linguistics and the Third Reich: Mother Tongue Fascism, Race, and the Science of Language* (London, UK: Routledge, 1999).

4. Leon Poliakov, *The Aryan Myth: A History of Racist and Nationalist Ideas in Europe* (New York: Barnes and Noble, 1996), 22. See also: Stephen J. Gould's treatment of this issue in *The Mismeasure of Man* (New York: W. W. Norton, 1981).

5. Poliakov, 35.

6. Poliakov, 98.

7. Dan Stone, *Breeding Superman: Nietzsche, Race and Eugenics in Edwardian and Interwar Britain* (Liverpool, UK: Liverpool University Press, 2002), 114.

8. Philip Wylie, *Gladiator* (1931; rpt. Lincoln, NE: University of Nebraska Press, 2004).

9. Naam, *Human*.

10. Naam, Ibid., 227.

11. Naam, Ibid., 232.

12. Michio Kaku, "Living in a Post-Human World," *Big Think* video, 1:34, Big Think, 2011, http://bigthink.com/videos/living-in-a-post-human-world.

13. Hughes, *Citizen Cyborg*, 131.

14. Moravec, *Children*, 158.

15. Moravec, Ibid., 125.

16. Alicia Chang, "Stem Cells Reverse Blindness Caused by Burns," *Salon*, June 23, 2010, http://www.salon.com/2010/06/23/stem_cells_blindness_vision/ (June 26, 2010). Freeman

17. "Subretinal electronic chips allow blind patients to read letters and combine them to words," E. Zrenner, et al., *Proceedings of the Royal Society,* November 2010, accessed February 22, 2013, http://www.rspb.royalsocietypublishing.org/content/early/2010/11/01/rspb.2010.1747.full.

18. Kristina Grifantini, "Personal Exoskeletons for Paraplegics: A mobile device helps patients with spinal cord injuries walk," *MIT Technology Review*, September 22, 2010. http://www.technologyreview.com/biomedicine/26328/?p1=A1&a=f.

19. "New 'Iron Man' Special Forces Exoskeleton Stops Bullets with Liquid Armor," *Futurism* (June 6, 2016) https://futurism.com/2018-will-be-big-on-special-forces-exoskeleton-tech/ .

20. Naam, *Human*, 5.

21. Naam, Ibid., 9.

22. Naam, Ibid., 10.

23. Julian Savulescu, "Unfit for Life: Genetically Enhance Humanity or Face Extinction," YouTube video, 59:21, from a lecture at the *Festival of Dangerous Ideas*, Sydney, AU, 2009, https://www.youtube.com/watch?v=PkW3rEQ0ab8.

24. Alexis Madrigal, "Gandhi Pills? Psychiatrist Argues for Moral Performance Enhancers," *Wired Science*, *Wired*, September 9, 2008, http://www.wired.com/wiredscience/2008/09/gandhi-pills-ps/.

25. John R. Shook, "Can We Make More Moral Brains?" *Free Inquiry* (December 2011/January 2012).

26. Stephen Adams, "Blood Pressure Drug 'Reduces In-built Racism,'" *The Telegraph*, March 7, 2007, http://www.telegraph.co.uk/health/health-news/9129029/Blood-pressure-drug-reduces-in-built-racism.html.

27. Xavier Symons, "Savulescu Warns that 'Love-diminishing' Drugs could be used for Gay Conversion Therapy," *Bio-Edge*, October 13, 2013, www.bioedge.org.

28. Bostrom, "Transhumanist Values."

29. Nick Bostrom, "In Defense of Posthuman Dignity," *Bioethics* 19, no. 3, 202–214.

30. Hauskeller, 41.

31. Warner, 28.

32. Warner, 19.

33. Coupe, 97.

34. Coupe, 96.

35. Naam, *Human*, 233."

36. Chaim Perelman and L. Olbrechts-Tyteca, *The New Rhetoric: A Treatise on Argumentation*, trans. John Wilkinson and Purcell Weaver (Notre Dame, IN: University of Notre Dame Press), 147.

37. Naam, *Human*, 233.

38. NickBostrom, "Why I Want to Be Posthuman When I Grow Up," (2006) Nick Bostrom's Homepage, 2. http://nickbostrom.com/posthuman.pdf. 108.

39. Bostrom, "Why I Want," 2.

40. Bostrom, Ibid., 5.

41. Warner, 72. Warner refers to the "lone hero" as "the pattern of modern man."

42. Bostrom, "Why I Want," 5; Sandberg, 9.

43. Warner, xx.

44. Nick Bostrom, "Are You Living in a Computer Simulation?" *Philosophical Quarterly* 53, no. 211, (2003), 243–255.

45. Midgley, *Myths*, 159. Midgley quotes Gregory Stock, *Redesigning Humans* (London, UK: Profile Books, 2002), 173.

46. Quoted in Midgley, *Myths*, 158. Robert Sinsheimer, "The Prospect of Designed Genetic Change," *Engineering and Science*, April 1969, 8–13.

47. Midgley, *Myths*, 155.

48. Immanuel Kant, *Critique of Pure Reason*, Book II, Chapter III, section I.

49. Tirosh-Samuelson, "Engaging Transhumanism," 19–20.

50. Warner, 19.

51. Bishop, "Transhumanism," 707.

52. Francis Fukuyama, "Transhumanism," *Foreign Policy Magazine*, October 23, 2009, http://foreignpolicy.com/2009/10/23/transhumanism/.53.Fukuyama.).

CHAPTER 9

1. Terasem Movement, accessed January 30, 2017, http://www.terasemcentral.org/. On Rothblatt and her career, see: Lisa Miller, "The Trans-Everything CEO," *New York Magazine* (September 7, 2014). See also: M. Rothblatt, *Virtually Human: The Promise—and the Peril—of Digital Immortality* (New York: St. Martin's, 2014).

2. See: Jay Yarow, "Google is Launching a Company that Hopes to Cure Death," *Business Insider*, http://www.businessinsider.com/google-is-launching-a-company-that-hopes-to-cure-death-2013-9.

3. Levi Sumagaysay, "Tech Billionaires and Human Immortality," *SiliconBeat, Mercury News*, March 6, 2015, http://www.siliconbeat.com/2015/03/06/quoted-tech-billionaires-and-human-immortality/.

4. Carole Haber, "Life Extension and History: The Continual Search for the Fountain of Youth," *The Journals of Gerontology* A 59:6 (June 2004), B515–22. http://biomedgerontology.oxfordjournals.org/content/59/6/B515.long (July 28, 2004).

5. Marquis de Condorcet, *Outlines of an Historical View of the Progress of the Human Mind* (1795; English trans. Philadelphia, 1796), *The Liberty Fund*. http://oll.libertyfund.org/?option=com_staticxt&staticfile=show.php%3Ftitle=1669&chapter=800&layout=html&Itemid=27 (June 15, 2012).

6. See: George M. Young, *The Esoteric Futurism of Nikolai Federov and His Followers* (New York: Oxford University Press, 2012).

7. Hagemeister, "Russian Cosmism," 188.

8. Frederik Pohl and Hans Moravec, "Souls in Silicon," *Omni*, November 1993, 66–76. For a treatment of cinematic efforts to eliminate death, see: "How Hollywood Killed Death," http://www.nytimes.com/2014/04/20/magazine/how-hollywood-killed-death.html?_r=0.

9. On commercial interest in longevity, see: Ted Anton, *The Longevity Seekers: Science, Business, and the Fountain of Youth* (Chicago, IL: University of Chicago Press, 2013). For a sociological analysis of mortality and immortality, see: Zygmunt Bauman, *Mortality, Immortality, and Other Life Strategies* (Palo Alto, CA: Stanford University Press, 1992).

10. Kenneth Burke, *The Rhetoric of Religion: Studies in Logology* (Berkeley, CA: University of California Press, 1970), 209.

11. For an analysis of the Christian and Transhumanist views of death, see: Todd T. W. Daly, "Diagnosing Death in the Transhumanism and Chris-

tian Traditions," in *Religion and Transhumanism: The Unknown Future of Human Enhancement*, ed. C. Mercer and T. J. Trothen (Santa Barbara, CA: ABC Clio, 2014), 83-96.

12. Frye, 42.

13. Midgley, *Science*, 13.

14. Warner, xix.

15. Jacob Weisberg, "Turn on, Start Up, Drop Out," *Slate*, October 16, 2010, http://www.slate.com/articles/news_and_politics/politics/2010/10/turn_on_start_up_drop_out.html.

16. Peter Thiel interviewed by Francis Fukuyama, *The American Interest*, March/April, 2012, http://www.the-american-interest.com/article.cfm?piece=1187.

17. J. D. Bernal, *The World, the Flesh and the Devil: An Enquiry into the Future of the Three Enemies of the Rational Soul* (1929, rpt. Bloomington, IN: Indiana University Press, 1969), http://cscs.umich.edu/~crshalizi/Bernal/. Bernal's comments are reminiscent of Hans Moravec's statement: "The most important thing about each person is the data, and the programs in the data that are in the brain." (Quoted in Hayles, 245).

18. "Robert Ettinger Dies at 92: Cryonics Pioneer", *Los Angeles Times*, August 1, 2011, http://www.latimes.com/news/obituaries/la-me-robert-ettinger-20110801,0,6175424.story.

19. Robert Ettinger, *Man Into Superman* (New York: Avon, 1972).

20. Ricoeur, *Reader*, 490.

21. Alcor Life Extension Foundation, "Frequently Asked Questions." Alcor Life Extension Foundation, accessed February 7, 2011, http://www.alcor.org/FAQs/faq01.html#dead.

22. Daniel Oberhaus, "The Art of Not Dying," *Motherboard*, Vice Media, November 28, 2014, http://motherboard.vice.com/read/the-art-of-not-dying-or-being-frozen-until-you-can-come-back.

23. John Smart, "The Brain Preservation Prize: Why Inexpensively Preserving Our Brains After Death is a Good Thing for Ourselves and Society, And What You Can Do to Help," presented at the *Humanity+ Summit*, June 12, 2010, Brain Preservation Foundation, accessed June 13, 2012, http://www.brainpreservation.org.

24. Kenneth Hayworth, "Proposal for a Brain Preservation Technology Prize," Brain Preservation Foundation, accessed June 18, 2010, http://www.brainpreservation.org/documents/proposalforbrainpreservationtechnologyprize.pdf.

25. Joseph Mali, *The Rehabilitation of Myth: Vico's New Science* (Cambridge, UK: Cambridge University Press, 1992), 150.

26. Frye, 118.

27. Brain Preservation Foundation, accessed July 4, 2010, http://www.brainpreservation.org/.

28. John Smart, *Humanity+ Summit*. Harvard University (June 12-13, 2010).

29. Coupe, 73.

30. Eliot, *Prose*, 177–178.

31. Robert Highfield, "How to Live Forever," *Telegraph*, January 14, 2008, http://www.telegraph.co.uk/news/science/science-news/3321714/How-to-live-forever.html.

32. Richard Alleyne, "Scientists Take a Step Closer to an Elixir of Youth," *Telegraph*, November 20, 2008, http://www.telegraph.co.uk/health/healthnews/3489881/Scientists-take-a-step-closer-to-an-elixir-of-youth.html.

33. Gautam Naik, "Aging Ills Reversed in Mice," *Wall Street Journal* online edition, *Wall Street Journal*, http://online.wsj.com/article/SB1000142405274870378570457564296420924180.html?mod=googlenews_wsj.

34. The Immortality Institute, accessed November 26, 2006, http://www.imminst.org/. The organization is now called Large City. De Garis was at one time an advisor to the group.

35. SENS Foundation, accessed August 18, 2015, www.sens.org.

36. Warner, 28.

37. Aubrey de Grey and Michael Rae, *Ending Aging: The Rejuvenation Breakthroughs that could Reverse Human Aging in our Lifetimes* (New York: St. Martin's Griffin, 2007), 3–4.

38. De Grey, 312.

39. Agar, 9.

40. Coupe, 8–9.

41. Mali, 3.

42. Coupe, 178.

43. Ricoeur, *Reader*, 490.

44. Kurzweil, *Singularity*, 198–199.

45. Mike Hodgkinson, "You Will be Able to Upload Your Brain," *The Independent*,September 27, 2009, http://www.independent.co.uk/news/science/by-2040-you-will-be-able-to-upload-your-brain-1792555.html. Kurzweil, *Singularity*, 284.

46. Lanier, *Gadget*, 77.

47. Tirosh-Samuelson, 39.

48. Hauskeller, 42.

CHAPTER 10

1. I. J. Good, "Speculations Concerning the First Ultraintelligent Machine" in *Advances in Computers*, ed. F. Alt and M. Rubinoff v. 6 (New York: Academic Press, 1965), 31–88 . http://www.acceleratingfuture.com/pages/ultraintelligentmachine.html.

2. Marvin Minsky, *The Society of Mind* (New York: Simon and Shuster, 1989); See also, *The Emotion Machine: Commonsense Thinking, Artificial Intelligence, and the Future of the Human Mind* (New York: Simon and Shuster, 2007).

3. Roger Penrose, *The Emperor's New Mind: Concerning Computers, Minds and the Laws of Physics* (New York: Oxford University Press, 1989), 11.

4. Penrose, 447. For Penrose's discussion of the possibility of Strong AI, see Penrose, 17–23.

5. "Bill Gates on AI doomsday" *RT: Question More*, RT, January 29, 2015, http://www.rt.com/news/227279-artificial-intelligence-opinions-differ/.

6. Coupe, 121.

7. Verene, 77.

8. Verene, 83.

9. Alan M. Turing, "Computing Machinery and Intelligence," *Mind*, 1950, 59, 433–460.

10. Turing, Ibid. Section 6: Contrary Views on the Main Question.

11. Good, "Speculations."

12. James Barrat, *Our Final Invention: Artificial Intelligence and the End of the Human Era* (New York: Thomas Dunne, 2013), 104.

13. Sharon Gaudin, "IBM's Watson's Ability to Converse is a Huge Advance for AI Research," *Computerworld*, IDG, February 15, 2011, http://www.computerworld.com/s/article/9209661/IBM_s_Watson_s_ability_to_converse_is_a_huge_advance_for_AI_research.

14. Jon Russell, "Google: Defeating Go champion shows AI can 'find solutions humans don't see,'" *TechCrunch*, AOL, March 17, 2016, https://techcrunch.com/2016/03/17/google-defeating-go-champion-shows-ai-can-find-solutions-humans-dont-see/.

15. Hughes, 5.

16. Frye, 203, 208.

17. Priya Ganapati, "Reverse-Engineering of Human Brain Likely by 2030, Expert Predicts," *Wired: Gadget Lab*, Wired, August 16, 2010, http://www.wired.com/gadgetlab/2010/08/reverse-engineering-brain-kurzweil/.

18. Human Brain Project, accessed August 18, 2015, http://www.humanbrainproject.eu/.

19. David Smith, "Building an Electronic Human Brain," *Israel 21C*, May, 2010, http://israel21c.org/technology/building-an-electronic-human-brain-2/. A team at the University of Waterloo has announced significant progress on a similar project. See: "Waterloo Researchers Create 'World's Largest Functioning Model of the Brain'" Kurzweilai Artificial Intelligence, Kurzweil Network, November 30, 2012, http://www.kurzweilai.net/waterloo-researchers-create-worlds-largest-functioning-model-of-the-brain.

20. Frye, 33–34.

21. Smith, "Building."

22. Henry Makram, "A Brain in a Supercomputer," *TED* video, 14:50, posted October 2009, http://www.ted.com/talks/henry_markram_super-computing_the_brain_s_secrets.html. The cortical column model of the brain's functioning is gaining ground. See, for example, Ray Kurzweil's discussion in *How the Create a Mind* (New York: Viking, 2012).

23. Jon Brodkin, "IBM Cat Brain Simulation Dismissed as 'Hoax' by Rival Scientist," *New York Times*, November 24, 2009.

24. Bryan Appleyard, "Top Scientists' Predictions for the Next Decade," *London Times*, December 27, 2009, http://www.thesundaytimes.co.uk/sto/news/article193725.ece.

25. Frye, 118.

26. Smith, "Building."

27. Smith, "Building."

28. Michio Kaku, *Physics of the Future: How Science will Shape Human Destiny and our Daily Lives by 2100* (New York: Anchor, 2012), 58.

29. Goertzel, "Manifesto."

30. Zoltan Istvan, "Are We Heading for a Jesus Singularity?," *Huffington Post Blog*, HuffingtonPost.com, March 21, 2014.

31. Hugo de Garis, "Think About It." YouTube video, 2:28, posted September 5, 2007, accessed December 13, 2011, http://www.youtube.com/watch?v=2A_5-Van9m4.

32. *Transcendent Man*, directed by Barry Ptolemy (2011).

33. Mali, 150.

34. de Garis, "Think About It."

35. Nick Bostrom, *Superintelligence: Paths, Dangers, Strategies*, (New York: Oxford University Press, 2014).

36. Bostrom, *Superintelligence*, 22.

37. Warner, 28.

38. Bostrom, *Superintelligence*, 29.

39. Bostrom, Ibid., 43.

40. Bostrom, Ibid., 56.

41. Bostrom, Ibid., 92.

42. Bostrom, Ibid., 78.

43. Bostrom, Ibid., 95.

44. Bostrom, Ibid., 100.

45. Bostrom, Ibid., 101–104.

46. Bostrom, Ibid., 117.

47. Bostrom, Ibid., 259.

48. Bostrom, Ibid., 260.

49. Joseph Weizenbaum, *Computer Power and Human Reason: From Judgment to Calculation* (New York: W. H. Freeman and Co., 1976).

50. Hayles, 287.

51. Hayles, 288.

52. Weizenbaum, 277.

53. Lanier, *Gadget:*, 49.

54. Jaron Lanier, "First Church of Robotics," *New York Times*, August 9, 2010, http://www.nytimes.com/2010/08/09/opinion/09lanier.html?_r=0.

55. Lanier, *Gadget*, 45; "Robotics."

56. Richard Fisher, "Is it OK to Torture or Murder a Robot?" *BBC Future*, BBC, November 27, 2013, http://www.bbc.com/future/story/20131127-would-you-murder-a-robot.

57. Ashrafian, "Intelligent Robots must Uphold Human Rights," *Nature* (March 24, 2015). http://www.nature.com/news/intelligent-robots-must-uphold-human-rights-1.17167.

58. Wesley J. Smith, "AI Machines: Things, Not Persons," *First Things*, April 10, 2015, http://www.firstthings.com/web-exclusives/2015/04/ai-machines-things-not-persons.

59. Hayles, 239.

60. Hayles, 243.

Chapter 11

1. Quoted in Hughes, *Cyborg*, 165.

2. *The Transhumanist Declaration* (1998), Humanity+, accessed August 11, 2015, http://humanityplus.org/philosophy/transhumanist-declaration/.

3. Nick Bostrom, "Human Genetic Enhancements: A Transhumanist Perspective," *The Journal of Value Inquiry* 37 (2003): 493. See also: "Transhumanist Values," http://www.nickbostrom.com/ethics/values.html#_ftn1.

4. 100 Year Starship, accessed January 30, 2017 , www.100yss.org.

5. Coupe, 8.

6. Ricouer, *Reader*, 490.

7. Coupe, 8–9.

8. Amara D. Angelica, "NASA Ames' Worden reveals DARPA-funded 'Hundred Year Starship' program," *Kurzweil Accelerating Intelligence,* October 18, 2010. http://www.kurzweilai.net/nasa-ames-worden-reveals-darpa-funded-hundred-year-starship-program accessed January 30, 2017. Pete Worden, "Hundred Year Starship Announcement," *The Long Now Foundation,* October 28, 2010, accessed June 11, 2012, http://blog.longnow.org/02010/10/28/100-year-starship-announcement/.

9. Bostrom, *Superintelligence,* 101–104.

10. William Sims Bainbridge, "Religion for a Galactic Civilization 2.0," *Institute for Ethics and Emerging Technologies Newsletter* (1989, rpt. 2009). http://ieet.org/index.php/IEET/more/bainbridge20090820/.

11. Young, *Cosmists,* 49.

12. Hagemeister, 198.

13. Hagemeister, 188.

14. Hagemeister, 189–190.

15. Hagemeister, 195.

16. Verene, 83.

17. J. D. Bernal, *The World, the Flesh and the Devil: An Enquiry into the Future of the Three Enemies of the Rational Soul* (1929, rpt. Bloomington, IN: Indiana University Press, 1969). http://cscs.umich.edu/~crshalizi/Bernal/ (May 10, 2012).

18. Teilhard, 286.

19. Virgin Galactic, accessed February 19, 2011, http://www.virgingalactic.com/.

20. Paul McDougall, "SpaceX Dragon Capsule Lands Safely," *Information Week,* December 9, 2010, http://www.informationweek.com/story/showArticle.jhtml?articleID=228800001.

21. Bigelow Aerospace, "Congratulations SpaceX," June 4, 2012, accessed Jun3 22, 2012, http://www.bigelowaerospace.com/Congratulations-SpaceX.pdf.

22. Diamandis and Kotler, 123–124.

23. Ted Greenwald, "The X Man," *Wired,* July 2012, 88.

24. Greenwald, 92.

25. Greenwald, 94.

26. Greenwald, 96.

27. Anissimov, "Top Ten Transhumanist Technologies," Lifeboat Foundation, accessed March 1, 2011, http://lifeboat.com/ex/transhumanist.technologies.

28. Frye, 119–120.

29. Frye, 120.

30. Coupe, 155. Coupe quotes Ricoeur, *The Conflict of Interpretations* (Evanston, IL: Northwestern University Press, 1974), 410.

31. Associated Press, "Hawking says Humans Must go into Space," MS-NBC.com, NBC, June 6, 2006, . http://www.nbcnews.com/id/13293390/ns/technology_and_science-space/t/hawking-says-humans-must-go-space/#.WIu2LH2GOT8

32. United Press, "Man Must Colonize Space," UPI.com, UPI, January 6, 2012,

http://www.upi.com/Science_News/2012/01/06/Hawking-Mankind-must-colonize-space/UPI-64431325871534/#ixzz1yZxQVutv.

33. Martin Rees, *Our Final Hour: A Scientist's Warning: How Terror, Error, and Environmental Disaster Threaten Humankind's Future in This Century—On Earth and Beyond* (New York: Basic Books, 2003), 170.

34. Midgley, *Myths*, 5.

35. Rees, 180.

36. Rees. 181.

37. Coupe, 6.

38. Rees, 181.

39. Rees, 182, 183.

40. Gerard K. O'Neill, *The High Frontier: Human Colonies in Space* (New York: Wiliam Morrow, 1977).

41. Freeman Dyson, *Imagined Worlds* (Cambridge, MA: Harvard University Press, 1998), 159.

42. Dyson, 154.

43. Dyson, 154.

44. Dyson, 153.

45. Dyson, 150.

46. J. Richard Gott III, *Time Travel in Einstein's Universe: The Physical Possibilities of Travel Through Time* (London: Phoenix, 2002), 229.

47. Gott, 231. See: Robert Zubrin, *Entering Space: Creating a Spacefaring Civilization* (Jeremy P. Tarcher, 1999), and *The Case for Mars: The Plan to Settle the Red Planet and Why We Must* (New York: Free Press, 1996). On the Mars Direct program, see: The Mars Society, accessed August 12, 2015, http://www.marssociety.org/home/about/mars-direct. The Society's website states:

> Mars Direct is a sustained humans-to-Mars plan developed by Dr. Robert Zubrin that advocates a minimalist, live-off-the-land approach to exploring the planet Mars, allowing for maximum results with minimum investment. Using existing launch technology and making use of the Martian atmosphere to generate rocket fuel, ex-

tracting water from the Martian soil and eventually using the abundant mineral resources of the Red Planet for construction purposes, the plan drastically lowers the amount of material which must be launched from Earth to Mars, thus sidestepping the primary stumbling block to space exploration and rapidly accelerating the timetable for human exploration of the solar system."

48. A. K. Herath, "Cyborgs Needed for Escape from Earth," *Astrobiology Magazine*, September 16, 2010, http://www.astrobio.net/exclusive/3617/cyborgs-needed-for-escape-from-earth.

49. Manfred Clynes, Nathan Kline, "Cyborgs and Space," *Astronautics* (1960;repr., Scribd, September 16, 2010, accessed June 25, 2012, http://www.scribd.com/doc/2962194/Cyborgs-and-Space-Clynes-Kline.

50. Carl Sagan, *The Cosmic Connection: An Extraterrestrial Perspective* (New York: Dell, 1973), 69.

51. Warner, 19.

52. Ricouer, *Reader*, 490.

53. Midgley, *Science*, 26.

CHAPTER 12

1. Waters, 293.

2. Francis Fukuyama, "Transhumanism," *Foreign Policy Magazine*, September 1, 2004.

3. Robert Sparrow, "A Not-So-New Eugenics: Harris and Savulescu on Human Enhancement," *The Hastings Center Report* 41, no. 1, (January–February 2011): 38.

4. Michael Sandel, "The Case Against Perfection," in *Human Enhancement*, ed. Julian Savulescu and Nick Bostrom (Oxford: Oxford University Press, 2009), 89.

5. Bishop, 715.

6. Hauskeller, 40.

7. Hauskeller, 40.

8. Hauskeller, 43.

9. Hauskeller, 43.

10. Hauskeller, 43.

11. Hauskeller, 44.

12. Hauskeller, 44.

13. Coupe, 73.

14. Coupe, 88. Coupe quotes Kermode "The Sense of an Ending," in *Studies in the History of Fiction* (London: Oxford University Press, 1967), 7.

15. Jean Bethke Elshtain, "Is There a Human Nature? An Argument against Modern Excarnation," in *After the Genome: A Language for our Biotechnological Future*, ed. Michael J. Hyde and James A. Herrick, (Waco, TX: Baylor University Press, 2013), 73.

16. Bethke Elshtain, 73–74.

17. Bethke Elshtain, 74.

18. Bethke Elshtain, 74–75. On this point, see also news of plans by Dr. Sergio Canavero to perform a full body transplant, alternately referred to as a head transplant: "30-Year-Old Russian Man Volunteers for World's First Human Head Transplant," *Medical News Today*, June 16, 2015, http://www.medicalnewstoday.com/articles/292306.php.

19. A helpful explanation of the CRISPR/Cas9 process can be found at: A. Reis, et al., "CRISPR/Cas9 and Targeted Genome Editing: A New Era in Molecular Biology," *New England Biolabs Expressions* 1 (2014), https://www.neb.com/tools-and-resources/feature-articles/crispr-cas9-and-targeted-genome-editing-a-new-era-in-molecular-biology.

20. Juan Enriquez, "The Glory of Big Data," *Popular Science*, Special Issue, November 2011.

21. Rob Stein, "Geneticists Breach Ethical Taboo By Changing Genes Across Generations," *National Public Radio* (October 24, 2012), http://www.npr.org/blogs/health/2012/10/24/163509093/geneticists-breach-ethical-taboo-by-changing-genes-across-generations.

22. David Cyranoski and Sara Reardon, "Chinese Scientists Genetically Modify Human Embryos," *Nature* 22 (April 2015), http://www.nature.com/news/chinese-scientists-genetically-modify-human-embryos-1.17378.

23. Francis Fukuyama, "Transhumanism," *Foreign Policy Magazine*, October 23, 2009, http://foreignpolicy.com/2009/10/23/transhumanism/.

24. Tirosh-Samuelson, 34.

25. Bethke Elshtain, 75.

26. Bethke Elshtain, 76.

27. Midgley, *Myths*, 23.

28. Midgley, Ibid., 13.

29. Lanier, *Gadget*, 25.

30. Sheila Heti, "Mary Midgley: Moral Philosopher," *The Believer*, February 2008, http://www.believermag.com/issues/200802/?read=interview_midgley.

31. See, for example, the work of ethicist Julian Savulescu: "Procreative Beneficence: Reasons Not to Have Disabled Children," *The Sorting Society*, ed. L. Skene and J. Thomson (Cambridge, U.K., and New York: Cambridge University Press, 2008); "New Breeds of Humans: The Moral Obligation to Enhance," *Ethics, Law and Moral Philosophy of Reproductive Biomedicine* 1,

no. 1 (2005): 36–39; "Procreative Beneficence: Why We Should Select the Best Children," *Bioethics* 15, no. 5 (2001): 413–26.

32. Lanier, *Gadget*, 75.

33. Hugo de Garis, "Think About It."

34. Sebastian Seung, *Connectome: How the Brain's Wiring Makes Us Who We Are*, (New York: Mariner Books, 2012), 276.

35. Lanier, "Robotics."

36. Sandberg, 6. Sandberg quotes "The Truths of Terasem," (2002) http//:terasemfaith.net.

37. Giulio Pirsco, "Transhumanist Religion 2.0," accessed July 12, 2012, http://www.kurzweilai.net/transhumanist-religion-2-0. See also, Giulio Prisco, "Transcendent Engineering, *Terasem Journal of Personal Cyberconsciousness*, accessed September 23, 2012 December 2011, http://www.terasemjournals.com/PCJournal/PC0602/prisco.html.

38. Giulio Prisco, "The Cosmic Visions of the Turing Church," presented at the *Transhumanism and Spirituality Conference*, Salt Lake City, Utah, October 1, 2010.

39. See: the Mormon Transhumanist Association http://transfigurism.org/, The Christian Transhumanist Association http://www.christiantranshumanism.org/, The Turing Church http://turingchurch.com/giulio-prisco/, and Terasem Faith Movement http://www.terasemfaith.org/.

40. Bishop, 718.

41. Lanier, *Gadget*, 18.

42. Midgley, *Science*, 13.

BIBLIOGRAPHY

"30-Year-Old Russian Man Volunteers for World's First Human Head Transplant." *Medical News Today*. Medilexicon International, June 16, 2015. www.medicalnewstoday.com/articles/292306.php.

Adams, Stephen. "Blood Pressure Drug 'Reduces In-built Racism.'" *The Telegraph*, March 7, 2007. www.telegraph.co.uk/health/healthnews/9129029/Blood-pressure-drug-reduces-in-built-racism.html.

Agar, Nicholas. *Liberal Eugenics: In Defense of Human Enhancement*. Hoboken, NJ: Wiley-Blackwell, 2004.

Alcor Life Extension Foundation. "Frequently Asked Questions." Alcor Life Extension Foundation, Accessed January 27, 2017. www.alcor.org/FAQs/.

Allen Institute for Brain Science. Accessed January 27, 2017. www.alleninstitute.org/.Alleyne, Richard. "Scientists Take a Step Closer to an Elixir of Youth." *The Telegraph*, November 20, 2008, www.telegraph.co.uk/health/healthnews/3489881/Scientists-take-a-step-closer-to-an-elixir-of-youth.html.

Anissimov, Michael. "Top Ten Transhumanist Technologies." Lifeboat Foundation, 2007. lifeboat.com/ex/transhumanist.technologies.

Anton, Ted. *The Longevity Seekers: Science, Business, and the Fountain of Youth*. Chicago: University of Chicago Press, 2013.

Appleyard, Bryan. "'Top Scientists' Predictions for the Next Decade." *London Times*, December 27, 2009. www.thesundaytimes.co.uk/sto/news/article193725.ece.

Ashrafian, Hutan. "Intelligent Robots Must Uphold Human Rights." *Nature* 519, no. 7544 (March 2015).www.nature.com/news/intelligent-robots-must-uphold-human-rights-1.17167.

Associated Press. "Hawking Says Humans Must Go into Space," MSNBC.com. NBC Universal, June 6, 2006. www.msnbc.msn.com/id/13293390/ns/technology_and_science-space/t/hawking-says-humans-must-go-space/#.T-i6MJGd6So.

—. "Robert Ettinger Dies at 92: Cryonics Pioneer." *Los Angeles Times,* August 1, 2011. www.latimes.com/news/obituaries/la-me-robert-et-tinger-20110801,0,6175424.story.

Bainbridge, William Sims. "Religion for a Galactic Civilization 2.0." *Institute for Ethics and Emerging Technologies Newsletter.* IEET, August 20, 2009. ieet.org/index.php/IEET/more/bainbridge20090820/.

Barrat, James. *Our Final Invention: Artificial Intelligence and the End of the Human Era.* New York: Thomas Dunne, 2013.

Bauman, Zygmunt. *Liquid Modernity.* Cambridge: Polity Press, 2000.

—. *Mortality, Immortality, and Other Life Strategies.* Redwood City, CA: Stanford University Press, 1992.

Bennett, Benjamin. "Nietzsche's Idea of Myth: The Birth of Tragedy from the Spirit of Eighteenth-Century Aesthetics," *Proceedings of the Modern Language Association.* 91, no. 3. May, 1979: 420–433.

Bennett, Oliver. *Cultural Pessimism: Narratives of Decline in the Postmodern World.* Edinburgh: Edinburgh University Press, 2001.

Bernal, J. D. *The World, the Flesh and the Devil: An Enquiry into the Future of the Three Enemies of the Rational Soul.* New York: Dutton, 1929. Reprint, Bloomington: Indiana University Press, 1969.

"Bill Gates on AI Doomsday 'I Don't Understand Why We Aren't Concerned.'" *RT: Question More.* RT, January 29, 2015. www.rt.com/news/227279-artificial-intelligence-opinions-differ/.

Bishop, Bryan. "Emotiv EPOC EEG Headset Hacked." *H+ Magazine,* September 13, 2010. hplusmagazine.com/2010/09/13/emotiv-epoc-eeg-headset-hacked/.

Bishop, Jeffrey. "Transhumanism, Metaphysics, and the Posthuman God." *Journal of Medicine and Philosophy* 35 (2010): 700–720.

Bostrom, Nick. "In Defense of Posthuman Dignity." *Bioethics* 19, no. 3 (2005): 202—14.

—. "Are You Living in a Computer Simulation." *Philosophical Quarterly* 53, no. 211 (2003): 243–255.

—. "Human Genetic Enhancements: A Transhumanist Perspective." *The Journal of Value Inquiry* 37 (2003): 493–506.

—. "Transhumanist Values." *World Transhumanist Association.* Accessed May 29, 2012. www.transhumanism.org/index.php/WTA/more/transhumanist-values/.

—. "Why I Want to be a Posthuman When I Grow Up." Nick Bostrom's Homepage.www.nickbostrom.com/posthuman.pdf.

—. *Superintelligence: Paths, Dangers, Strategies.* New York: Oxford University Press, 2014.

Boyden, E. S. "In Pursuit of Human Augemtation." *MIT Technology Review*, September 17, 2007. www.technologyreview.com/blog/boyden/21839/.

Brodkin, Jon. "IBM Cat Brain Simulation Dismissed as 'Hoax' by Rival Scientist." *New York Times*, November 24, 2009. www.nytimes.com/external/idg/2009/11/24/24idg-ibm-cat-brain-simulation-dismissed-as-hoax-by-rival-39598.html.

Burke, Kenneth. "Myth and Ideology." *Accent: A Quarterly of New Literature* 7 (Summer 1947).

—. "Revolutionary Symbolism in America." Unpublished manuscript, 1935. In *The Legacy of Kenneth Burke*, edited by Herbert Simons and Trevor Melia, 267–280. Madison, WI: University of Wisconsin Press, 1989 .

—. *The Rhetoric of Religion: Studies in Logology*. Los Angeles: University of California Press, 1970.

Campbell, Joseph. *The Hero with a Thousand Faces*. New York: Pantheon, 1949. Reprint, New York: MJF Books, 1997.

Cannon, Lincoln. "Trust in Posthumanity and the New God Argument." Presented at the *Transhumanism and Spirituality Conference*, 2010. Transcript, *Lincoln Cannon* (blog), October 3, 2010. Accessed May 23, 2012. lincoln.metacannon.net/2010/10/transcript-of-presentation-at.html.

Chang, Alicia. "Stem Cells Reverse Blindness Caused by Burns." *Salon*, June 23, 2010. www.salon.com/2010/06/23/stem_cells_blindness_vision/.

Clarke, Arthur C. *Childhood's End*. New York: Ballantine Books, 1953.

—. *Profiles of the Future: An Inquiry into the Limits of the Possible*. New York: Harper & Row, 1962.

—. *The City and the Stars*. New York: Harcourt, 1956.

Clynes, Manfred, and Nathan Kline. "Cyborgs and Space." Scribd, September 16, 2010, www.scribd.com/doc/2962194/Cyborgs-and-Space-Clynes-Kline.

Coupe, Laurence. *Myth*. New York: Routledge, 1997.

"CRISPR/Cas9 and Targeted Genome Editing: A New Era in Molecular Biology." *New England Biolabs Expressions*, no. 1 (2014). www.neb.com/tools-and-resources/feature-articles/crispr-cas9-and-targeted-genome-editing-a-new-era-in-molecular-biology.

Cupitt, Don. *The World to Come*. London: SCM Press, 1982.

Cybernetics: The Macy-Conferences 1946–1953. Edited by Claus Pias. Zürich: Diaphanes, 2003.

Cyranoski, David, and Sara Reardon. "Chinese Scientists Genetically Modify Human Embryos." *Nature*, April 22, 2015. www.nature.com/news/chinese-scientists-genetically-modify-human-embryos-1.17378.

Daly, Todd T. "Diagnosing Death in the Transhumanism and Christian Traditions." In *Religion and Transhumanism: The Unknown Future of Hu-*

man Enhancement, edited by C. Mercer and T. J. Trothen, 83–96. Santa Barbara, CA: ABC Clio, 2014.

Damasio, Antonio. *Descartes' Error: Emotion, Reason, and the Human Brain.* New York: Penguin, 2005.

Dardel, Eric. "The Mythic." In *Sacred Narrative: Readings in the Theory of Myth*, edited by Alan Dundes, 224–243. Berkeley and Los Angeles: University of California Press, 1984.

Davies, Charles M. *Heterodox London: Phases of Free Thought in the Metropolis.* London: Tinsley Brothers, 1874. Reprint, New York: A. M. Kelley, 1969.

Dawkins, Richard. *The Selfish Gene.* New York: Oxford University Press, 1976.

de Chardin, Teilhard. *The Future of Man.* Translated by Norman Denny. New York: Harper and Row, 1964.

—. *The Phenomenon of Man.* Translated by Bernard Wall. New York: Harper and Row, 1959. Originally published as *Le Phenomene Humain*, 1955.

de Condorcet, Marquis. *Outlines of an Historical View of the Progress of the Human Mind.* Translated from the French. Philadelphia: M. Carey, 1796. Reprint, The Liberty Fund, n. d. oll.libertyfund.org/?option=com_staticxt&staticfile=show.php%3Ftitle=1669&chapter=800&layout=html&Itemid=27.

de Garis, Hugo. "Globa: Accelerating Technologies Will Create a Global State by 2050." *Kurzweil Accelerating Intelligence.* Kurzweil Network, January 19, 2011. www.kurzweilai.net/globa-global-state-by-2050.

—. "Think About It." YouTube video, 2:28. Posted September 5, 2007. Accessed January 27, 2017. www.youtube.com/watch?v=2A_5-Van9m4.

de Grey, Aubrey and Michael Rae. *Ending Aging: The Rejuvenation Breakthroughs that Could Reverse Human Aging in Our Lifetimes.* New York: St. Martin's Griffin, 2007.

Di Gregorio, Mario A. *From Here to Eternity: Ernst Haeckel and Scientific Faith.* Göttingen: Vandenhoeck and Ruprecht, 2005.

Diamandis, Peter H. "Who I am and What I Believe." September 9, 2015. YouTube video. https://www.youtube.com/watch?v=gGJIsX45nl8. Accessed January 30, 2017.

Diamandis, Peter and Steven Kotler. *Abundance: The Future is Better than You Think.* New York: Free Press, 2012.

Dupuy, Jean-Pierre. *On the Origins of Cognitive Science: The Mechanization of the Mind.* Translated by M. P. Debevoise. Cambridge, MA: MIT Press, 2009.

Dvorsky, George. "The Most Significant Tech of the Next 20 Years." IEET, November 4, 2010. ieet.org/index.php/IEET/more/dvorsky20101104.

—. "The Most Significant Technological Developments of the Next Twenty Years." *Sentient Developments* (blog), November 3, 2010. www.sentientde-velopments.com/2010/11/most-significant-technological.html.

Dyson, Freeman. *Imagined Worlds*. Cambridge, MA: Harvard University Press, 1998.

Eliade, Mircea. "Cosmogonic Myth and 'Sacred History.'" In *Sacred Narrative: Readings in the Theory of Myth* Edited by Alan Dundes, 137–151. Berkeley and Los Angeles: University of California Press, 1984.

Eliot, T. S. *Selected Prose*. Edited by F. Kermode. London: Faber and Faber, 1975.

Elshtain, Jean Bethke. "Is there a Human Nature? An Argument against Modern Excarnation." In *After the Genome: A Language for our Biotechnological Future* Edited by Michael J. Hyde and James A. Herrick. Baylor University Press, 2013.

Enriquez, Juan. "The Glory of Big Data." *Popular Science*, November 2011.

Ettinger, Robert. *Man Into Superman*. New York: Avon, 1972.

Fisher, Richard. "Is it OK to Torture or Murder a Robot?" *BBC Future*. BBC, November 27, 2013. www.bbc.com/future/story/20131127-would-you-murder-a-robot.

FM-2030. *Are You a Transhuman? Monitoring and Stimulating Your Personal Rate of Growth in a Rapidly Changing World*. New York: Warner Books, 1989.

Frye, Northrop. *Anatomy of Criticism: Four Essays*. Princeton, NJ: Princeton University Press, 1957.

Fukuyama, Francis. "Transhumanism." *Foreign Policy Magazine*, September 1, 2004.

Ganapati, Priya. "Reverse-Engineering of Human Brain Likely by 2030, Expert Predicts." *Wired*, August 16, 2010. www.wired.com/gadgetlab/2010/08/reverse-engineering-brain-kurzweil/.

Garreau, Joel. "Environmentalism as Religion." *The New Atlantis*28 (Summer 2010).

—. *Radical Evolution: The Promise and Peril of Enhancing Our Minds, Our Bodies—and What It Means to Be Human*. New York: Doubleday, 2005.

Gaudin, Sharon. "IBM's Watson's Ability to Converse is a Huge Advance for AI Research." *Computerworld*. IDG Communications, February 15, 2011. www.computerworld.com/s/article/9209661/IBM_s_ Watson_s_ ability_to_converse_is_a_huge_advance_for_AI_research.

Gilliam, Jim. "The Internet is My Religion." Filmed at the Personal Democracy Forum, 2011. YouTube video, 12:26. Posted June 9, 2011. www.youtube.com/watch?v=-4WKle-GQwk .

Gliboff, Sander, and H. G. Bronn. *Ernst Haeckel, and the Origins of German Darwinism: A Study in Translation and Transformation.* Cambridge, MA: MIT Press, 2008.

Goertzel, Ben. *A Cosmist Manifesto. A Cosmist Manifesto* (blog), Accessed January 21, 2011., cosmistmanifesto.blogspot.com/.

Good, I. J. "Speculations Concerning the First Ultraintelligent Machine." In *Advances in Computers,* edited by F. Alt and M. Rubinoff, 31–88. Academic Press, 1965. www.acceleratingfuture.com/pages/ultraintelligent-machine.html.

Gott, J. Richard III. *Time Travel in Einstein's Universe: The Physical Possibilities of Travel through Time.* London: Phoenix, 2002.

Gottschall, Jonathan. *The Storytelling Animal: How Stories Make us Human.* Boston and New York: Houghton Mifflin, 2012.

Gould, Stephen J. *The Mismeasure of Man.* New York: W. W. Norton, 1981.

Graham-Rowe, Duncan. "Wheelchair Makes the Most of Brain Control." *MIT Technology Review,* September 13, 2010. www.technologyreview.com/news/420756/wheelchair-makes-the-most-of-brain-control/.

Graham-Rowe, Duncan. "World's First Brain Prosthesis Revealed." *New Scientist,* March 12, 2003. www.newscientist.com/article/dn3488-worlds-first-brain-prosthesis-revealed.html\.

Green, John C. "The Interaction of Science and Worldview in Sir Julian Huxley's Evolutionary Biology." *Journal of the History of Ideas* 23 (1990).

Greenwald, Ted. "The X Man." *Wired,* July 2012.

Grifantini, Kristina. "Personal Exoskeletons for Paraplegics: A mobile device helps patients with spinal cord injuries walk." *MIT Technology Review,* September 22, 2010. www.technologyreview.com/biomedicine/26328/?p1=A1&a=f.

Grossman, Lev. "Singularity." *Time,* February 21, 2011.

Haber, Carole. "Life Extension and History: The Continual Search for the Fountain of Youth." *The Journals of Gerontology* 59, no. 6 (June 2004): 515–22. biomedgerontology.oxfordjournals.org/content/59/6/B515.long.

Haeckel, Ernst. *The Riddle of the Universe at the Close of the Nineteenth Century.* Translated by Joseph McCabe. New York: Harper and Brothers, 1900.

Hagemeister, Michael. "Russian Cosmism in the 1920s and Today." In *The Occult in Russian and Soviet Culture,* edited by Bernice Glatzer Rosenthal. Ithaca: Cornell University Press, 1997: 195–202.

Haldane, J. B. S. *Possible Worlds.* London: Chatto and Windus, 1937.

Harris, John. *Enhancing Evolution: The Ethical Case for Making Better People.* Princeton, NJ: Princeton University Press, 2009.

Hauskeller, Michael. "Reinventing Cockaigne: Utopian Themes in Trans-humanist Thought." *The Hastings Center Report* 42, no. 2 (April 2012): 39–47.

Hayles, N. Katherine. *How We Became Posthuman: Virtual Bodies in Cybernetics, Literature, and Informatics.* Chicago: University of Chicago Press, 1999.

Hayworth, Kenneth. "Proposal for a Brain Preservation Technology Prize." The Brain Preservation Foundation, June 18, 2010, www.brainpreservation.org/documents/proposalforbrainpreservationtechnologyprize.pdf.

Heims, Steve J. *Constructing a Social Science for Postwar America: The Cybernetics Group, 1946-1953.* Cambridge, MA: MIT Press, 1999.

Herath, A. K. "Cyborgs Needed for Escape from Earth." *Astrobiology Magazine,* September 16, 2010. www.astrobio.net/exclusive/3617/cyborgs-needed-for-escape-from-earth.

Herritt, Robert. "Google's Philosopher." *Pacific Standard,* December 30, 2014,http://www.psmag.com/navigation/nature-and-technology/googles-philosopher-technology-nature-identity-court-legal-policy-95456/.

Heti, Sheila. "Mary Midgley: Moral Philosopher." *The Believer,* February 2008. www.believermag.com/issues/200802/?read=interview_midgley.

Hickey, Walter. "These twenty Advanced Military Projects Will Change Your Life." Business Insider. Business Insider, July 27, 2012. http://www.businessinsider.com/darpa-military-projects-that-will-change-your-life-2012-7?op=1#ixzz22416TypT.

Highfield, Robert Highfield. "How to Live Forever." *The Telegraph,* January 14, 2008. www.telegraph.co.uk/news/science/science-news/3321714/How-to-live-forever.html.

Hodgkinson, Mike. "You Will be Able to Upload Your Brain." *The Independent,* September 27, 2009. www.independent.co.uk/news/science/by-2040-you-will-be-able-to-upload-your-brain-1792555.html.

Hughes, James. *Citizen Cyborg: Why Democratic Societies Must Respond to the Redesigned Human of the Future.* Cambridge, MA: Westview Press, 2004.

Human Brain Project. Accessed August, 18 2015. www.humanbrainproject.eu/.

Hutton, Christopher M. *Linguistics and the Third Reich: Mother Tongue Fascism, Race, and the Science of Language.* New York: Routledge, 1999.

Huxley, Julian. *Evolution: The Modern Synthesis.* London: Allen and Unwin, 1942.

——. "The Evolutionary Vision." *Evolution after Darwin: Issues in Evolution,* vol. 2. Chicago: University of Chicago Press, 1960

——. *New Bottles for New Wine.* New York: Harper, 1957.

Huxley, T. H. "Evolution and Ethics." *Collected Essays IX: Evolution and Ethics and other Essays*. London: Macmillan, 1893. http://aleph0.clarku.edu/huxley/CE9/E-E.html#cite20.

Istvan, Zoltan. "Are we Heading for a Jesus Singularity?" *Huffington Post* (blog). TheHuffingtonPost.com, March 21, 2014. http://www.huffingtonpost.com/zoltan-istvan/are-we-heading-for-a-jesu_b_5002863.html.

J. Craig Venter Institute. "First Self-Replicating Synthetic Bacterial Cell." J. Craig Venture Institute, May 20, 2010, http://www.jcvi.org/cms/press/press-releases/full-text/article/first-self-replicating-synthetic-bacterial-cell-constructed-by-j-craig-venter-institute-researcher/home/

Kaku, Michio. "Living in a Post-Human World." *Big Think* video, 1:34. Accessed 2011. bigthink.com/videos/living-in-a-post-human-world.

Kaku, Michio. *Physics of the Future: How Science Will Shape Human Destiny and Our Daily Lives by 2100*. New York: Anchor, 2012.

Kant, Immanuel. *Critique of Pure Reason*. J. F. Hartknock: Riga, 1781.

Kellim, S., et al. "Decoding Spoken Words using Local Field Potentials Recorded from the Cortical Surface." *The Journal of Neural Engineering* 7, no. 5 (October 2010).

Kelly, Kevin. *What Technology Wants*. New York: Penguin, 2011.

King, Leo. "Mind-Controlled Drone Scientists Work On Groundbreaking Flight." Forbes. Forbes Media, February 25, 2015. www.forbes.com/sites/leoking/2015/02/25/mind-controlled-drone-scientists-work-on-groundbreaking-flight/.

Koch, Christof. *Consciousness: Confessions of a Romantic Reductionist*. Cambridge, MA: MIT Press, 2012,

Kraft, Nicole. "Brain-To-Brain Communication Achieved, Telepathy A Reality." *SourceFed*. Discovery Communications, November 10, 2014. sourcefed.com/brain-to-brain-communication-achieved-telepathy-a-reality/.

Kurzweil Accelerating Intelligence. "'Neural Dust' Brain Implants could Revolutionize Brain-machine Interfaces." Kurzweil Network, July 17, 2013. www.kurzweilai.net/neural-dust-brain-implants-could-revolutionize-brain-machine-interfaces-and-large-scale-data-recording.

—. "New Genes Linked to Brain Size, Intelligence." Kurzweil Network, April 16, 2012. www.kurzweilai.net/new-genes-linked-to-brain-size-intelligence.

Kurzweil, Ray. *How to Create a Mind: The Secret of Human Thought Revealed*. New York: Viking, 2012.

—. *The Age of Spiritual Machines: When Computers Exceed Human Intelligence*. New York: Penguin, 2000.

—. *The Singularity Is Near: When Humans Transcend Biology.* New York: Viking, 2005.

Lanier, Jaron. "First Church of Robotics." *New York Times*, August 9, 2010. www.nytimes.com/2010/08/09/opinion/09lanier.html?_r=0.

—. *You Are Not a Gadget: A Manifesto.* New York: Knopf, 2010.

Levi-Strauss, Claude. "The Structural Study of Myth." *The Journal of American Folklore* 68, no. 270 (1955): 428–444.

Li, Shan. "Mind Reading Is on the Market." *LA Times*, August 8, 2010. articles.latimes.com/2010/aug/08/business/la-fi-mind-reader-20100808.

Lukashevich, Stephen. *N. F. Fedorov (1828–1903): A Study in Russian Eupsychian and Utopian Thought.* Cranbury, NJ: Associated University Press, 1977.

Madrigal, Alexis. "Gandhi Pills? Psychiatrist Argues for Moral Performance Enhancers." *Wired*, September 9, 2008. www.wired.com/wiredscience/2008/09/gandhi-pills-ps/.

Makram, Henry. "A Brain in a Supercomputer." *TED* video. Filmed July 2009. *TED* video, 14:50. Posted October 2009. www.ted.com/talks/henry_markram_supercomputing_the_brain_s_secrets.html.

Mali, Joseph. *The Rehabilitation of Myth: Vico's 'New Science.'* Cambridge: Cambridge University Press, 1992.

McCullough, Warren. "'Mysterium Iniquitiatus' of Sinful Man Aspiring into the Place of God." *Embodiments of Mind.* Cambridge, MA: MIT Press, 1965.

McDougall, Paul. "SpaceX Dragon Capsule Lands Safely." InformationWeek. UBM, December 9, 2010. www.informationweek.com/story/showArticle.jhtml?articleID=228800001.

McKay, Donald J. *The Clock Work Image: A Christian Perspective on Science.* Downers Grove, IL: Intervarsity Press, 1974.

Midgley, Mary. *Evolution as a Religion: Strange Dreams, Stranger Fears.* London: Methuen, 1985.

—. "Gene-juggling." *Philosophy* 54 (October 1979).

—. *Science as Salvation: A Modern Myth and Its Meaning.* New York: Routledge, 1992.

—. *The Myths We Live By.* New York: Routledge, 2011.

Miller, Lisa. "The Trans-Everything CEO." *New York Magazine*, September 7, 2014.

Milo, Peter V. "Scientists Successfully 'Hack' Brain to Obtain Information." *CBS Seattle.* CBS News, August 25, 2012. seattle.cbslocal.com/2012/08/25/scientists-successfully-hack-brain-to-obtain-private-data/.

Minsky, Marvin. *The Society of Mind.* New York: Simon and Shuster, 1989.

—."Will Robots Inherit the Earth?" *Scientific American*, October 1994. www.scientificamerican.com/article/will-robots-inherit-the-earth/.

Moravec, Hans. *Mind Children; The Future of Robot and Human Intelligence.* Cambridge, MA: Harvard University Press, 1988.

—. *Robot: Mere Machine to Transcendent Mind.* New York: Oxford University Press, 2000.

More, Max. *The Principles of Extropy*, Extropy.org, May 28, 2004. http://lists.extropy.org/pipermail/extropy-chat/2004-May/006399.html

Moreno, Jonathan. *Mind Wars: Brain Research and National Defense.* New York: Bellevue Literary Press, 2012.

Moskowitz, Sam. *Explorers of the Infinite: Shapers of Science Fiction.* New York: Hyperion Press, 1963.

Naam, Ramez. *More Than Human: Embracing the Promise of Biological Enhancement.* New York: Broadway Books, 2005.

—. *Nexus.* Nottingham: Angry Robot Books, 2013.

Nagel, Thomas. *Mind and Cosmos: Why the Materialist Neo-Darwinian Conception of Nature is Almost Certainly False.* New York: Oxford University Press, 2012.

Naik, Gautam. "Aging Ills Reversed in Mice." *Wall Street Journal*, November 28, 2010. online.wsj.com/article/SB10001424052748703785704575642964209242180.html? mod=googlenews_wsj.

Nakamur, Lisa. *Cybertypes: Race, Ethnicity and Identity on the Internet.* New York: Routledge, 2002.

National Institutes for Health BRAIN Initiative. Accessed on July 25, 2015. http://braininitiative.nih.gov/about.htm

O'Neill, Gerard K. *The High Frontier: Human Colonies in Space.* New York: Wiliam Morrow, 1977.

Oberhaus, Daniel. "The Art of Not Dying." *Motherboard*, Vice Media, November 28, 2014. motherboard.vice.com/read/the-art-of-not-dying-or-being-frozen-until-you-can-come-back.

Penrose, Roger. *The Emperor's New Mind: Concerning Computers, Minds and the Laws of Physics.* New York: Oxford University Press, 1989.

Perelman, Chaim and L. Olbrechts-Tyteca. *The New Rhetoric: A Treatise on Argumentation.* Translated by John Wilkinson and Purcell Weaver. Notre Dame, IN: University of Notre Dame Press.

Philips, Paul. "One World, One Faith: The Quest for Unity in Julian Huxley's Religion of Evolutionary Humanism." *Journal of the History of Ideas* 68, no. 4 (October 2007): 613–633.

Pickering, Mary. *August Comte: An Intellectual Biography.* New York: Cambridge University Press, 2006.

Plotz, David. "Total Recall: The Future of Memory." *Slate*, March 11, 2003, www.slate.com/articles/health_and_science/superman/2003/03/total_recall.single.html

Pohl, Frederik and Hans Moravec. "Souls in Silicon." *Omni*, November 1993, pp. 66–76.

Poliakov, Leon. *The Aryan Myth: A History of Racist and Nationalist Ideas in Europe.* New York: Barnes and Noble, 1996.

Prisco, Giulio. "The Cosmic Visions of the Turing Church." Presented at the Transhumanism and Spirituality Conference, University of Utah, October 1, 2010. www.slideshare.net/giulioprisco/transpirit2010.

—. "Transcendent Engineering." *Terasem Journal of Personal Cyberconsciousness,* December 2011. www.terasemjournals.com/PCJournal/PC0602/prisco.html.

—. "Transhumanist Religion 2.0." Kurzweil Accelerating Intelligence (blog). KurzweilAINetwork, July 12, 2012. www.kurzweilai.net/transhumanist-religion-2-0.

Reed, Edward S. *From Soul to Mind: The Emergence of Psychology from Erasmus Darwin to William James.* New Haven, CT: Yale University Press, 1997.

Rees, Martin. *Our Final Hour: A Scientist's Warning: How Terror, Error, and Environmental Disaster Threaten Humankind's Future in This Century—On Earth and Beyond.* New York: Basic Books, 2003.

Ricoeur, Paul. *A Ricoeur Reader: Reflection and Imagination.* New York: Harvester/Wheatsheaf, 1991.

—. *The Symbolism of Evil.* Translated by Emerson Buchanan. Boston: Beacon Press, 1967.

Rosenthal, Bernice Glatzer. "Introduction." *The Occult in Russian and Soviet Culture.* Edited by Bernice Glatzer Rosenthal. Ithaca: Cornell University Press, 1997.

Rothblatt, Martine. *Virtually Human: The Promise and Peril of Virtual Immortality.* New York: St. Martins, 2014.

Russell, Bertrand. *Has Man a Future?* New York: Simon and Schuster, 1961.

Russell, Jon. "Google: Defeating Go Champion Shows AI Can 'Find Solutions Humans Don't See.'" TechCrunch. AOL, March 17, 2016. techcrunch.com/2016/03/17/google-defeating-go-champion-shows-ai-can-find-solutions-humans-dont-see/.

Sagan, Carl. *The Cosmic Connection: An Extraterrestrial Perspective.* New York: Dell, 1973.

Sandberg, Anders. "Transhumanism and the Meaning of Life." In *Religion and Transhumanism: The Unknown Future of Human Enhancement Religion*, edited by Calvin Mercer and Tracy J. Trothen. Santa Barbara, CA: Praeger, 2015.

Sandel, Michael. "The Case Against Perfection." In *Human Enhancement*, edited by Julian Savulescu and Nick Bostrom. New York: Oxford University Press, 2009.

Savulescu, Julian. "New Breeds of Humans: The Moral Obligation to Enhance." *Ethics, Law and Moral Philosophy of Reproductive Biomedicine* 1, no. 1 (2005): 36–39.

—. "Procreative Beneficence: Why We Should Select the Best Children." *Bioethics* 15, no. 5 (2001): 413–26.

—. "Procreative Beneficence: Reasons Not to Have Disabled Children." *The Sorting Society*. Edited by L. Skene and J. Thomson. New York: Cambridge University Press, 2008.

—. "Unfit for Life: Genetically Enhance Humanity or Face Extinction." Filmed at the *Festival of Dangerous Ideas*, 2009. YouTube video, 59:21. Posted on March 21, 2014. www.youtube.com/watch?v=PkW3rEQ0ab8.

Schactman, Noah. "Air Force wants Neuroweapons to Overwhelm Enemy." *Wired*, November 2, 2010. www.wired.com/dangerroom/2010/11/air-force-looks-to-artificially-overwhelm-enemy-cognitive-capabilities/.

Seo, Dongjin, et al., "Neural Dust: An Ultrasonic, Low Power Solution for Chronic Brain-Machine Interfaces." Cornell University Library, July 8, 2013. arxiv.org/abs/1307.2196.

Seung, Sebastian. *The Connectome: How the Brain's Wiring Makes Us Who We Are*. New York: Mariner, 2012.

Shaw, George Bernard. "The New Theology." *The Christian Commonwealth*, May 1907. http://en.wikisource.org/wiki/The_New_Theology_%28Shaw%29.

Sheridan, Kerry. "Coming Soon: A Brain Implant to Restore Memory." Medical Xpress. Science X, May 1, 2014. medicalxpress.com/news/2014-05-brain-implant-memory.html.

Shook, John R. "Can We Make More Moral Brains?" *Free Inquiry*, December 2011/January 2012.

Silver, Lee M. "Reprogenetics: How Reproductive and Genetic Technologies Will Be Combined to Provide New Opportunities for People to Reach Their Reproductive Goals." In *Engineering the Human Germline*, edited by Gregory Stock and John Campbell. New York; Oxford University Press, 2000.

Singer. Emily. "Watching a Single Thought Form in the Brain." *MIT Technology Review*, September 6, 2006. www.technologyreview.com/biomedicine/17458/?mod=related

Sinsheimer, Robert. "The Prospect of Designed Genetic Change." *Engineering and Science*, April 1969, pp. 8–13.

Smart, John. "The Brain Preservation Prize: Why Inexpensively Preserving Our Brains After Death is a Good Thing for Ourselves and Society, And What You Can Do to Help." *Humanity+ Summit*, June 12, 2010. http://www.brainpreservation.org.

Smith, David. "Building an Electronic Human Brain." *Israel 21C*, May 2010. israel21c.org/technology/building-an-electronic-human-brain-2/.

Smith, Huston. *Why Religion Matters*. New York: HarperCollins, 2001.

Smith, Kerri. "Mind-reading Technology Speeds Ahead." *Scientific American*, October 23, 2013, www.scientificamerican.com/article/mind-reading-technology-speeds-ahead/.

Smith, Wesley J. "AI Machines: Things, Not Persons." *First Things*, April, 10 2015. www.firstthings.com/web-exclusives/2015/04/ai-machines-things-not-persons.

Sparrow, Robert. "A Not-So-New Eugenics: Harris and Savulescu on Human Enhancement." *The Hastings Center Report* 41, no. 1, January–February 2011.

Stapledon, Olaf. "The Splendid Race." *An Olaf Stapledon Reader*. Syracuse: Syracuse University Press, 1997.

Stein, Rob. "Geneticists Breach Ethical Taboo by Changing Genes across Generations." *National Public Radio*, October 24, 2012. www.npr.org/blogs/health/2012/10/24/163509093/geneticists-breach-ethical-taboo-by-changing-genes-across-generations.

Stock, Gregory. *Redesigning Humans*. N.p.: Profile Books, 2002.

Sumagaysay, Levi. "Tech Billionaires and Human Immortality." *Siliconbeat* (blog), *Mercury News*, March 6, 2015. www.siliconbeat.com/2015/03/06/quoted-tech-billionaires-and-human-immortality/.

Symons, Xavier. "Savulescu Warns that 'Love-diminishing' Drugs Could Be Used for Gay Conversion Therapy." *Bio-Edge*. New Media Foundation, October 13, 2013. www.bioedge.org.

Thomson, Helen. "Electrical brain stimulation improves math skills." *New Scientist*, November 4, 2010. www.newscientist.com/article/dn19679-electrical-brain-stimulation-improves-math-skills.html.

Tirosh-Samuelson, Hava. "Engaging Transhumanism." In *Transhumanism and Its Critics*, edited by Gregory R. Hansell and William Grassie. Philadelphia, PA: Metanexus Institute, 2011, pp.19–52.

Trafton, Anne. "Neuroscientists Plant False Memories in the Brain." *MIT News*. MIT, July 25, 2013. http://news.mit.edu/2013/neuroscientists-plant-false-memories-in-the-brain-0725 .

Turing, Alan M. "Computing Machinery and Intelligence." *Mind* 59, no. 236 (October 1950): 433–460.

Tyler, William J. "Remote Control of Brain Activity Using Ultrasound." *Armed with Science* (blog). US Defense Department, September 1, 2010. science.dod-live.mil/2010/09/01/remote-control-of-brain-activity-using-ultrasound/.

Venter, J. Craig. "Life: A Gene-centric View." *Edge: The Third Culture*. Edge, January 2008. http://www.edge.org/documents/dawkins_venter_index.html.

—. "A DNA Driven World," *BBC Richard Dimbleby Lecture*, December 4, 2007, http://www.bbc.co.uk/pressoffice/pressreleases/stories/2007/12_december/05/dimbleby.shtml

—. *Life at the Speed of Light: From the Double Helix to the Dawn of Digital Life*. New York: Viking, 2013.

United Press International. "Hawking: Man Must Colonize Space." UPI.com, January 6, 2012. www.upi.com/Science_News/2012/01/06/Hawking-Mankind-must-colonize-space/UPI-64431325871534/#ixzz1yZxQVutv.

Verene, Donald Phillip. *Vico's 'New Science': A Philosophical Commentary*. Ithaca: Cornell University Press, 2015.

Warner, Marina. *Six Myths of Our Time: Little Angels, Little Monsters, Beautiful Beasts, and More*. New York: Random House, 1994.

Waters, Brent. "Flesh Made Data: The Posthuman Project in Light of the Incarnation." In *Religion and Transhumanism: The Unknown Future of Human Enhancement*, edited by Calvin Mercer and Tracy J. Trothen, 291–302. Santa Barbara, CA: Praeger, 2015.

Watson, James. *The Double-Helix: A Personal Account of the Discovery of the Structure of DNA*. New York: Touchstone, 2001.

Weisberg, Jacob. "Turn on, Start Up, Drop Out." *Slate*, October 16, 2010. www.slate.com/articles/news_and_politics/politics/2010/10/turn_on_start_up_drop_out.html.

Weizenbaum, Joseph. *Computer Power and Human Reason: From Judgment to Calculation*. New York: W. H. Freeman and Co., 1976.

Whyntie, Jen. "One Rat Brain 'Talks' to Another Using Electronic Link." *BBC Radio*, February 28, 2013, www.bbc.co.uk/news/science-environment-21604005.

Wright, Robert. "Building One Big Brain." *New York Times*, July 6, 2010. opinionator.blogs.nytimes.com/2010/07/06/the-web-we-weave/.

Wylie, Philip. *Gladiator*. 1930. Reprint, Lincoln, NE: University of Nebraska Press, 2004.

Yarrow, Jay. "Google is Launching a Company that Hopes to Cure Death." *Business Insider*, October, 15, 2013, www.businessinsider.com/google-is-launching-a-company-that-hopes-to-cure-death-2013-9.

Young, George M., Jr. "Federov's Transformations of the Occult." *The Occult in Russian and Soviet Culture.* Edited by Bernice Glatzer Rosenthal, Ithaca: Cornell University Press, 1997.

—. *The Russian Cosmists: The Esoteric Futurism of Nikolai Fedorov and His Followers.* Oxford: Oxford University Press, 2012.

Zrenner, E., et al. "Subretinal Electronic Chips Allow Blind Patients to Read Letters and Combine Them to Words." *Proceedings of the Royal Society* 466, no. 2123 (November 2010). www.rspb.royalsocietypublishing.org/content/early/2010/11/01/rspb.2010.1747.full.

Index

ABOUT THE AUTHOR

James A. Herrick (PhD University of Wisconsin, MA University of California-Davis) is the Guy Vander Jagt Professor of Communication at Hope College in Holland, Michigan. He is the author of *The Making of the New Spirituality*, *Scientific Mythologies*, *The Radical Rhetoric of the English Deists*, *Argumentation* and *The History and Theory of Rhetoric*, and co-editor of *After the Genome: A Language for our Biotechnological Future*. Herrick writes and speaks about the history of rhetoric, new religious movements, and popular narratives about science and technology.

Photograph of the author by Chris deVries.
Used by permission.

CPSIA information can be obtained
at www.ICGtesting.com
Printed in the USA
BVOW04s0814100317
478246BV00001B/5/P